Alfred Holbrook

Reminiscences of the Happy Life of a Teacher

Alfred Holbrook

Reminiscences of the Happy Life of a Teacher

ISBN/EAN: 9783337056049

Printed in Europe, USA, Canada, Australia, Japan

Cover: Foto ©ninafisch / pixelio.de

More available books at **www.hansebooks.com**

REMINISCENCES

OF THE

HAPPY LIFE

OF A

TEACHER.

BY

ALFRED HOLBROOK.

CINCINNATI:
Elm Street Printing Company, Nos. 176 & 178 Elm St.
1885.

Entered according to Act of Congress, in the year 1885, by
ALFRED HOLBROOK,
In the Office of the Librarian of Congress, at Washington, D. C.

PREFACE.

AFTER my children had teased me for many years to write out the incidents of my life, and I had demurred, it was suggested by one of them: "Why, papa, wouldn't you like to have the life of your father, with his experiences?" "Most assuredly." "Then think how your children and grandchildren will prize your experiences and your triumphs."

To this I succumbed, and set about writing these "reminiscences."

They may or may not be valuable, or interesting to some of my seventy thousand pupils. I hope they may.

Writing amid the pressure of business cares, I have endeavored to introduce such facts as may exemplify my theory of Education, of Teaching and School Management. Possibly the narrations of those difficulties, common more or less to all teachers, and the ways by which such difficulties were converted into means of my continued success, may arouse some discouraged teacher "to take heart again" and feel that he can use similar plans to save and bless his pupils, to establish his own goings.

For my innovations upon the general plan of education, I have come in for the personal denunciations and maledictions of many college men from time to time. I can safely say that while I have freely attacked the usages and abuses so prevalent in colleges, I have never permitted myself to speak disrespectfully or unkindly of any college man. On the other hand, there are very few college men that I do not most thoroughly respect, and among my best friends I have always numbered many college graduates. But they are those who have acquainted themselves with my work, and who have discovered more good than evil in my efforts to do my duty in my own way.

CONTENTS.

CHAPTER I.
GENEALOGY.

How I found the line of my ancestry—Descent and descendants—Of good Puritan stock—Conjugal devotion—My first recollections of Melissa Pierson—Holbrooks and Piersons settle on the Western Reserve—Melissa's return in after years—Melissa Craft and Melissa Pierson two rare examples of piety—Their influence on my life.

CHAPTER II.
AT GROTON, MASSACHUSETTS.

A pupil under Elizur Wight—My father's Scientific Lectures—John Todd's story-telling—Early mechanical training—A coincidence.

CHAPTER III.
LIEE IN BOSTON.

My father a Yale graduate; a student under Prof. Silliman—Failure of Colleges in scientific training then and now—The first Manual Labor School—Lyceum System introduced—The origin of Holbrook's apparatus—Why I did not go to College—Day's Algebra mastered in morning hours—My experience in the best school in Boston—Lowell Mason and his sons—Daniel Webster in a storm—Dr. Lyman Beecher's church burned—His power—A remarkable snow-storm—A sad love story—My father's educational labors—He secured the first geological survey in the United States.

CHAPTER IV.

MY TEACHERS.

I am taught to read a chapter in the Bible at three years of age—Early punishments—Old time district school—My father a good Normalite—Victims of the *College fetich*—My only whipping at school—Distinguished teachers: Elizur Wight, Dr. John Todd, Dr. Samuel Beech, Zephaniah Swift—The Puritan Sabbath—Repeal of the Blue Laws—I am guilty of breaking the Sabbath - Grandfather Swift's home a "Ministers' Tavern" —Signing the Temperance pledge—Rum-drinking deacons—A sad case—My childhood recollections of College Professors— Puritan customs—Grandfather Holbrook's high moral character and business energy—*My father as my teacher*—His "drawing out" system—Our familiarity with prominent places, men and books—Sights in the Boston Museum—Reading, and reading— (A story to tell)—Object-lesson teaching - My father's advanced views of Education—My attitude toward colleges and college men—My educational views an inheritance—Some lessons in mechanics and business practices.

CHAPTER V.

STAMFORD.

A short chapter of stories.

CHAPTER VI.

MY FIRST SCHOOL.

Engaged at seventeen years of age, on my own conditions, to teach a country school—My examination quickly accomplished —Efficacy of muscular Christianity shown in my first day's teaching—Pouring in and drawing out methods tested--The first *preliminary drill* in class-work—The first blackboard used— Am I the teacher or my patrons?—Boarding 'round—How we enjoyed it—Teaching a delight in its triumphs—Our Literary Society—School Directors' dodges—A lesson in learning and teaching the modern languages.

CHAPTER VII.

MY EXPERIENCES IN NEW YORK CITY.

Preparatory work in engineering—Social environments—Religious discussions—Theater-going—Five Points—Ill health—Horace Greeley—Evenings employed in reading—Attendance upon lectures—Conversation with an intelligent Catholic—Arthur Tappan—New York fire, 1836—Mr. Finney's preaching; effects upon me.

CHAPTER VIII.

MELISSA AND I.

Our early training—Our love story—Her character and work.

CHAPTER IX.

A REMINISCENCE IN BEREA.

First Institutes in Ohio—My first Institute—Eastern and Western hospitality forty years ago—Melissa's prophets' chamber.

CHAPTER X.

SOME REMINISCENCES OF JOHN BALDWIN.

Berea community—Lyceum village—Discovery and sale of Berea grindstone—I am entrapped—Resignation—Removal to Chardon—Gifts of house and lot—A characteristic incident of Mr. B—His keen appreciation of good school management—Encounter with the doctors—Our last meeting.

CHAPTER XI.

EXPERIENCES AT CHARDON, O.

Self-reporting system discussed—A woman's enterprise—Gov. Corwin's oratory—Providential interference in my behalf—Dishonesty a growing evil among teachers—Purchase of $2,500 worth of apparatus—Ill health the cause of closing school—Partnership with Dr. Nicholls.

(*Contents continued on p. 358.*)

Reminiscences of Alfred Holbrook.

CHAPTER I.

GENEALOGY.

In tumbling over the rubbish, one rainy day, in the garret of the house in which I was born, built by my great-great-grandfather, early in the eighteenth century, I found a copy-book, written by my grandfather, Daniel Holbrook. Besides many pages of manuscript, written from copies apparently, at school, there were other pages of miscellaneous matter, chiefly historical, relating to the settlement of Derby, Connecticut, and the part the Holbrook family had had in the growth of the town.

My grandfather wrote a large, round, beautiful hand, more legible than print. The manuscript was probably over sixty years old, and it is nearly sixty years since I found it.

The genealogy of the Holbrooks was given thus, somewhat: Among the twenty-three families that formed the first organization of the township of

Derby, I find Stephen Pierson and Deacon Abel Holbrook. This was in 1675. These twenty-three families had already settled a minister, built him a house, also a meeting-house, costing £100, pledged him a support by taxation on their lands, besides paying their proportion in supporting a minister at Milford, whence most of them had removed.

This ancestor, Abel Holbrook, had previously been accustomed to worship at Milford, taking his wife and baby there and back every Sabbath, a distance of eight miles through the woods. Their custom was to ride one horse; the couple taking turns in riding and walking, the one riding carrying the child. This method of traveling was called "to ride and tie."

Our family comes from John Holbrook, (one of three brothers), who emigrated from Derby, England, and settled at Oyster Bay, Long Island, 1652. Deacon Abel Holbrook settled on the farm extending over Sentinel Hill and through Pleasant Valley in Derby, Connecticut, 1676. Deacon Daniel Holbrook married 1729. Deacon Daniel Holbrook, second, my grandfather, married 1766. He was a Colonel in the Revolutionary War. Josiah Holbrook married Lucy Swift, 1815; children: Alfred (the writer of this) and Dwight. Alfred married Melissa Pierson, March 24, 1843; children: Josiah, R. Heber, John B., Agnes Irene, Anne Lucy, and Alfred Holbrook. The youngest, Alfred Holbrook, was drowned when fifteen years of age. The others are living, and engaged with their father in the National Normal University. The mother died, May, 1884.

My grandfather, Colonel Holbrook, states that Captain Bradley, in his regiment, was shot through the head, in the defense of East Haven. I have often seen the hat he wore, penetrated with the bullet-holes, hanging in the house of his son, Captain Bradley, of Derby.

The present Holbrooks may consider themselves as coming from good Puritan stock, an unbroken line of deacons. Some of my Derby recollections may be interesting to my family and other immediate friends. My mother died when I was two years old, consequently I do not remember her. I only remember hearing my father speak of her once: "I never came into the house or into her presence, anywhere, that she did not welcome me with her sweet and beautiful smile."

My parents were both good singers, and led their parts in the church-choir of Derby. My aunts have told me that "my father sang my mother's favorite hymn at her burial by himself," but he was never heard to sing afterward. He never married again, though, in my opinion, he was a very handsome and attractive man, and might have married a fortune at several different times, as I was told.

When my father had built a house on Sentinel Hill, and had moved into it, Aunt Irene Pierson occupied the Holbrook homestead in Pleasant Valley, while her husband was at work on the home farm. It thus happened, that my wife, Melissa, and I, were born in the same room in the Holbrook mansion. My first recollection of her is that I was seated by a little, flaxen-ringletted girl in school for punishment, when about seven years old. The punishment thus given by Miss Julia Ann Tomlinson, was not severe; whether it proved effectual I am unable to state.

Melissa left Derby with her parents when eight years old. They came to Kirtland, Ohio, and settled on a farm the mother had received as her patrimony from the Holbrook estate. The farm is still occupied by her son, Julius Pierson.

Some forty years after the family left Derby, my wife and I returned. I was continually surprised at the familiar acquaintance which she exhibited with every street, brook, bridge, every old house and old family in Derby. I had left Derby twelve years later. This was the first time either had returned to Derby since coming West. My recollections of my childhood are very pleasant. My aunt, Mrs. Melissa Holbrook Craft, had taken me when my mother died, and provided for, and trained me, till my father called me to Boston.

She was a woman of most implicit trust in her Savior. With small means she rendered help and sympathy to all who were in want or distress. Such self-denial in all personal comforts for increasing the means of helping others, I have never seen in any other, excepting one. Besides feeding and clothing me, her house was the home at different times for various others who had been unfortunate. She was often told that she would scarcely eat or wear anything which she could give away. She lived to an advanced age, and never wanted for any good thing, was always thankful, and never was entirely deprived of the privilege of giving consolation and aid to some whom she thought more needy than herself.

The only other woman I ever knew whom I thought as self-sacrificing, as trustful, as devoted in her piety, as ready in her sympathy, and earnest in her benevolence, was her namesake, Melissa Holbrook Pierson Holbrook, my wife.

The influence of two such Melissas, one in childhood, the other in manhood, was surely of divine appointment, and has ever been regarded as such.

CHAPTER II.

EXPERIENCE IN GROTON, MASSACHUSETTS.

IN 1827, my father sent for me to meet him in Groton, Massachusetts. He was giving a course of scientific lectures there, and I was entered as a pupil in the Groton Academy. Elizur Wright was the Principal. We boarded with Rev. John Todd, the noted preacher and evangelist. The competition of Mr. Todd and father in story-telling was amusing and exciting. It was a common saying in the streets of Groton, "Did you go to hear Todd tell stories last Sunday?" The question had reference to his preaching. I was eleven years old, and Mr. Todd was the first preacher I had ever listened to with interest or profit. His sermons abounded in illustrations, anecdotes, humor and wit, and were just as interesting to children as to adults. He had gathered the orthodox members of the old Congregational Church, who had virtually been expelled by the Unitarians from the church their fathers had erected, and was building a new edifice. The dedication was noted by the harnesses of the members being cut, their linchpins being removed, and by kegs of sulphur being rolled into the vestibule. All of which were evidences of Mr. Todd's power as a preacher and organizer. I will give one of Mr. Todd's Andover experiences as related by him at the dinner table.

A senior student returning to the seminary from a village, where he had supplied a pulpit, related to his room-mate and others that he had been waylaid in a patch of woods just out of the village, and had been robbed of his watch and pocketbook. It was all the worse that his pocketbook contained all the money he had—the five dollars he had received for preaching.

Several of the students volunteered to go with him the next morning to the place of his misadventure, hoping to aid in tracking and apprehending the highwayman.

On arriving at the place, they found an orchard on one side of the road, a pump standing by the fence, with the handle projecting toward the road. The pocketbook and watch were lying on the ground, near the pump, where the frightened theologue had thrown them as he started to run from the robber.

Besides giving me the advantages of school, my father hired a watchmaker to give me daily training in the use of tools. The knowledge and skill there obtained, and the practical economy there acquired, in making poor tools and defective materials accomplish their ends, have been of the greatest possible advantage in every position in which I have since been placed.

I there learned there was excitement and interest in overcoming difficulties, rather than in being overcome by them.

I remember hearing my father say for my encouragement: "Anybody can work with good tools, but it takes pluck to manage poor ones, and a genius to perform his work with none at all."

The pluck was developed, if anything. My worthy mechanic teacher gave me his poorest tools to work with, until I had demonstrated that I would not spoil his good ones.

At the same time, father bought me a box of drawing instruments, and set me to work in mechanical drawing. I was much interested in this, and have ever since made use of the power there and then acquired in the training of the hand, eye and mind together, in all demands for mechanical calculation and invention. The calls for just such skill and contrivance as that early training gave me, have been varied and numberless, all my life long. It was just the training that a good Providence only could foresee was necessary in the independent, revolutionizing course I have been led to pursue in all matters pertaining to education. It was this practical combination of mechanism and science, which my father still continued in Boston, that has made it possible for me to sustain myself amid the poverty, and against the maledictions and denunciations of otherwise good men, in developing a practical system of training, which has, to a large extent, in my humble opinion, already done much to modify educational work everywhere, and which will, with other providential means, speedily revolutionize the entire scope and plan of college instruction.

My father, about this time, commenced the manufacture of the apparatus in Boston, Massachusetts, which has since borne his name.

While attending school in Groton, my roommate and I occasionally took walks in the country. There is a beautiful lake east of Groton, some three miles, as I recollect it. One evening, returning from this lake, around which we had been picking huckleberries, we passed an orchard full of fine fruit. The ground was covered under many of the trees. We concluded to enter the orchard and help ourselves to some of the apples. Passing around among the trees, we filled our pockets, eating the meanwhile. Being just ready to return to the road with our supplies, we heard a voice angrily calling after us. My first impulse was to run, but being too plucky for that, I walked toward the man who was bawling at us. He met me half way, saying: "My boy, why didn't you run away like a thief, with that other fellow?" My roommate had scampered away down into the cranberry swamp, adjoining the orchard.

"I would rather pay for the apples I have taken."

"Pay for them? No, no. Come and get all the apples you want; only come and ask me, and I will find the best ones for you."

"Thank you, sir."

"But you tell that little rapscallion if he ever comes this way again, I'll horsewhip him."

More than fifty years after, a Miss Shattuck entered school here, from Groton, Massachusetts. Enquiring of her one day whereabouts in Groton she lived, she replied: "About two miles east of the old church." On the road out to the lake?" "Yes." "Did your house stand on the north side of the road, with an orchard and cranberry swamp on the south side?" "Yes. Why?" Then I told her the story of Charley Richards and myself stealing apples, and what the farmer said. "That is just like my grandfather; I have heard many such things of him, though I do not remember him."

CHAPTER III.

EXPERIENCE IN BOSTO]

My father, Josiah Holbrook, was a graduate of Yale in 1814. He was engaged with Professor Silliman as a student and laboratory worker in introducing chemistry as a practical science to his classes. He thus became interested in practical scientific work. The difficulty was, that as treated in Yale and other colleges, it was entirely beyond the public schools, where it was most needed. In fact, to this day, laboratory work is, in most colleges, deferred to the senior year, and even then hardly five per cent. of any graduating class engage in it. The class as a class listen to the lectures and witness the experiments, with what results is well known. Not one college graduate now in twenty really knows anything certainly or practically of the natural sciences, or is able to converse technically or intelligently on scientific subjects. On leaving college, father began applying his scientific knowledge to farming, in the training of about twenty young men to the application of scientific principles in their daily labor. They were also pursuing the ordinary college curriculum. This was the first manual labor school that I have any knowledge of. The young men obtained such a power in study on this practical plan, that several of them afterward became eminent in the different professions.

But the manual labor system was a financial loss to the originator. It has been a failure in the hundreds of attempts made since my father's experience.

His next enterprise was the organizing of lyceums, and to this end he invented and constructed simple and inexpensive articles of chemical and philosophical apparatus, reducing the price of an outfit from thousands to tens of dollars, thus bringing the actualities of scientific laboratory work within the reach of lyceums and the pupils of public schools. The apparatus now in use in our public schools, and in many colleges, was invented by my father, and first manufactured in his shops in Boston. Very few additional articles comparatively have been introduced since he left the business, even in electricity.

It thus will be seen that Josiah Holbrook was a practical educator, and was among the first to advocate the study of natural science. This training of the mind and hand together he urged as the most effectual method of mental and manly development.

When fifteen years of age, and all my schoolmates were going to college, I asked my father when I was going to college. He replied: "Alfred, I do not expect to send you to college. You are getting a better education now than any college can give, as colleges are now managed. I can give you double the amount of money required for a college course in some other way; but I do not wish you to waste so much time, and run such a risk of ruin as I did. I barely escaped, and I am not willing to expose my son to the temptations and dangers that I experienced in college life."

So I did not go to college, though I could not but think then that I was not very well used. I have since, however, fully concurred in my father's judgment.

Soon after this conversation, he proposed, as I was working ten hours per day in his apparatus manufactory, that I should rise at five o'clock and study an hour or two before breakfast, promising that he would make a room comfortable for me to study in, *i.e.*, lighted and warmed. Said I, "Pa, will you call me?" "No," he replied, "you will have to wake yourself; but when you have mastered Day's Algebra I will make you a present of a watch." "Will you help me?" "No, you can master it yourself." "I don't know; I'll try," said I, and accepted the proposition.

So in about a month I was wearing my watch. This was in the winter of 1830–31. I wore that watch for ten years or more.

No stimulus but the power of study has ever been needed since that time to rouse me at any fixed time in the morning to pursue my studies.

It encouraged me greatly when one day I overheard my father say, in advocating his plan of education (manual labor), that "Alfred was making better progress in his studies while working ten hours daily in the shop than most boys who were attending school and doing nothing else."

It was in the second year of my Boston life that I asked father to let me attend Mr. Pile's school. It was the most popular school in Boston at that time, for fitting boys for Harvard or Yale. More than this, I had become acquainted with Lowell Mason's two boys, about my age, and they were attending there. Father smiled, saying, "Alfred, you will not like it there; it will only be a hindrance to you." "But pa, I would like to try it, and if I don't like it, I won't be obliged to continue, I suppose." "Well, all right; here are ten dollars to pay your tuition; the experience you will get there may be worth something to you."

I attended one week, and asked father if I might quit, saying, "Why, I can learn more in one day, besides doing my work, than they go over there in three." "I am glad you are satisfied," said father; "the ten dollars were a good investment." I was studying Virgil at the time, with no regular recitation to father. He, however, occasionally quizzed me, to satisfy himself that my progress was safe and thorough. On such occasions, though his criticisms were rigid and exacting, I enjoyed them, and not unfrequently asked him to examine me in my studies. His reply was almost always something like this: "You are doing well enough. I want you to become independent of me as a student, just as far and as soon as possible."

By this kind and happy management my father aroused in me a controlling devotion to study and love of work. It has been my own salvation, and, I trust, the effectual means of saving and blessing thousands of others.

Speaking of the sons of Lowell Mason, Mr. Winthrop B. Smith, the founder of *the* Schoolbook House of the West, before he retired from business, told me the following (he was a roommate of mine in Boston):—

"I always stop with William Mason, one of the firm of Mason Bros., when in New York. Once, on arriving about 10 A. M., I went directly to Dr. Mason's room, where he was sitting at his piano, composing a piece of music. He welcomed me pleasantly, inquired how long I would remain in the city, etc. I went out about my business, but returned to dinner. As we were sitting at the table the doctor came down and greeted me most cordially, saying, 'It is a long time, Mr. Smith, since I have seen you; I fear you don't always call when in New York,' showing that he was unconscious of having welcomed me earlier in the day. On mentioning this to William, who was not at dinner, he replied: 'Oh, father is very much absorbed in music. It was only last month, when the panic (of 1857) struck us, and we were unable to meet our engagement at the bank, that I went to father's room, saying, "Father, I want you to go to Boston and get twenty thousand dollars; we are not able to raise the money here, and we must have it or have our note protested." Father replied: "Well, William, please don't interrupt me; I have an idea here that I am trying to work out; don't disturb me, I am afraid I shall lose it." "But father, we have to have the money, or we are all ruined. You must go to Boston and get it for us. We can't do anything there, and you can." (The doctor had been a bank director in Boston.) 'So,' continued William, 'I had to get father's coat and boots, and almost drag him to the cars.' He returned in due time with the money. Handing it to me, he said: "There, William, I hope you will never disturb me again; I have lost the idea, and fear I can not recover it. Never do it again, William." ' "

The second centennial of the settlement of Boston occurred in 1830. It was celebrated as Boston only can do such things. A procession was formed at the State House; the Governor and his staff led on horseback; and were followed by the "ancient and honorable artillery." Distinguished citizens and invited guests then came in carriages. Two bands furnished music for the march. John Quincy Adams was the speaker of the day. The

Old South Church was jammed to its utmost capacity; there was no more standing-room even in the second gallery. The long stanchions, extending from the floor thirty feet to support these galleries on three sides of the house, possibly gave the idea of insecurity. The Old South was the oldest church then standing in Boston. This fact was taken into consideration also. After the oration, which I heard standing near the pulpit on the lower floor, an anthem was being performed, accompanied by the great organ—the largest then on the continent. One of the back seats in the upper gallery, on which six or eight men were standing, broke with a crash. A panic ensued. Everybody rushed for the nearest door. Screams of women were heard as they were crushed in the stairways. The organist, by some fortuity, intensified the general fright by placing both his arms on the keys, several heavy stops of the organ being in connection. In the midst of all this chaos and rage of the elements, a thundering voice was heard—"There is no danger; the house is as firm as the everlasting hills!" Quiet was instantly restored; the panic was over; all returned to their places; the anthem proceeded, and the exercises closed as usual. It was the voice of the god-like that stilled the storm—it was Daniel Webster's.

My father's office was at the corner of Washington and School Streets. His office and salesrooms for his apparatus occupied the whole of the second story. Carter & Hendee occupied the ground floor as a book-store. It was *the* book-store of Boston then; it is a book-store still. The same old two-story building stands there now, while contiguous, and all around in every direction, are seen immense structures of five and six stories. This old corner is an interesting locality to me and my children when we visit Boston. All who visit Boston take in the Old South, corner of Washington and Milk Streets, as one of the sights. It is now the repository of all the odd, queer, out-of-date articles gathered from old garrets and other stowaway places, illustrating the social usages and bygone customs of earlier days. It is an interesting place to spend an hour in.

The first Sabbath night after I arrived in Boston, being then 14 years of age, I was aroused by the clang of the Old South bell, about midnight. My room was as light as day, though it was a stormy and moonless night. I had never seen a "fire" before. The cry of "fire" ringing through the streets, the jingle of the bells on the fire-engines, and the bawling of the trumpets all contributed to my alarm; but I had nothing else to do than to lie quiet till my father, sleeping in another room, should order me out; though I thought the room felt hot already. No father's voice was heard. I began to think he had gone out and forgotten his boys, and was just about to get up and take care of myself and get out if the fire would let me, when I heard some one say, who had just entered the house, that Dr. Beecher's church was burning. Now I had already learned that his church was more than a mile distant from Sewall Place, where we were boarding; my fears subsided, I dropped off to sleep, and knew no more till morning, when, of course, we all visited the ruins.

Now, it was rather a singular circumstance that, as we considered Dr. Beecher the head and front of the first temperance movement, we should see in the streets near the ruins, piles and piles of casks of all sizes, labeled wine, brandy, etc., etc. It was, however, explained in a measure, when we learned that the cellars of the church were not under Dr. Beecher's control. They had been used, possibly, by some of his church-members as storerooms for this kind of merchandise. I afterward attended Dr. Beecher's services. He, with his congregation, worshiped at the Park Street Church. Lowell Mason was the organist and choir leader. It was rather amusing to hear those say who attended there nearly every Sabbath, on returning from preaching, that Beecher had preached the most powerful sermon they ever heard. For once this would have been well enough; but as a recurring fact that any man had done the most powerful thing ever heard of, was to me a little funny, to say the least. That winter the doctor gave a course of Sunday evening lectures on Catholicism. Multitudes went away from the house on every such occasion, unable to find standing room even.

The preacher himself found entrance at a back window, and was aided by the police in making his way to the pulpit. The Catholic Bishop attempted to answer Beecher. I was present at one of these attempts—the only time I ever made a part of a cathedral congregation. The jam was fearful. Though the night was intensely cold, the house was hot and foul with exhalations of tobacco and whisky. A woman fainted near the altar. She had to be sent out over the heads of those crowding the aisles. A priest cried out, "Open the windows in the galleries!" All the upper windows of the immense building were opened. Though the night was clear without, the cold air entering and sweeping through the moist atmosphere produced a dense cloud, extending through all the upper part of the building. It was a phenomenon. But shortly a fall of snow covered all on the lower floor—the only snow-storm I ever saw in clear weather, or inside of a cathedral.

We were accustomed to obtain most of our hardware for the manufacture of apparatus from Bradley's hardware establishment on Washington Street, just north of the Old South Church. I became well acquainted with the head clerk, Thompson. Mr. Bradley had advanced him from an errand boy to the position of confidential clerk. Contrary to the wishes of his employer, he had formed an attachment for his daughter, and the attachment was ardently reciprocated. Every influence was used by the parents to prevent the match; the daughter was sent away to school, was sent to Europe, but every such means, as usual in such cases, only seemed to endear the young people to each other the more. They both declared, and always, they would never marry without her parents' consent. Their objection to the young man as a son-in-law was not known. It was conjectured that they had formed a more ambitious alliance for their daughter with one of the first families of Boston, but this was only conjectured. That there was no objection to his moral or business character, was apparent from the fact that Mr. Bradley proposed to Thompson that if he would give up his design upon the daughter he would send him to New Orleans and set him up in the hardware business there.

Thompson accepted the proposition. The goods were purchased, a vessel was chartered and Thompson was to sail with the goods on a certain night. It was supposed that he had gone with the vessel.

The next morning the boy who usually opened and swept the store, was unable to open the door. There was a key, or other obstruction, in the lock. He reported at once to Mr. Bradley, who hastened to the store and effected an entrance. Nothing was disturbed on the shelves or the cases or drawers below. The boy went up into the several stories and found everything all right. He came down and reported accordingly. He was asked if he had gone into the garret, for Mr. Bradley found his own key in the door inside, and he feared something terrible. The boy went to the garret, and there found Thompson and Miss Bradley hanging from a rafter dead in each other's arms.

So ended this love story. It was a matter of universal horror, and yet of condolence. But the discussion of the catastrophe frequently ended with something like this, Why didn't they run away and get married? or, Why couldn't the old folks trust the young man with their daughter, when they were willing to trust him with everything else?

It was finally ascertained that the parents' objection to the young man was, that he was an infidel, and they felt they could not consent to place their daughter and her children under such influences.

After my father had accumulated over $20,000 in cash and in stock from his apparatus business, he planned a tour through all the States, with the design of arousing a general and national interest in his views and plans of education. Hoping to secure legislative action favorable to the general organization of lyceums in every town and village, he visited nearly every capital and addressed the legislature convened, or a committee appointed for the purpose. His letters expressed great encouragement that his plans would be generally adopted, and that lyceums, through the legislative action promised, would become as common as public schools, and would exert an influence for immeasurable good in turning the minds of the people to scientific inquiry and investigation, thus developing in an unprecedented manner the agricultural, manufacturing and mining resources of every State and community. He had already secured the law for the first geological survey in the United States. It was accomplished in part by placing a small cabinet of fifty minerals on the desk of each Senator and Representative in the Massachusetts State House. I had the pleasure and the advantage of selecting and preparing these cabinets under my father's direction.

CHAPTER IV.

MY TEACHERS.

My first teacher, whom I do not remember as such, was my aunt Theodosia Swift, my mother's oldest sister. I heard my aunts and others say that my father, not long after my birth, offered this aunt a new silk dress as soon as Alfred learned to read in the Testament, and that this my first teacher obtained before Alfred was three years old. Of this I know nothing further than by report. The first teacher that I do remember, was a Miss Julia Ann Tomlinson, who taught a summer-school in the old Academy at Derby, which stood on Science Hill, near where the old First Congregational Church stood, in my early recollections. Miss Julia Ann was very popular with the children. Not infrequently she gave us little prizes, of ribbons round the neck with some coin attached, sometimes little pictures and drawings which she made herself, more frequently perhaps, kisses, both for boys and girls, and she was always remembered by all her pupils with kindness and affection. Her modes of punishment were not specially peculiar for that day. I remember very well of wearing the foolscap, and of sitting on the dunce-block, but it was a rare misdemeanor that brought down upon me, as a culprit, the punishment of sitting beside a little flaxen-haired girl two years younger than myself.

I suppose, though I don't remember distinctly, that there was a good deal of whimpering by the punishee, but whether it was sham or in earnest, I am not able to tell now. But it seems to me that I do remember the picture of the little lassie who was made the means of punishment. But this may be more a matter of imagination than of memory. Years afterward, she certainly was not a punishment or a bugbear; but the greatest blessing that heaven ever bestowed upon a man. She was the mother of all my children. Some years after this happened, when my wife and I were visiting Derby, and called upon Mrs. Julia Ann Tomlinson Blakeman, my recollections of her methods of discipline were not fully corroborated by her statement of the case. Nor did the rod of affliction who was with me, realize that she had ever been made use of for such a disciplinary purpose. Nevertheless, I am confident that all those things took place in the manner above described, but there is one thing Mrs. Blakeman declared to be true, which I had forgotten, and that is, she did put the split quill on my nose at a certain date for a distinct offense.* What the offense was, she was unable to recall, but it was something terrible which she would not tell, if she could remember.

My next teacher and the only district-school teacher with whom I ever came in contact, I shall call Dr. Goodson. He was employed by district authorities to bring the school into order, after the pupils had behaved so badly that they became unmanageable under a college graduate from Yale College. Dr. Goodson was a thoroughgoing teacher, after the principles then in vogue. His methods of government were whipping for whispering, whipping for throwing spit-balls, whipping for tardiness, whipping for staying out late at recess, standing in the corner for not getting lessons in time, standing in the corner and holding a book out at arm's length, for playing "baker's dozen" and "three men Morris;" and sometimes, in rare cases when these varieties of discipline failed to have their effect, the "foolscap" was applied, and the "dunce-block" was resorted to, and the split quill placed upon the nose of the offender while sitting on the dunce-block. For leaving seats, laughing aloud, and other like improprieties, all these were combined as being necessary to correct waywardness and stubbornness. Looking out of the windows was also forbidden, and received the penalty of standing up in the corner with the face toward the corner. Other teachers of those days were accustomed to apply the ferule, but our school being near a row of quince trees in an adjoining garden lot, Dr. Goodson found it more convenient and salutary to apply quince tree sprouts to the back of the offender. In extreme cases, the culprit was compelled to take off his coat, and one or more of those quince sprouts were applied, according to the heinousness of the offense. At the coming of the first ice, the boys all remained out to slide, the girls passing in at the call of the ruler rapped on the side of the house. At the second or third rap, it being louder than the previous one, the boys went in. There were about twenty involved in this disregard of regulations and good order. We were all called up for the administration of suitable penalty. We were marshaled in line upon the longest clear crack in the floor of the room, each toeing the crack. The tallest boy, Jim Smith, taller than the teacher himself, stood at the head of the row; Alfred, the least of all, stood at the foot. One of the good boys, who had not gone out to play at all, but had remained in to study, was sent to the aforesaid quince trees, with orders to bring in two or three dozen whips. The good faithful Doctor applied one whip most conscientiously to the back of each of the several boys, until, coming to the last one, he said, in sympathy and consideration, "Why, Alfred, you are so little, I guess I will let you go this time." Now, the Doctor was an honest, Christian worker. Whatever he did was done most faithfully and conscientiously, and especially that of whipping the boys, so that I was very glad just

3

at that moment that I was so little. So much for public school discipline.

The methods of instruction were such as were prevalent in those days. We were all required to do the sums printed in Daboll's Arithmetic, and to get the answers, the slates being examined as often as they were filled with figures. If any one was puzzled and needed help, it was customary for him to go and stand by the Doctor's desk, until his turn came, when his example would be solved on the Doctor's slate, examined by the pupil, and the pupil required to work out the same example, himself, on his own slate at his own desk. This individual system, which is so much lauded nowadays by a certain class of institutions, was then, over sixty years ago, in full and successful operation, doing its best to make pupils thorough, "and not keeping any pupil back, to accommodate the slow ones in the class." To be thorough, every one must work every example and get every answer, and every example thus wrought, must be examined by the Doctor, before further progress could be made. I am a little fearful that the present advocates of the individual system are not quite so thorough, faithful and patient as was my old teacher. Dillworth's spelling-book had just gone out of date, and Webster's had just come in.

The only classes that I remember of being taught as classes in Dr. Goodson's school, were the reading and spelling classes. Great attention was paid in those times to the ability to spell all the words in the spelling-book, commencing at "baker." And if there was any keeping after school for the purpose of making up lost time, and inflicting punishment for laziness or stupidity, it was to learn our spelling lessons. Willet's geography, with its old, blurred and dim maps, was in use, but I was not sufficiently advanced to study geography with Dr. Goodson. However, the same individual system was pursued in the geography class, and he heard a pupil recite whenever he felt like it, or the pupil was prepared. The directions given to the pupils in common, and to individuals especially, in the reading class, were such as these: "You must not read so fast." "You must not skip your words." "You must pronouce every word distinctly." "You must mind your stops; if you don't do better I will count for you at every stop, one for every comma, two for every semi-colon, three for every colon, and six for every period." These are my most salient recollections of my district school experience, so far as indoor work was concerned. The plays of those times, more than sixty years ago, were very similar to the plays of the present time. Some of these were "base-ball," in which we chose sides, "one hole cat," "two hole cat," "knock up and catch," "blackman," "snap the whip," skating, sliding down hill, rolling the hoop, marbles, "prisoner's base," "football," mumble the peg," etc.

In the school-room, the only apparatus was slate

and pencil, ferule, and the quince tree whip. No blackboards, no desks, save an inclined wide board in front of the seats stretched along the side of the house, with a shelf underneath the long desk; no prepared fuel, the boys being required to cut and bring in wood by turns. The stove had been very recently introduced; the open fireplace still remained to receive the debris of the catastrophies and mischief of the day, and the remnants of the dinner baskets, etc. Such were the facilities and appointments of my only district school.

The privileges are implied in these questions, "May I speak?" "May I go out?" "May I go to the fire?" "May I get some water?" "May I sit with John?" "May I borrow a pencil?" All of which interrogations were mostly complied with, by our really kind and faithful teacher. It was customary in those early days in all schools in New England to use the Testament as a reading book. And when Sallie Morris, an adopted girl, read, "And he rebuked the winds, and there was a great *clam*," we were not so pious or devout that we could not smile aloud on that, and like occasions. When the aforesaid boy, Jim Smith, who did not enjoy his school-work especially, and for that reason was not a remarkably prompt and ready reader, requested me, sitting beside him one morning, to help him when he came to the hard word Jerusalem in the sentence, "Christ went up," etc., and I helped him by saying, "*a bean-pole*," Jim brought down the house, to use a modern expression. For this successful accomplishment I might have had my bones broken, if I had not had a sufficiency of protection and protectors.

Those school days were on the whole profitable, and the children, for aught I know, made about as good improvement as is found in the more recent forms of punishment, incitement and discipline outside of true normal training.

My next teacher was my father, who, having been absent from Derby for three or four years, in the business of scientific lecturing, in the various towns and villages of New England, returned, and in company with Truman Coe, his brother-in-law, took possession of the old academy, and organized, developed and built up very rapidly, a large and prosperous school. I remember, quite distinctly, the boys and young men from all parts of the United States, and from nearly all the leading towns and cities of New England. My experiences in this school, under my father's direction, were altogether delightful and profitable. He gave courses of lectures with apparatus of his own construction, upon physics and chemistry, and had classes in botany and astronomy, in all of which classes I found myself (being the youngest, then about nine years of age) deeply interested and thoroughly absorbed. Woodbridge's Geography was introduced at this period; classes were formed in all the different branches, and regular recitations were conducted, with a system of grading; although I do not remember that any special prizes were offered, save that these grades were reported to the parents of the boys and girls in attendance. The boys and girls were incited to collect minerals from the the bowlders which abound in all that region, my father aiding them in analyzing, naming and classifying them. I was as eager as a boy well could be in the examination of all the odd places where others were not accustomed to go. One day, in digging and searching in a deep old ravine on Science Hill, I came upon a peculiar-looking bowlder, which excited my curiosity. I made out to break it open. The yellow, glittering substance which revealed itself to my astonished eyes, excited me beyond measure. Taking a small fragment of the golden discovery in my hand, and running at the very top of my speed to the academy, with great excitement I presented to father this wonderful find of "solid gold," not telling him where I had found it. "Well, Alfred," said father, "you have made a discovery, but you never heard of the great discovery they made at Jamestown, Virginia, did you?" "No, sir. What was it?" "Why, they did worse than you; they loaded a ship with the same kind of material you have here, and took it to England, supposing that they had all made their fortunes. But sad was their disappointment when they found that instead of gold it was merely 'Fool's Gold,' sulphuret of iron. So you are not the first one that has been made a fool of by that mineral." It is not necessary to say that my feelings collapsed, though I was hardly willing to take the word of my father against my own eyes. But he convinced me by taking some portion of it and pounding it, when the hammer reduced it to mere dust. Taking then a gold coin which he happened to have in his pocket, he showed me there was quite a difference between true gold and the false.

It was customary for father to make excursions with the pupils, about the neighborhood, for the purpose of finding every variety of mineral that existed in the bowlders, also specimens for botanical analysis. These excursions were enjoyed exceedingly. I remember an excursion to Monroe, Connecticut, where I afterward taught. The object of this excursion was to investigate a mine where fluor spar and copper were said to be found. The place was reached and thoroughly examined, and some inferior specimens of fluor spar were obtained, but much better specimens, were purchased from those in the neighborhood. Our most interesting excursion was on the first steamboat ever on the Housatonic River, having been brought there by Captain Thomas Vose, with the design of plying between Derby and New York City. Our excursion only extended as far as Stratford, at the mouth of the Housatonic River. The object of the excursion was the finding of seashells upon the beach, of digging clams, and if possible to find the *habitat* of oysters. By some defect in the machinery, we failed to reach our destination. Nevertheless, it was a delightful day, and all the students and others enjoyed it immensely. A circumstance happened in the dining-saloon, which I heard my father relate afterward several times, in his conversations, as a rare instance of self-control.

Now, sea-captains like Captain Vose, who had retired but very recently from the sea, are not proverbial for the gentleness, purity or piety of their expressions, even on comparatively slight provocations. Captain Vose was not above the average of his class, as his neighbors well knew; but on this occasion, as the servant was carrying out on a large tray as many dishes as he could manage, by some means or other he let the tray and its contents fall, shattering the dishes, and scattering the fragments. Captain Vose, being present, instead of ripping and tearing with his oaths and curses, as was expected, simply remarked: "John, I am really afraid it will take you too long to gather up all these pieces; I think I will have to help you."

The popularity of the school increased, and considerable patronage was drawn from New York City, the West Indies and Canada. Many students came from wealthy families, and their use of money was lavish, and in most cases quite detrimental to their progress, health and personal habits. The only difficulty that I remember that my father had with any of these young men, was with young Poindexter, from Georgia. He was accustomed to bet heavily on any species of gambling on which he could find others willing to bet with him. One Saturday afternoon, he offered to bet $25 with anybody against $5, that he could shoot a ball through a suspended silk handkerchief fluttering in the wind. There was a drinking fellow about, who was foolish enough to take up the bet, or at least said he would bet $5 against $25 that Poindexter could not do it. Poindexter failed in the experiment, and, as it happened, did not have the $25 to pay the bet with. But in order to ease off the matter, he bet the same fellow that he could not take up an empty flour barrel, lying near, and carry it to the top of the hill, and never lay it down. It was but a short distance to the top of the hill. This was $1 against $25. "Beers Hotchkiss," as we always called the fellow, started with the barrel toward the top of the hill, with his usual springhalt when he was tipsy. The boys at the same time cried: "Beers, *never* lay it down, remember! *Never* lay it down!" "Oh, you go to h——, I will take care of that." And so he ascended the hill with the crowd accompanying him. He then found a spike projecting from the side of a house, on which he hung his barrel, and won the second bet. Poindexter was so chagrined, and the boys laughed at him so heartily, that he charged around extensively, and did considerable damage, he himself not being entirely free from the effects of liquor. The matter came up to my father for adjudication, and the citizens, with some of the leading pupils, declared that such conduct should not be passed by, that the young man ought to be expelled. He was a disgrace to the school, and a nuisance to the town, etc. While of course father did not in any sense apologize for Poindexter, or extenuate the folly and wickedness of his conduct, he declared that whoever had been wronged should prosecute him. It was not his business to control Poindexter, or any other pupils, in any relations other than those immediately connected with the school.

My recollections of the closing of the school are very faint, but this I know, that at the close of the second year, father left the school, and commenced his career, the establishing of lyceums.

My next teacher was Mr. Saunders, a recent graduate of Yale, who had opened a private school in Derby Narrows during my absence. With him I commenced the study of Latin and algebra. The book I used, which father had given me, was Colburn's Primary Algebra, in which all the subjects were developed by examples rather than by rules. No answers were given to the problems. Mr. Saunders had never studied this text-book, and when I thought he would be puzzled with any knotty problem to be solved, I took some pride in working it out myself, and after I had done so, asking Mr. Saunders to work it for me. There was a student who had been suspended from West Point boarding at Mrs. Allen's house, the same place where Mr. Saunders boarded. He informed me that Mr. Saunders had come to him several times to solve the said examples. When I told the West Pointer that I had solved them, but was amusing myself by seeing Mr. Saunders stalled, he would hardly believe me, but took it upon himself to test my assertions and satisfy himself that I had solved every example that Mr. Saunders had brought him. We, from that time, formed a kind of conspiracy against the teacher, to see how much shuffling and prevarication we could get out of him. Mr. Saunders was preparing to be a minister, and we were wicked enough to make use of our opportunity to place him (in our estimation) in a very unfavorable light. But the power developed in the combination of circumstances connected with it seemed to assure me that I could pursue mathematics to any extent without the aid of any teacher. I was then but twelve years of age. This power has been tested since, and I need hardly say that I have never called upon any one for help in reading any of the mathematical authors that I have used in the various classes that I have taught since. Of course I do not narrate this circumstance to vindicate or show my approval of the principle, or want of principle, which evoked this mathematical power, but I narrate it to show how Mr. Saunders, as my teacher, wrought in me a decided advance, and by his training, or want of training, established a degree of independence which, perhaps, no honest teacher, as teachers are mostly accustomed to manage, would have done.

I commenced the study of Latin also, at least of Latin grammar, with Mr. Saunders. There were several other pupils in the class, young ladies and gentlemen, also my brother Dwight, living then at my grandfather's. The study of Latin grammar was chiefly memorizing paradigms of nouns, adjectives, pronouns, verbs, etc.; also rules, remarks, observations, exceptions and explanations in an endless array. My younger brother was in the same class, and rather than submit to such continued demands upon his patience and industry, without seeing any possible returns, he preferred to submit to a feruling once or twice a day. Nor was he ever persuaded afterward to give any serious study to Latin, or any other branch, such was the determined hostility that he conceived to study under this abominable management. But this was the common and accepted method of teaching Latin in those days, and virtually continues to the present day, to a large extent, with most teachers who have been trained in colleges or by college teachers. Well may such an abuse of the human mind, merely to follow the long sanctioned usage of college instruction, be called the *college fetich.*

The only time that I was ever whipped in school was by this same college teacher, Mr. Saunders. It happened on this wise: As was the custom, I was writing in my copy-book after the copies set by the teacher, when my seat-mate, a man of twenty years, commenced pulling my copy-book away from me. Of course, I held on to it. Mr. Saunders, seeing the contest, and feeling that he ought to check the disorder occasioned, and that it was necessary to make an example of somebody, called me up (the little, weak one), and belabored one hand after the other most cruelly, with a heavy ferule, giving the real cause of the disturbance scarcely a reproof. The indignation of the students was beyond control, and Mr. Saunders found himself the object of increased disfavor and hostility until he was compelled to close the school.

Soon after this I was called by my father to Groton, Mass., where I found him boarding with the Rev. John Todd. I was entered as a student of Groton Academy, under the instruction of Mr. Elizur Wright. Both these gentlemen have since become celebrated, each in his line; the Rev. Todd as a noted evangelist and popular preacher, and by his founding several educational institutions. His biography, written by his son, is more exciting and interesting than any novel. Mr. Todd was my special admiration as a preacher, story-teller, mechanic and friend. His interest in my studies was a great incitement to the highest possible effort. I was placed in classes consisting almost entirely of adults preparing for teaching and for college, about three weeks after they had commenced their study in arithmetic, English grammar and natural philosophy. My pride and ambition were to pass a better examination than any of these young ladies and gentlemen at the close of the term, and such was the energy and industry aroused by the combined management of Mr. Todd and Mr. Wright, that when the term expired I was assured by Mr. Wright that I stood among the very first in this class of adults, being myself a little spindling boy of twelve years. I remember Mr. Wright as the best teacher, aside from my father, that I ever had. His ingenuity in planning methods of exciting enthusiasm in his students, and his genial bearing toward us all, had a peculiar influence upon me, who had just come from under a regime so austere and unreasonable and unjust as that of Mr. Saunders. It is true, Mr. Wright's methods were college methods, chiefly memorizing the text-book and working the examples and getting the answers; but the spirit of the school, and the respect that all the pupils had for the kindness and genial spirit of our teacher, made work which had before been very repulsive quite attractive and exciting. I don't remember that he ever punished a pupil or kept one after school, or, in fact, had any special occasion even for administering rebuke. Mr. Wright in those days was an acceptable member of the Congregational Church, of which John Todd was the pastor. Since then, however, he has been a leader in all sorts of infidel operations.

Another of my worthy teachers, who was not professionally such, was Dr. Samuel Beech, of Stamford, Connecticut. He married my aunt, Mary Swift, and was a popular physician in Stamford and for all that region. My health failing the second time in Massachusetts, I returned to Derby. When sufficiently recovered, I was invited by Dr. Beech to spend some time with him. Soon after going there, I obtained the position of assistant postmaster in the distributing office of that place. My business training in the post-office has been of very considerable value to me ever since. An immense amount of mail matter passed through this post-office, coming from all quarters, and being distributed from this Central District Office. The worthy postmaster, a Mr. Brown, was a farmer of very considerable business ability, an ardent Democratic politician, and a very genial gentleman. He made my position a very pleasant one. Several clerks were employed during the hours of distribution of mail. I was, however, in charge of the office at other hours, and with the help of another clerk, kept the books of the office. Long tiers of boxes and pigeon-holes were ranged in cases for the distribution of the mail matter. On one occasion, the postmaster being present, aiding us in the distribution, having taken from the mail-bag a package too large to handle, placed part of it, some twenty or thirty letters, on the top of one of these cases. This pile of letters remained there for three weeks, and might have remained there much longer, had I not taken into my head to dust off the tops of these cases.' The pile of letters was discovered, and was found to be valuable letters, all from New Orleans to Boston, containing, nobody knows how much of money and drafts. How much interference with business this accident occasioned, one can only conjecture; but doubtless much delay and disappointment to all parties concerned.

Dr. Beech was especially kind, and cordially interested in my well-being. A very intelligent and well-read gentleman; he delighted to draw me out on all subjects on which I was competent to talk, frequently taking me in his sulky on his professional visits, and occupying the time of our rides in the most agreeable and exciting lines of conversation. His object was undoubtedly to aid me in rapid, correct and coherent expression. This was not, however, done in the line of instruction, but rather for the purpose of mutual entertainment, he being a man of forty and I a boy of sixteen years. The Doctor had been a great reader himself, and had traveled more or less, and was familiar with current literature, and had a good library. He did not spare any of these resources in making my stay with him interesting and useful. After the distributing post-office was removed to New York City, the Doctor, wishing to furnish me something to do, purchased quite an extensive circulating library, and a considerable stock of drugs, putting me in charge of both. This, he said, would furnish me an opportunity of extending my reading, as the books he selected were such as I desired to read. Almost daily, or whenever an opportunity offered, he was ready to converse with me upon any topic which I had read, or any subject in which he was interested.

Having previously become acquainted with Dr. Jennings, and having known something of his theory about medicine, I took it upon myself to venture the opinion that all medicines were injurious any further than they excited the imagination of the patient, and by that means affording help to the working of the resources of nature in restoration to health. This was a new subject of discussion and comment, the Doctor maintaining and demonstrating, I have no doubt to his own satisfaction, that medicines under his own prescriptions were generally effectual as remedies. He cited numerous examples where disease had continued for weeks and months, and yielded immediately to his application of the proper remedies. I still maintained on my side of the argument that in every such case it might be possible that the disease had reached its crisis about the time that the medicine had been administered, and that the patient would probably have recovered quite as quickly, if not more quickly, if the supposed remedy had not been used. Thus the Doctor and I kept up the discussion, always returning to it whenever other subject matter failed. The Doctor was very patient with my pertinacity, and perhaps did not more than half believe that I was in earnest, nor was I very sure of my ground. The Doctor, however, was one of my most interesting teachers, and aided me very much, as was his object, in enlarging my talking vocabulary. I had written considerably before this, but never enjoyed so desirable an opportunity of expressing myself coherently and argumentatively with a competent interlocutor. I remember the Doctor with a great deal of satisfaction and gratitude.

In illustrating the Doctor's character still further, I will briefly relate an incident occurring after he removed to Bridgeport, Connecticut. The leading physician in Bridgeport had been a Dr. Summers, an ardent politician. The dissatisfaction which prevailed among the leading families of Bridgeport, with the moral character of Dr. Summers, was perhaps what led them to invite Dr. Beech from Stamford to Bridgeport. He speedily secured a good practice in Bridgeport, to the no small discomfiture of Dr. Summers, who spared no opportunity of traducing and abusing Dr. Beech behind his back. He had his emissaries here and there and everywhere with special instructions to misrepresent the Doctor's practice, and to set in circulation false reports, not only against his professional work, but also against his personal character. But the Doctor's friends were on the alert, and the efforts of Dr. Summers recoiled upon himself.

A traveler had stopped at the hotel where Dr.

Summers was accustomed to hold forth, and where, indeed, he had his office, and was taken sick there. Dr. Beech was called to attend to the case. As he entered the office of the hotel to inquire where the patient could be found, he saw Dr. Summers. Walking up to him, he very genially offered his hand, and passed the compliments with him as he would with any other gentleman, regardless of all the vile work of Dr. Summers. As Dr. Beech passed out of the office, the bystanders expressed their surprise that the two doctors should meet so kindly, who were at swords' points—they only having heard Summers' side of the matter. Summers replied: "Oh, well, Beech is such a —— —— gentleman, that I can't do a thing with him, anyhow. I might as well let him run and do his worst."

Another instance of Dr. Beech's penetration and general information I remember very distinctly. My Aunt Mary and I were sitting at the dinner table, when Dr. Beech, coming in hastily, said: "Alfred, there is a gentleman over here at the hotel, a splendid-looking man, a magnificent specimen; I want you to go and see him; I never saw so remarkable a head in all my life." I went over immediately with the doctor, and we passed through the hall toward the door into the dining-room. The moment I saw the stranger, I recognized him as Daniel Webster, and announced the fact to Dr. Beech, saying, also, that I had my suspicions that it was he; for I thought there was no other man in America, or elsewhere, who had the intellect which his physiognomy indicated. I had seen Mr. Webster frequently in Boston.

My grandfather Holbrook I never knew, as he died about the time of my birth; but my maternal grandfather, Zephaniah Swift, holds a venerated place among my teachers. Among my earliest recollections are my pleasant visits and play-days with Aunt Persis and Uncle Urbane. They were respectively two and four years older than I; but we were much together in my childhood life, as schoolmates and as playmates. Although our Sabbaths were of the Puritan cast, subject to the rigorous restraints coming down from the previous Puritan ancestors, and it was unlawful to whistle and wicked to find one's self in any kind of amusement, or in reading any books that were not of the most devout character; yet, by some means, we managed to make our Sabbaths quite tolerable, and it was really a treat for me to spend the Sabbath at my grandfather's with this uncle and aunt. Then again, there were spinning visits and social visits and Thanksgivings as extra occasions, when all Puritan restraints seemed to be forgotten, and young, joyous life seemed to make reprisals for its subjugation on Sabbath and fast-days.

Now, it was both unlawful and wicked to play ball on fast-day, and none of my associates in town were ever known to engage in such unholy enterprises and sinful amusements on fast-days;

but other wicked boys, with whom I had nothing to do, made it their special delight and boast to get together in some quiet, concealed place, and enjoy themselves, more especially because it was a violation of law. Not infrequently, however, they found the constable after them, or other officers of the peace. On one occasion I remember hearing one of those bad boys relate with great gusto a trick they served the constable, who had gone after them. They managed to place themselves on the remote side of a deep ditch, across which they had thrown a couple of planks. These planks they had carefully sawed underneath, so that any one stepping upon them would be sure to go down with the planks into the water. They, of course, were playing near the planks, and when the officer came they took to their heels, but did not retreat so far but that they could see the fun and hear the officer call for help. They gathered about him and offered to help him out if he would agree not to apprehend them. The water was very cold, and after he had floundered around for awhile, the boys found a rail, and helped him out.

Soon after, this blue law, perhaps the only one in the Connecticut Code, was repealed. Then the boys thought no more of playing on fast-days than on any other. The testimony of my grandfather and grandmother, and of all my aunts and uncles, against such wickedness, and the expressions of contempt, mingled with pity, in which they depicted those engaged in these law-breaking amusements, no doubt had their influence in training us children and grandchildren to a respect for the laws and for the proprieties of life. Our Sabbaths, however, always ended at sundown, having begun the night previous at sundown. No cows were milked before sundown on Sabbath, nor other chores done, but Saturday night all work was completed and laid aside before sundown. This arrangement at my grandfather's, which was also adhered to by all my Presbyterian relatives, involved me once in a sad dilemma. It was in the springtime, when hoop-rolling was having its turn, an amusement in which I thought I excelled, and therefore enjoyed, being able to roll the hoop farther and faster than any of my competitors. So it happened one cloudy Sunday afternoon, when I had not consulted the clock or the almanac very carefully to ascertain what time the sun was setting, or was about to set, I was out on the street rolling my hoop. This being duly reported to my grandparents, caused them a great deal of grief. That their grandson should be so lawless, and have so little respect for their feelings, as to roll a hoop in the public streets on Sabbath day, was almost more than they could bear. This happened when I was about eight or nine years of age, as nearly as I can remember. I only relate it to show the interest that my grandparents took in my moral training. When I came to explain to them that I was mistaken about the time, and thought the sun was down, and had no design whatever of breaking the Sabbath, and would not have done so for anything, their grief was mollified and their good will restored.

My grandfather's house was frequently called the "Ministers' Tavern." It was certainly a place of very frequent resort for ministers of all classes, especially for those who had earned the opprobrious title of "Everlasting Candidate." I have known such individuals to remain at my grandfather's for weeks, and be treated with all courtesy and kindness. One especially, Mr. Griswold, I hold in anything but sacred remembrance. It was customary for the boys to occupy one side of the gallery of the Presbyterian Church and the girls the other. It was a hard task for the boys to give their continued attention to the long, prosy sermons of those days, and it was not an uncommon thing for a group of boys in the gallery to engage in some more edifying, or at least, more amusing, occupation than that of listening to the preacher. On one occasion like this, when Mr. Griswold was occupying the pulpit, some one or two boys giggled loud enough to attract Mr. Griswold's attention. Shutting his Bible with a violent noise, he said: "Boys, boys, boys! there in the gallery, make less noise! I am afraid you will wake your parents below!" No doubt the parents were aroused by this time.

Mr. Griswold had a peculiar management of his eyes. It seemed to us boys that, while one eye was directed to his manuscript, which he read in continuity, the other eye was wandering around the galleries, looking after the boys, to see what they were about. After this attack upon our peace and amusements, we became a little more discreet, and, perhaps, practiced more concealment in our arrangements for our amusements.

My grandfather took immediate action upon the subject of temperance as soon as Dr. Lyman Beecher's twelve sermons reached him. He spared no effort to secure the signatures to the pledge against the use of distilled liquors from all the members of his church and congregation. To this end he invited Mr. Brewster, of carriage-making fame, from New Haven, and a Mr. Gilbert, a reformed drunkard, to lecture in his church on the subject of temperance. These were the first temperance lectures I ever heard. Mr. Brewster, being an educated man, gave an ornate and somewhat effective exhortation on the subject of temperance, but Mr. Gilbert carried the audience with him. In relating his experiences, his fall, his sufferings, and the wrongs he had inflicted on his family and on the church, his deliverance by means of the pledge, he swayed the audience, though an uneducated man, as I had never known before; now in tears and sobs all over the house, then again in irrepressible laughter. The result of these lectures was, that when the pledge was circulated, every member of my grandfather's church signed the pledge, except two deacons, Deacon S—— and

Deacon C——. Grandfather had previously used his personal influence as far as possible with these gentlemen. Each one had his own special reason for not signing the pledge, and they were such reasons as are prevalent at this time. "I don't want to sign away my liberty; I don't drink except when I need it; I have no objection to others signing it if they feel it necessary. If I ever feel so, I will sign the pledge. As I now feel, it will be declaring that I have lost control of myself, and am obliged to pledge myself in order to keep from drinking too much, which certainly is not the case." The more my grandfather talked with these gentlemen, the more he became convinced that they, more than any others, needed the restraining influence of the pledge, and that they were both, to a greater or less degree, the slaves of cider brandy. Hoping still to reach them and to extricate them from the snare in which he found them, grandfather employed Dr. Hewitt, of Bridgeport, a powerful preacher, to fill his pulpit on a certain Sabbath, and to preach or lecture on temperance in the evening. Practicing perhaps a little wiliness, it was not announced on what subject Dr. Hewitt would preach in the evening, my grandfather fearing that since so much had been said and done with and for the deacons, that they would fail to be present if they knew that Dr. Hewitt was to preach on temperance, especially as they would know, of course, that the preaching was aimed chiefly at them. A large congregation assembled, Dr. Hewitt's reputation as an orator being sufficient to fill a house anywhere. The deacons were present. What his text was, I do not remember, but the sermon was a temperance sermon, and effectual in a manner that grandfather hardly anticipated. It was one of those sermons that everybody listens to with unremitting attention and cumulative interest. The application of his sermon was something like this: "Brethren, from all these considerations which I have presented, you will agree with me that that one of our fellow-citizens, who does not permit his name and his influence to be used to check such a dire flood of iniquity and destruction as is sweeping over the land, and carrying with it so many thousands of victims, is, to say the least, chargeable with a want of good citizenship and of patriotism. But if there should be any member of this church, or of any other church of Christ, who refuses to use his utmost endeavors for the benefit of his fellow-men and for the salvation of those for whom Christ has died, and for whom he has pledged himself to work on every occasion and opportunity that the Lord and Master shall give him to save the sinner from death and his soul from eternal destruction, we can hardly say for such a church-member, who refuses to sign the pledge, that he is using his full privilege, as a living member of the church of Christ, to honor his Master. Such being the case, what shall we say of that deacon, ordained for special service as leader in the ranks of Christian wokers, as an assistant of the pastor in his blessed work, as a man who shall be 'void of offense,' and 'as a lively stone in the house of God'—what shall we say of that deacon who refuses to give his name and his entire influence and character, however much self-denial it may require of him;—what shall we say, I repeat it, of such a deacon, who proves such a recreant to the vows of his ordination, and his love for his Savior and of his love for souls?" With this climax the Doctor held himself silent for perhaps half a minute, when he hissed a whisper, which was distinctly heard in the most remote part of the building, like this: "Thank God, rum-drinking deacons will not live forever." With this the sermon closed. The two deacons never appeared in the church again. Deacon C—— never was known to attend any church or any religious services anywhere, to his death. He died a drunkard. Deacon S——, after some lapse of time, attended the Episcopal services; whether or not he joined the Episcopal Church, I do not know. He died in consequence of a slight wound, which the doctors said might have healed in a few days, but so filled with alcohol was his entire system, that this wound could not be healed; inflammation and gangrene set in, and speedily resulted in death. So that grandfather's efforts in behalf of his deacons, at least removed them out of the way as stumbling blocks, to the possibly more rapid hastening of their lamentable end.

The Mr. Gilbert, of whom I was speaking, continued for seven years as a most effective worker in the temperance cause. Before he gave himself up to drink, he had been a worthy mechanic, had accumulated property, had secured a good home; but in consequence of yielding to this passion, had lost control of a good business, mortgaged his home for all it was worth, lost his standing in society, and given up his membership in the Methodist Church. When, however, he reformed, and became an outspoken temperance man, an indefatigable and powerful worker in the cause, he was taken back into the church, and restored to his former standing as a local preacher. He also recovered his property, and was enjoying his position in society, his leadership in politics, and his control of a lucrative business, as before he had abandoned himself to drink; in fact, he seemed to be more than reinstated in his former prosperity and standing. His house was the home of the Methodist ministers, and his daughter was engaged to a young circuit-rider. At the wedding, wine was introduced; wine, ciders and fermented drinks not yet being tabooed by the pledge. As the wine was passed around once or twice, Mr. Gilbert refused it. His daughter, noticing the fact, took a wineglass from the table, ran across the room to her father, and asked him if he would not take some wine with the rest of the party. He replied, "No, daughter, I do not wish for any wine." "But," said she, "Father, I was never married before, I never expect to be married again; you will take some wine now at the first wedding that has ever taken place in your house; I am sure you will take some wine with me, papa." He took the wine and drank it, and in a few minutes went across the room and took another glassful, and then another and another, until, before the party retired, it was found the good man was drunk. This mastery of liquor over his will-power, thus reestablished by his daughter's persuasions, continued, so far as I know, to his death. Remark is superfluous.

My grandfather's house was the frequent resort of the President and Professors of Yale College. There I was accustomed to listen to the conversation of those worthy and dignified gentlemen; for as well as I can remember, I found it convenient whenever any such distinguished company was expected to be there, my Aunt Persis apprising me and urging me to go home with her. Thus, in early life, up to the time of my leaving Derby, I enjoyed the best opportunities of seeing and knowing the very finest specimens of human intellect and dignity. From the first, I enjoyed the conversations that went on at the table and elsewhere, and spared no pains or reasonable opportunity to be present as a listener. Then again, I was sent with the horse and buggy to New Haven, to bring out one of the professors to fill grandfather's pulpit, when his other duties prevented him from writing his sermon. Thus, my early standards, through my grandfather's kindness in always permitting me to enjoy such associations, in the way of my education, were the best possible for those times.

I remember very well when grandfather brought the first copy of Webster's Unabridged, two large quarto volumes, home from New Haven. Happening to be there when they arrived, they were a great treat, and were considered a perfect treasure-house, the more so as my grandfather spared no means of incitement to enhance my interest in the study of these volumes. I read scores of pages consecutively, time after time, as I had opportunity, of these volumes, studying as I was able, the etymology of the words, the various significations being especially interesting in the examples given of the authorities for the special meanings and uses of words. In fact, my grandfather humorously called me the little bookworm, and in the same spirit of humor, pretending to be at a loss now and then for the pronunciation of a word, or for its signification, or for the best word to use for the expression of an idea, would come to me very gently and meekly to get my opinion about it. Of course, I did the best I could, and was always encouraged by his kindness and appreciation of my childish efforts to grapple the mighty problems in precision and taste, which he delighted to throw upon me.

The usages of his family were a part of my training. In family prayers, which grandfather always conducted himself, after the reading of a chapter, verse by verse, all around the whole circle of children, grandchildren, employés and visitors, the whole family stood, in my earliest recollections, while prayer was being offered, each leaning upon his chair. Before every meal, too, the blessing was asked, the family all standing, each behind his chair. After the meal, the family rising and taking the same position as before, thanks were returned, and seldom did any one leave the table before the "returning of thanks." At the table, the food being placed upon central dishes, each helped himself, save perhaps the youngest children and grandchildren, who were served by the grandmother, or one of the aunts. It was not considered good form to eat butter while meat was on the plate. The general butter-plates were so arranged that each cut off as much butter with his own knife as he would spread for the time being upon his piece of bread. The cutting off of a larger mass of butter, and placing it upon the side of the plate, rather than that each should help himself continuously from the common plate, was an innovation. No butter-knives were used in those days, and individual butter-plates were unknown. No napkins were seen in the hands or laps of any, but each one used his own handkerchief when necessary, at the table. No butter was used on cake, and no sugar or sirup on pie. Nothing that any animal could eat must be thrown in the fire. It was wasteful and wicked. Cider was more generally drank at the table for dinner, coffee for breakfast, and tea for supper. Not infrequently, however, our coffee was grown in the rye-field, and being properly browned, made us a very palatable drink, certainly not very stimulating.

The best people of New Haven, Andover, Boston and New York were entertained at my grandfather's hospitable board. There seemed to be no end to his acquaintance with Congregational ministers, in those days called Presbyterians. For the most part, these gentlemen were to the children and grandchildren especially, welcome, and being all college graduates, much of the time of the visits was occupied in the narration of college experiences. And thus, in early days, did I get the feeling that college life was not one of special earnestness, or of high-toned moral power. For most, even in those days, that I heard of college life from these ministers and professors, was the narration of college tricks upon teachers, fellow-pupils, or citizens. With special gusto would most of these reverend fathers speak of the manner in which they "came it" over the professors in passing muster at recitations and examinations, and get their grades (honorably or passably) without deserving them.

I remember very well the square case containing twelve bottles filled with the best of liquors, and the manner in which the bottles were applied to for the filling of the decanters which were used on various occasions, with liberality proportioned to the dignity, position or fame of the visitor.

My grandfather himself, though not a total abstinence man, rarely, according to my remembrance, partook of any stimulant, nor did he furnish it to any of his work-hands, excepting in haying, in harvest, or when the help of neighbors was required; as, for instance, at the raising of a barn, the digging of a well, or some extra work of this kind. All these usages, in my childish estimation, were the right thing to do, and were doubtless according to the best usages of the best society, although they have been very much modified since in most intelligent families. Thus, my grandfather, with the usages of his family, and his wide acquaintance, was one of my earliest and most venerated teachers.

My Grandfather Holbrook, whom I never saw, as he died a short time previous to my birth, was also indirectly one of my early teachers, especially as he was quoted constantly by my aunts and others as a man of unswerving principle, of great public spirit, of determined purpose and of a pure life. Many of his peculiarities were related in my hearing. These ever excited a high degree of veneration, and, no doubt, had a very positive influence in determining me to lead a pure, useful and progressive life. His service in the Revolutionary War was narrated—his raising a company among his fellow-citizens; his being appointed colonel of a regiment and his meeting the British forces at East Haven, where a large band of marauders had landed, burned and destroyed all within their reach; his success in driving them back to their ships, and his ever rejecting the military title and preferring that of "Deacon," thus recognizing his office in the church as more worthy of regard than his position in the army. From the report of his children and others I learned that he was the leading spirit in every good enterprise of the times. As agriculture was his principal business, he was engaged in one improvement after another, introducing the best seeds, having the most profitable crops and the most valuable stock upon his own farm, and thus inciting his neighbors to like improvement. When plaster of Paris was first introduced as a valuable manure, in order to influence his neighbors and fellow-citizens to use this fertilizer, he sowed a quantity upon one of his meadows, which was visible at a considerable distance in all directions from the hills. On another meadow, similarly situated, he sowed a quantity in the form of the letters D-a-n-i-e-l H-o-l-b-r-o-o-k. By the superior verdure and growth his name could be read on that meadow for miles in nearly all directions. His farm, whether named by himself or others, was called "Happy Valley." It not only embraced the valley, but hundreds of acres around over the hills in three directions. My father was a determined anti-Mason. Inquiring of him one day why he was so opposed to the Masonic fraternity, he told me that his first opposition arose from the reports of my grandfather Holbrook, who had been a leading Mason of the Derby Lodge. He had quietly abandoned the lodge and all connection with it many years before his death, giving as his reason that the lodge urged many of its claims in opposition to those of the Church of Christ, and that he felt that the established order and privileges of the Christian religion were immeasurably more effective for the progress of society and for the safety of the individual than anything that Masonry could or would furnish. For these reasons he abandoned the lodge and clung to the church. Another reason he offered was, that the great majority of the members of the lodge, in their frequent meetings, no women being present, were induced, out of a feeling of good fellowship, to use more wine and brandy than was prudent or right.

My grandfather was one of the first who invested in lands in New Connecticut, now called Western Reserve. He was engaged in this line of purchase with other leading citizens, among whom was Deacon Tomlinson, of Great Hill. General Cleveland was their agent. He located himself at the port now called Cleveland after him, and had the general control of all those lands then purchased by the citizens of Derby. Several different townships were purchased. One in Loraine County was named Holbrook after my grandfather; another was named Kirtland after a gentleman who took the place of General Cleveland. It was in this township that my Uncle

David and three of my aunts, with their husbands and families, afterward settled on lands coming from my grandfather's estate. It was related by my aunts that if either Deacon Tomlinson or Deacon Holbrook received a letter on Saturday containing information in which the other was interested, when they met on Sabbath at the public services, neither communicated to the other even the fact that he had received such a letter, but deferred the matter entirely until the next day, when the one who received the letter rode a distance of six or eight miles to confer with the other upon the subject-matter of the letter.

One of my grandfather's farms was located in Choosetown, afterward called Humphreysville, now Seymour. This farm was tilled by a negro slave, by the name of Richard. Of course this was before any laws looking toward manumission were enacted. Richard was a very pious and reliable negro. How much my grandfather paid for him, or whether he was born in the family from slaves previously purchased, I am not able to say; but he was very much respected and considered entirely reliable and worthy of all confidence by grandfather and his family. It was grandfather's custom as often, perhaps, as once a week, to visit this farm and give Richard such directions as were necessary, and to furnish such other help as was needed to carry on the work of the farm profitably. One Monday morning, grandfather, arriving at the Choosetown farm, looked around over the various fields, saw that they were in good condition, the fences all in order, the cattle and the horse in their proper pasture lot, and crops all flourishing, but no Richard was to be seen anywhere on the property. Riding up to the cabin prepared for Richard's comfort, he heard, inside, Richard's voice, apparently engaged in devotion. Alighting from his horse, he opened the door and found Richard reading his Bible. He looked up with some amazement, waiting for the master to address him. "Well, Richard, how are things getting along here?" "All right, massa, all right; t'ank de Lord!" "Are you well, Richard?" "Yes, massa, all right, all right; bress de Lord!" "Well, how are your oxen, are they doing well?" "All right, massa; t'ank de Lord!" "Have you been out at work this morning?" "No sah, no sah; can't work Sabba' day." "Why, Richard, it is not Sabbath; it is Monday." "Monday, massa! Monday! why I worked all day Sabba' day! Can't work to-day, massa; can't cheat de Lord out ob one day. Please, massa, worked all day yes'aday; can't cheat de Lord, massa." "Well, Richard, you need not work to-day. Serve the Lord as much as you feel you ought. I will come up again to-morrow and see you." This circumstance may, perhaps, show the relation which existed in New England between the slaves and their masters in the time of New England slavery.

MY FATHER AS MY TEACHER.

I have related elsewhere father's interest in my mechanical training with Mr. Colburn, and his furnishing me with a set of drawing instruments, and his requiring me to copy certain engravings of machinery. And I may continue here by explaining how he excited an interest in drawing by his presenting various problems in geometry, involving accurate drawings of the figures, also in conic sections, also in freehand-drawing, in arranging a set of drawings, illustrating every form of leaf, of flower and of fruit. Now, these my early attempts at drawing were, by my father's management, rather as appealing to my feeling of good-will, pride and ambition than as requirements; in truth, my father *never required* anything of me; I do not remember that he ever gave me a word of censure or rebuke.

When my brother and I were called to Boston, and came under his immediate continuous control, he spared no means or opportunity to interest us in practical science in all its workings. Our work in the apparatus manufactory seems to me now to have been directed more to our instruction than to the profit derived from our labor, and yet I was very proud when I heard father tell a visitor that Alfred was worth as much to him in the shop as any hand he employed, although I was then only fourteen years of age. Not infrequently did he engage in excursions with the children of this or that public school, for the collection of specimens of various rocks found in the suburbs of Boston, either as bowlders, or *in situ.* Thus, I became at a very early period familiar with the geology of the neighborhood, from close and continued observation under my father's direction. By exchanges, we obtained large quantities of valuable specimens of ores, crystals, geodes and other beautiful and valuable minerals, from all parts of the world. A general national exchange of minerals and other valuable articles was an original and favorite idea of my father. His correspondence for this purpose was immense. A part of this correspondence was in the form of circulars, which I folded and directed, and of course read and studied. It was by these means that I early acquired a ready power of discrimination of nearly all possible minerals at sight, aiding myself now and then by blowpipe analysis. Father, during my stay in Boston, occupied the Columbian Hall, opening upon School and Tremont Streets. Here his large collection of boxes was stored, and their contents examined and selected for his own cabinet, and other specimens, broken and labeled, were prepared for sending to all parts of the world. In another place, I have related how father accomplished the first geological survey made in the United States.

Besides the excursions with children, before spoken of, father made excursions with my brother and myself to more remote points, for instance to

Nahant, Dorchester Heights, to Charleston, government shipyards, Cambridge University, and various other places of interest, all of which were designed to enlarge our field of general information, and extend our course of reading, and train our powers of observation—designed, as I now see, to train and discipline our faculties in every conceivable direction.

On Sabbath, we were accustomed to read religious books, for instance, Dwight's Theology, (father was a great admirer of Dr. Timothy Dwight) and we were taken to listen to the most celebrated divines of Boston, among whom were Dr. Channing, John Pierrepont, and Dr. Lyman Beecher. In all of these walks, excursions, readings and listenings, we were incited to prepare ourselves to report at a favorable opportunity, on our views, and as to what our opinions were, after witnessing all these different exhibitions of natural scenery, human ingenuity and ability. Thus, without realizing father's design, we were trained to become intelligently familiar with the leading men of the times, whether in the pulpit or on the rostrum. I was once taken by my father through the Quincy Market, then the most beautiful market-house in the world. Being early in the season, we came to a fruit-stand, on which were displayed a number of pears. Father handed my brother a pear, gave me one, and took one himself, which he immediately bit, asking the fruit-vender the price. "Fifty cents apiece, sir," said the man.

"Well," said father, "I guess one of these will answer, and I will get some other kind of fruit for the boys." So father paid for the pear, and went to another stand, inquiring the price before purchasing. He then took occasion to tell us many anecdotes about "Billy Gray," one of which was on an occasion after he had amassed a fortune. Being in market one day getting his supplies, a young fellow came along and got his supplies, filled his basket, and inquired of the market-man if he knew of any boy that would take the basket home for him. Billy Gray standing near, and not being known to the young man, offered to take the basket for him, telling him he should charge him a dime. This was readily agreed to. Billy Gray started off with the baskets, finding it was on his way to his own palatial residence. The young man being anxious to know who the old man was who was carrying the two baskets, was told by the market-man that it was Billy Gray, one of the wealthiest men of Boston. Now, it so happened that the father of this young man was in Billy Gray's employ, the young man himself having been absent at college. Feeling chargrined at the result of his silliness in being ashamed to be seen carrying a market-basket through the streets of Boston, he speedily overtook Billy Gray, and asked that his basket should be returned, but Mr. Gray refused to give it up, inquiring who the young man was as if he did not know already, and then informed him that he had been accustomed in his early life to do just that kind of thing for his regular business, but he had not got too old nor too rich to carry a basket for himself or his neighbors if he got his pay for it.

My father was a very interesting conversationalist, and wherever he was, in my partial view, he was the leading thinker and talker. His office on the Corner of School and Washington Streets, was the frequent resort of the best men of Boston, if I may except the politicians. Such men as Channing and Pierrepont, S. V. S. Wilder, the Mayor of the city; H. V. R. Smith, General Butler, Sr., and all the leading educators and writers of Boston, I became acquainted with in their visits and conversations, which were chiefly upon educational topics, not infrequently taking a much wider range. Our week-day reading consisted mostly of such volumes as Goldsmith's "Animated Nature," Bigelow's "Technology," and other important works on practical science. The Boston Museum was a favorite place of resort, my father holding a free family ticket. He kindly went with us, directing our attention chiefly to the natural curiosities that had been collected from Europe, Asia and Africa in the lines of zoölogy, mineralogy and geology. One of these I remember to have seen with him—whether foreign or domestic, I am unable to say—was a flea chained up by one leg to a pin driven into the top of a table. This was an active specimen. Father raised the inquiry, "If a flea can jump eighteen inches at one spring, how far ought an elephant to jump, in proportion to his weight and size, at one leap?"

The first rattlesnake I ever saw was kept in a box, and was visible through a wire grating. We were permitted to run a stick through the grating to stir up the rattlesnake, and rouse him, if possible, to some kind of attention; but we found it very stupid, and apparently so little disturbed by our attacks, that we soon let him alone, and went elsewhere to find some more interesting amusement. One day after we had been stirring up his snakeship, we read in the *Evening Transcript*, which had then only just begun its career, that the keeper, on the same day, after we left, had been bitten by this same rattlesnake. Now, the keeper had been very kind and attentive to us two boys, and we felt an interest in his well-being. He told us afterward, on inquiring of him, that, as he was cleaning out the sand and other materials from the snake's box, with a rod, there remained a straw which he could not easily remove with his rod. The snake being in the remote part of the box, he put his thumb and finger under the grating to take hold of the straw, but no sooner was his thumb within reach of the snake, than he he struck instantly his fangs into the flesh. With some little difficulty the keeper withdrew his thumb. He passed to the table on which lay a hatchet, and as quickly as possible, cut his thumb off near the inner joint. The physician was at once called; such applications as were thought to be effectual, were made. His hand and arm immediately swelled to an enormous size, became the color of the rattlesnake's skin, and all hope was abandoned of saving the man's life. He was, however, saved, barely escaped, and, as in every such case, the annual return of that day brought with it the same symptoms, but each successive year with diminished virulence.

Speaking of the *Transcript*, it was customary with us at our boarding-place, Mr. Pelton's, in the old Province House Court, to read the evening paper, or to have it read, every evening after supper. One of the young lady boarders, taking up the *Transcript* one evening, commenced reading for the benefit of the company. As she proceeded, she read something like this: "At the dedication of the Masonic Temple yesterday, one of our solid men was noticed as a prominent figure standing against one of the columns in the midst of the vast assemblage. His splendid physique and lordly bearing, no doubt attracted the general attention of the audience. While apparently giving his attention to the proceedings of the dedication, it was noticed that he was seized with a sudden tremor; his rubicund countenance was blanched—his whole figure trembled with alarm. He continued feeling in every pocket about his person; it was evident some loss had befallen him. While this was going on, a laboring man was seen advancing toward him through the crowd. As he reached him, he handed a pocketbook rounded out with the contents, as it was supposed, of large bills of money. It was taken with eagerness, and the poor but honest man was rewarded with twenty-five dollars, no cents." As the young lady read on, no doubt most of her audience were inquiring within themselves what that "twenty-five dollars, no cents" meant. My father, as soon as the young lady had left the room, requested me to take up the paper and read that incident reported to have occurred at the dedication of the Masonic Temple. As I found it punctuated it read thus: "The poor but honest man was rewarded with twenty five—dollars? No!!—cents!"

Father was accustomed to relate his experiences during the visitations he made to the public schools. He made frequent use of a system of object lessons of his own invention and arrangement, interesting the children in such a way as to send them out into the fields and quarries in the neighborhood of Boston.

One of his object-lessons, as he reported, ran thus: "What is this I have in my hand, boys?" "Coffee, sir." "What use does your mother make of it?" "Makes '*tay*,' sir." Again, in an infant school, the teacher was engaged in teaching spelling; father asked to be permitted to hold the attention of the class for a moment. "Certainly," said the teacher. "Well, my boy, s-t-a-i-r-s, what does that spell?" "Don't know." "*Don't know?*" why what do you go up on when you go to bed?"

One little boy, brighter than the rest, sang out, "A ladder, sir!" "Very well, s-t-a-i-r-s don't spell ladder. I want to know if the rest can tell what it spells." Nobody could tell. Well, now, what is it that you go up to your chamber on?" "Don't go up to no chamber; we sleep down cellar." "Well, what do you go down cellar on?" "Go down on the steps, sir." Father, at last, had to tell the children; he could not draw it out of them by any of his devices. From these lines of procedure, in every variety it may well be inferred that my early training was valuable as a preparation for the work Providence designed for me. In all his educational labors, whether written or spoken, father was at least fifty years ahead of his times. Even now, I apprehend that, in the majority of the most wealthy and aristocratic institutions, his educational measures and plans would be considered quite visionary and fanatical; as iconoclastic and impracticable. In fact, after meeting with the National Association of Educators in New York City, in May, 1837, I remember hearing him say, with disgust, that he could find no sympathy or place of common standing with the leading educators in that association, of which he was one of the original founders. All measures that they proposed—that they discussed—he considered as, in a large measure, useless, tending to stupefy the mind rather than excite the ambition of the student, and any and everything he proposed was considered by the worthy gentlemen who constituted that association as utterly invalid and futile and visionary.

The world moves, nevertheless, even though the only places through which the turbid stream of the dark ages still flows are the most highly endowed and the most aristocratic of the colleges. It may be charged, as it has often been, that I am hostile to colleges and to college men. Not in the least. As was my father before, I am bitterly opposed to the evil practices, the antiquated usages, the repressive influences of colleges, as many of them are yet conducted. I have never attacked a college or officer of any college; I have done whatever seemed to me to be desirable and proper on all occasions, by writing, by speaking and by my own course in building an institution that should utilize all that is good in colleges and reject all that is acknowledged to be bad.

While I fight the iniquities of a system with no hostile feeling toward any man, I have often been made the target of most bitter personal attack and denunciation. I sent word to one worthy college president, who used a considerable part of his time in Teachers' Institutes in denouncing me as a charlatan and a humbug, that I could afford to pay him a moderate salary for these efforts to crush and ruin me. Why? In every Teachers' Institute in Ohio, and several other States, the most active workers in attendance are my pupils. They take up these statements made by such men, and either in private or before the Institute, show their falsity, and thus expose the bigotry and bitterness of those who make them. The result is always favorable to this institution, and the reverend speaker is thus the means of removing prejudices and sending me pupils who otherwise would never have come.

It will be seen by this time that I have come honestly by my opinions and practices; my doings and daring in grappling with the grand fetich of this age. I am proud of my father's memory, as an iconoclast, a humanitarian, a Christian, and more especially, thankful that I had the continued teaching and example of such a man.

On another page I have given my father's management of his boy, in part. I shall now try to describe the training he gave me under Mr. Keys, a mechanic he had found in one of his lecturing tours at West Boylston, Mass., in 1829 or 1830. Mr. Keys was a foreman in Flagg's machine shop at that place, and, like many of the Yankee employes, was well read, intelligent and ingenious. He was much interested in father's lectures on chemistry, astronomy and natural philosophy, and always remained after the lecture to inquire further, and to ask for the titles of the best books treating on these subjects.

Father became much interested in him, especially as Mr. Flagg, his employer, explained an important attachment that Keys had invented for power looms. It was this: before this Keys' improvement was applied, a girl was required to watch each loom in order to stop the loom and tie a thread whenever one was broken. As one neglect to do this would impair the value of the entire piece, the mill-owner was obliged to put a heavy money penalty upon the loom-girl who failed to take up and connect the ends of a broken thread. The strain on the girls was severe, and not infrequently brought on brain fever, or some other serious malady. Mr. Keys' kindness of heart and ingenuity were aroused to mitigate these evils—loss on the mill-owner and penalty on the girls.

His contrivance was very simple. He placed a cylinder, rotating by its connections directly under the cloth where the filling was being thrown by the shuttle. The cylinder was as long as the cloth was wide. Narrow creases were made about a third of an inch apart, and extending the whole length of the cylinder. A stiff steel wire, having a loop at the top, was so hung on each thread of the warp that when a thread broke the wire would drop upon the revolving cylinder and into one of the creases. This threw the loom out of gear and stopped it, thus automatically apprising the girl in charge of the fact of a broken thread, and stopping the loom till she could take up the thread and make all right again.

A girl could more safely attend to three looms with Keys' attachment than to one without it, and with no special tax upon her attention. Mr. Keys took out no patent for this most valuable improvement, though his employer advised him to do so. Mr. Flagg was a manufacturer of power looms. Whether the improvement is still in use, or has ever been superseded, I am unable to say.

When it was explained to me by my father, with devices of other men in machinery to save time and labor and mental strain, it not only excited my interest in labor-saving machinery and mechanism generally, which was never abated, but a special respect for Mr. Keys, my teacher in practical mechanics.

In starting an apparatus manufactory in Boston, my father selected Mr. Keys as the man to take charge of it. A number of other mechanics were employed; for there was no trade nor art, scarcely, that was not brought into requisition in the construction of scientific apparatus as devised by my father. Mr. Keys was the genius of the manufactory; my father found his suggestions valuable in devising and constructing orreries, tellurians, globes, electric machines and electric batteries, air-pumps and their attendant receivers, stopcocks and whatnots. All of these articles, such as were being used in Harvard, Yale and other colleges, had been previously imported from Europe. For example: Father took me over to Harvard one day, and showed me an orrery which, he said, was seldom or never used, that cost in Paris $5,000. Said he: "Alfred, I shall make an orrery that will be used, and will answer every purpose that this does, for $10."

And this was about a fair example of the revolution father's apparatus wrought for the advantage of colleges, but more for public and private schools. All colleges are now supplied with the Holbrook apparatus, though the manufacturers in Boston, New York, Philadelphia and Chicago do not to any extent recognize the name.

Mr. Keys, I thought, took a great interest in training me in all mechanical contrivances, in the use of all kinds of tools and machines. The manufacture of apparatus involved the most accurate and finished kinds of work in wood, in metal, in paper and cloth, in paints, varnishes, lacquers, and every other conceivable material and appliance. We had a forge and anvil in our shop, several different kinds of lathes, a full set of cabinet-maker's tools, an outfit for a tinner, and a clock-maker; besides, much of the work was carried out of the building to every variety of mechanic and artisan. Engravers, water-color painters, marblers and molders were brought into requisition; in fact, there was scarcely any kind or variety of mechanical or art work which I did not become more or less familiar with, and, to a considerable extent, an expert operative in it, partly because I enjoyed the work, but more because father intended that I should continue in it for my life business. Doubtless Mr. Keys and father held many a conversation as to what was best for me to engage in next and next, and so on. One thing more I learned from my father's connection with Mr. Keys.

After he left Boston, and had supplied us with large quantities of apparatus, which he made in West Boylston, in a shop which he had fitted up there, he died from typhoid fever.

His administrator brought in his book account against father of several thousand dollars.

Relying upon Mr. Keys' fidelity and accuracy, father had kept no regular accounts that could be authenticated in court. The receipts for money paid had always been sent him, but they were thrown carelessly, with other loose papers, into a drawer, and some had been destroyed. Several payments father remembered, which were not on Keys' books, and for which the receipts could not be found. The administrator insisted on the repayment of all charges for which no vouchers could be found, though several receipts were shown for payments not credited on Keys' books. This lesson has been of much value to me in insisting that my regular employes keep their own accounts, and whether they do or not, that I have vouchers for all payments made them.

CHAPTER V.

STAMFORD.

WHILE living in Stamford, Connecticut, 1832-3, I was occasionally amused by the performances of a queer fellow, who, it was said, had been disappointed in love. He was a great tobacco-chewer, and perhaps that had something to do with the addled condition of his brain. He was never seen to walk through the streets, but when he came to the town his passage was made by running a few rods at a time and stopping to take breath. He was often the butt of ridicule for the boys, and sometimes, from his marked devotional feeling in church, excited the attention and roused the spirit of merriment of those who were not seriously engaged in the worship of the sanctuary. He generally sat in the gallery of the church. It happened one Sabbath, I sat in the same vicinity, and was disturbed by the giggling and whispering of two boys in the front seats, just below us. The personage previously mentioned doubtless felt that his devotions were interfered with by these boys. My attention was turned from the boys to the manifest anger of this devout worshiper, as he endeavored several times to turn away his eyes from the boys to the preacher during the long prayer. He at length seemed to yield to the disturbance, in so far as to give his undivided attention to the boys, quite abandoning his devotions. Had I been more strictly devout myself, perhaps I should not have witnessed his performance. As it was, however, I was watching the indignation gathering in his eyes. His cheeks swelled with wrath and tobacco. When he could hold neither any longer, a flood of indignation and tobacco-juice burst forth into the faces of the disturbers of the peace. This irregular proceeding attracted the attention of all within the range of vision, and a smile of approval went in waves over their countenances. In relating this to the minister, a few days afterward, he said in reply: "The boys got just what they deserved, and I hope for once they were calmed into a reverent quiet and a proper respect for the feeling of others while engaged in Sabbath exercises. My eyes being closed, I was only conscious of some unusual state of feeling in my audience;" "but," said he, "a few Sabbaths ago, while a brother-minister was offering the long prayer, my attention was distracted, I confess, by the contortions of the countenance of this same young man, and for once I could not quite suppress a smile, even in the sacred desk, and during prayer. It so happened that a young man, with remarkably red hair, sat in the same place where these boys sat.

The peculiar fiery aspect of the head a little in front and beneath, attracted the attention of our friend. I noticed that he was exceedingly interested in the appearance, and after various contortions and evolutions and other manifestations of intense interest, I observed that he placed the index-finger of his left hand on top of the red head, (the possessor hardly aware of the use being made of his flaming locks) and turning it over as if it were a piece of iron in the forge, occasionally taking it away, and placing it on the back of the seat, hammered at it with his other fist. After he had reduced it toward the proper shape, and it became too much chilled, it was replaced for another heating in the glowing source of heat, and then subjected to further manipulation. I believe this is the only time that I ever lost possession of myself, and laughed in church."

With regard to this love-stricken youth, it was narrated in Stamford that his mother, being anxious to bring him out, made arrangements with her brother, a New York merchant, to have John visit the city, and spend a few weeks in wearing off his rusticity. Before the son took his departure, it is said, the mother carefully enjoined upon him, "John, you know you are not as smart as some people, especially, as some of your cousins in the city; you must do the best you can, and unless you can answer correctly and at once, it will be best for you not to make any answer at all. Now, remember, John, remember what I tell you; if you can't answer correctly and at once, make no reply whatever." So John found himself in the city, a guest in his uncle's family, and no doubt he was treated very hospitably. But, on the first Sabbath, when the family was assembled at dinner, and some of the clerks with them, one of them said to John, "Be so kind as to pass the biscuits." John passed the biscuits, but made no reply. The manner in which it was done rather interested the clerk, and he addressed several questions to the country boy, to which, John, following the injunctions of his good mother, made no reply. At length the clerk, turning to the one who sat by him, on the other side, whispered, loud enough for John to hear, "What is the matter with this fellow; he is a fool, isn't he?" John, hearing the allegation, started up and ran away from the table, saying, "There, mother, they have found it out, and I haven't said a word; but they have found it out." With this, he left the room, and all at the table in a roar.

Living in Stamford, was a remarkably handsome lawyer by the name of T——. Having married an heiress, he was sent by her to Yale College, to prepare for his chosen profession, the law. But having, probably, too much money at his control, and not having his wife there to hold him in check, he was engaged with other students in mischief, time and again, at the expense of the Professor of mathematics, who, from his earnestness to help the boys to do something for themselves, became very unpopular. Young T., on an occasion, had been interrupted in a clandestine performance in the recitation-room of this Professor. He had drawn a striking caricature upon the blackboard, and had just commenced writing the inscription underneath. He had proceeded so far as to write "A demon," but being interrupted by the sound of the professor's key placed in the lock, he made a precipitate escape through a window of the room. He was called up before the dons, in a Faculty meeting, to give an account of himself for thus denominating a worthy Christian gentleman. His defense was, that if he had been left alone a little longer, he would have given them the inscription he had designed, which was simply "A *demonstration*" that he was making upon the board and writing the proper inscription, but being interrupted at an unfortunate point, he had inadvertently given a more appropriate title to the gentleman than he had intended. He was expelled, not unwillingly probably to his wife and his ease. All he ever did in the practice of law, so far as I know, never led to any additions to his wife's possessions. I heard him say, however, that when "the boys" were engaged in card-playing in his rooms, one night, momentarily expecting a call from one of the professors on his round, they had prepared in their room a kettleful of mush, and had deposited a part of it in the pockets of an overcoat hanging by the door. When the expected knock was heard, the usual cry "Come in" was given, but the boys having everything arranged, were in a great flutter, and one of them had apparently deposited some of the contraband articles in the overcoat in such a manner as was intended to lead the Professor in that direction. The Professor thrust his hand into one of the pockets of the overcoat, but withdrew it much more rapidly than he had thrust it in, his hand being badly scalded by the mush prepared for that purpose, but when the boys were summoned before the Faculty to give an account of themselves, and being questioned by the President of the Institution, and no one being willing to reply or to implicate himself in this transaction, T. himself, according to his account, arose and remarked: "I am able to inform you gentlemen, although I know very little about the affair, who had a *hand* in it—It was the Professor himself."

CHAPTER VI.

MY FIRST SCHOOL.

In the fall of 1833, being then seventeen years old, and having come from West Boylston, Mass., and having recovered my health, I had not as yet engaged in any business. I was living at my grandfather's. One day, being occupied in a cornfield, gathering corn, I noticed a stranger coming toward me. He said: "Your name is Alfred Holbrook." "Yes, sir." "I understand you are a pretty good scholar, and I am in pursuit of a teacher for our village school." "I never taught any, and, of course, do not know whether I can teach or not. Where are you from, sir?" "From Monroe; I was directed to you as one who would like to get a situation." "I have no business in view, sir, and have never taught. I don't know whether I will make a good teacher or not. What wages do you pay?" "We expect to pay $12 per month." "You furnish board?" "Oh, yes; our teacher always boards round with us." "Well, sir, I have not been examined, and not having taught any, don't know whether I shall succeed. How long do you wish your school to continue?" "Six months, if everything works well; that is, if you give satisfaction." "Well, sir, if I pass examination and you will give $14 a month, provided I am not discharged before the time expires, and $12 a month for the time I really teach if I am discharged, I am willing to make the attempt." My condition of $14, provided I was not discharged, seemed to strike the gentleman rather pleasantly, as I noticed he smiled. He saw, of course, that he could discharge me half an hour before the time expired and pay me $12 a month if he chose. My object in offering this condition was, that I might put myself under the strongest possible inducement to work hard and give the best possible satisfaction. I had learned that I was subject to temptation, like other boys of that age, and thought it desirable to place myself under such conditions as would hold me to my business; such conditions as would appeal both to my pride and to my pocket also. My examination by the town authority was, to me, somewhat interesting. After being asked to spell one or two words, one of which was calico, and not being sure, I suggested it was spelled differently in different dictionaries. In my examination in geography, I was asked: "Who is the present king of Spain?" My answer was: "The present king of Spain is a woman, sir, if I remember rightly." He smiled and rejoined: "That is a good one. You know more about it than I do." This closed my examination.

At the appointed time I found myself at the house of Mr. Robinson, the gentleman with whom I had made the contract, having himself four children for the school. He said he would, if it were agreeable to me, prefer to have me board out the time with him, before I passed to other families in the district. He remarked that it would be proper for me calculate how long it would be necessary to board for each child attending school. When the calculation was made, I found that I would continue with this very worthy family for three weeks, and I found a very pleasant introduction to the society of Monroe through them and their special friends.

On opening my school according to contract on Monday, at 9 A. M., I found about twenty-five pupils in attendance, among whom was a bright, smart colored boy, about nineteen years of age. I requested the pupils to take their seats as they had been accustomed to. The seats were arranged somewhat in this manner: the benches extended entirely around the house; plain, continuous boards were ranged in front upon standards, so as to form a desk in common for about five pupils each. The colored boy, "Lew," occupied the middle seat, or the desk in front of the teacher's desk. As I proceeded with my work, and my first class was a reading class, they occupying the floor in a standing position, I noticed that the pupils who were not engaged in this class were preoccupied by some mischief, which led them to titter and whisper, and to fall into other forms of disturbance. Not perceiving the cause of this merriment, I restrained myself until I should ascertain why or how it happened. I soon discovered, from the direction of the children's glances, that the darkey, Lew, was the center of the mischief. He was a great mimic, and was taking off my performances to the amusement of the younger children. Immediately I addressed myself to Lew, in words something like these: "I discover that you are not inclined to be very studious, young man. I think you will make less trouble and find less trouble if you will apply yourself more closely to the book you have before you." His response was a good-natured grin, equivalent to "What are you going to do about it?" I continued: "If this disturbance is repeated, I shall be compelled to take charge of you myself." This was answered by a grimace of defiance, as much as to say, "Touch me if you dare!" Now he was two years older and twenty per cent. heavier than I was. I was afterward informed that he had broken up several previous schools by similar performances. The children generally sided with him, and he was a very popular individual, so far as they were concerned. I told the class with which I was engaged to take their seats. Said I: "Young man, I want you to come out here to me," and stepped toward him with no pleasant expression probably. He seized the desk with both his hands, as I grasped his collar with both of mine. I stood upon a small seat in front of the continuous desk, behind which he was seated. I gave him a jerk with whatever of energy and will-force I could apply, and the teacher, the darkey and the desk came over into the middle of the floor in a pile. It happened, however, that the teacher was on top. Said I: "Are you willing now to get up and behave yourself?" Said he, with an oath: "You get off of me." I replied: "I shall get off from you when you promise to behave, and not before." Said he: "I'll not behave as long as you are on top of me." I jumped up and began to kick him, yet holding him down on the floor. I treated him roughly; and when he began to whimper and the children around the room were crying and my strength was somewhat exhausted, I remitted my efforts and again inquired: "Will you get up now and take your seat and behave?" He replied, whimpering: "If you will let me get up I will go home." At that, I sat down upon him and pounded him, exerting the best energies I had in the practice of muscular Christianity. Presently he begged that I would let him up. He said that he would get up and go to his seat. Said I: "Will you behave and let these children alone?" He said: "I won't let you alone." So I thought it necessary to make another reformatory application. Inquiring again if he would get up, go to his seat and behave, he blubbered at last that he would. I let him up. He went to his seat and never gave me any more trouble. He proved one of the best pupils I ever had—a very good-natured boy; but he had been petted and spoiled by the people who raised him, and by the children whom he had amused. I was told by the family who raised him, with whom I afterward boarded, that it was really the best thing that ever happened to Lew, for he was really a good boy, so far as they were concerned. Now I do not wish my young friends, who may read this, to suppose that I give this incident as an example of skillful school management. On the contrary, it was abominable; but it was the best I knew under the circumstances, at that time. It secured for me the respect of my pupils, and of all their parents, so far as I learned. If I had the thing to do over again I should pursue an entirely different course. As it was, however, I had no further difficulty in government.

Having attended only one district school in my life, and that but for three months, the teacher being Dr. Goodson, I was led to practice the extreme of explanation, from his utter paucity in that article, as he never gave any explanations whatever, but held us closely to the text and letter of the book. In managing my classes—and, by the way, he never had any but reading classes, each pupil reciting in other subjects when called upon—I assumed that nothing should be done or said or recited that was not fully explained, either by the pupil or by the teacher. Of course, the teacher had nearly all the explanation to do. This was especially true in arithmetic. After managing the most advanced arithmetic class of about eight pupils in this manner for two weeks, I found that very little study was done by any member of the class, and that the recitation was about as irksome to them as it was trying and discouraging to me. I thought I was doing the best possible by demanding and giving explanations of every step in every process. At the close of a recitation of this class, occurring on the third week of school, at 12 o'clock, while walking to Mr. Robinson's, my boarding-place, I said to myself: "What is the matter with the arithmetic class? Arithmetic certainly ought to be made interesting, and the study exciting, and I am not accomplishing anything but my own defeat and the discouragement of my pupils; what is the matter? Is it because the subject is in itself so dry and repulsive? No; it is most useful and necessary. Is it, then, because this class is unusually mischievous and troublesome? No; these children are just as good as any other children. The trouble is not with the children. The difficulty, Alfred Holbrook, is with yourself; you don't know how to interest them; you don't know how to teach." The afternoon was passed much as usual—hearing the children read and recite their geography and work at their penmanship; a specially gloomy time was it all through. I went to my boarding-place at night very much disheartened, not knowing whether I ought to abandon the school or what I ought to do. I concluded that something must be done. I was too much excited and chagrined to eat my supper, or, indeed, to sleep any that night. Though I had never expected to teach, and, least of all, expected to make teaching my life-work, the idea of being defeated in anything I had undertaken from my own incapacity was more than I could bear. Some time in the early morning a revelation came to me. It was this: "You have been making a fool of yourself—try a better plan." This revelation was a new inspiration, and I was just as confident of the proper management of that class and school as I was after it was accomplished. I went to my school that morning a new creature. When the arithmetic class was called at half-past eleven, I said to the class: "Instead of reciting the lesson I assigned for the day, we will look at the next lesson, and see what is to be done." The subject-matter was the rule for the Division of Denominate Numbers. I commenced a PRELIMINARY DRILL on the rule, requesting the pupils to work an example step by step, as the rule directed, calling upon one pupil to work the example on the blackboard. By the way, so far as I know, this was the first blackboard ever used in a public school in the State of Connecticut. I had made it myself. It will be remembered this was in 1833. The children continued working the example step by step, as the rule directed, until one little brown-eyed girl looked up at me very prettily, and said: "Mr. Holbrook, why do we bring down that number there?" "Why, Mary, the book says so, doesn't it?" She pushed the inquiry no farther—she was too timid. Another, however, took up the inquiry: "I don't understand, Mr. Holbrook, why we multiply and bring down that number there. You told us we ought to understand it ourselves, and not take what the book says, and I don't understand it." "Oh, well," said I, "the book is all right, isn't it?" "I don't know; I don't understand it." "Well," said I, "go according to the book this time." One little fellow, the son of the Presbyterian minister, put his head around back of the one he was sitting with, and said to the next one in a whisper: "I don't believe he understands it himself." I had now accomplished my purpose. I had really aroused an interest in knowing the reason why. I had been forcing reasons down their intellectual throats in such a manner as to nauseate and repel. From that time onward my school was my joy and pride. This was my first discovery in pedagogics. This little Mary French, who started the question "why," was a very diligent student, and had gone through Woodbridge's Geography three or four times, and did not like to be in the class which had only gone through it once or twice, and wanted to know if I would not hear her recite separately. She said: "My ma told me to ask you if I could not recite by myself." I replied: "Mary, your mother does not control this school. Give her my compliments, and tell her I am teacher here." Now, it is not to be supposed that I would have any one imitate this piece of bad management. However, Mrs. French, being a sensible and good-natured woman, instead of making a fuss about such a message, took it kindly, and when she met me, thanked me for the course I had taken.

My next boarding-place in "boarding 'round" was at Mr. Munson's, a hatter, also a farmer and butcher, at least, so far as his own meat was concerned. The first supper that I took there consisted of boiled beef, hot bread and burnt rye coffee, all of which was rather novel, except the beef, which I think must have been an old cow, past twenty-five years of age. I took a piece in my mouth, but did not succeed in masticating it, so put it down under the side of my plate. There were seven children in this family, good children enough; I liked them all; but I did not like the idea of spending all my hours out of school at the family kitchen fire, as it was expected I would do. When I requested to be shown to bed, the eldest daughter was directed to show me to my room. Passing up-stairs, she went into their spare chamber, a large, comfortable room, neatly furnished, and I thought I was going to have very pleasant quarters in my new abode. It was a consideration, as I expected to board at this place five weeks. Instead of setting down the light in this room, she passed through into another, saying that I would find my bed in that room. She left the light and me to our own radiant reflections. I found a very hard bed, with insufficient clothing, the sheets being woolen blankets, which had been thoroughly fulled in washing, and were as hard as a board; and the whole, bed and all, under the garret stairs. I must confess I was somewhat disgusted. Nor did I think that the profession of teaching was so utterly menial that I ought to be treated worse than an ordinary hired hand. But I concluded to make the best of it, and to endure whatever came. I had enlisted for the cause and would prove no deserter. I waked happy the next morning; felt jolly in contriving some new artifice for my school. I really believe I made friends of these children and their parents: the only modification of my quarters being that I requested another bed-quilt or two.

I next boarded at Mr. Babbitt's. Now this was the most respectable family in town. Two sons were in business in New York; two handsome and very intelligent daughters were at home with their mother. A hired hand and the family servant, with the mother and daughters, made up the family. As I was taking my seat at the supper table for the first time with these young ladies, I found an atmosphere of culture, refinement and all the appointments of good society, and their very best set out for the entertainment of their teacher. In fact, the poorest of this family was better than the best that the Munson family ever furnished for the entertainment of their friends. My private room was the best the house contained, and was made comfortable for me in every respect to pursue my studies as I pleased. For instance: when I retired at night, on turning back the bed covers, I thought they were exceedingly light for that cold night; but, being too bashful to call for any more bed covers, I bravely crept under the cover, expecting to freeze before morning. I fell asleep, and on waking was perfectly comfortable. I inspected the covering under which I had slept so delightfully, and found it made of down. I congratulated myself that I had not committed the blunder of asking for more bed-clothing before I had given the down a trial. It is hardly necessary to say that all my time in this house was not spent in my studies in my room. The young ladies were too attractive and intelligent, and it seemed to me, exerted themselves most beautifully to entertain the boy-teacher that had been sent to them in the ordinary course of "boarding around." I regretted the time when I was compelled to find another boarding-place, especially as the young ladies urged me to continue a few days longer, saying that they hardly thought I had got my money's worth in such board as they provided. By the way, their table was most lavishly furnished.

My time being about to expire there, I requested the children to inquire of their parents when it would be convenient for me to board with them, respectively, or who would be ready to receive me next. The following morning there was an unusually bitter, cold, driving snow-storm; but about half an hour after school opened, we heard a stamping and wheezing and puffing in the hall. Not knowing what or who the arrival might be, I requested one of the children to open the door, when my young friend, Walter Carleton, made his appearance, nearly stiff with cold, but sufficiently excited with the news he was about to impart. "Well, Walter, what is it?" "My Aunt Maria says, Mr. Holbrook, that we are going to kill the old sow next Saturday, and she would like to have you come and board with us just as soon after that as you can." "Very well, Walter; tell your Aunt Maria I shall be there next Saturday night, unless I have other orders from her." I found my home with Aunt Maria and her worthy sister a very pleasant one. My acquaintance with those good maiden ladies was of real value. They were pious, devoted Christians, well read in all the literature of the times. They seemed to take a deep interest in my religious welfare, for which I was not sufficiently thankful at the time. On the second or third night of my boarding with them occurred the great meteoric storm of 1833. These devoted Christian ladies, from their own account of it afterward, met what they supposed to be the judgment day with excitement and terror, mingled with reverence and awe. Their description of their feelings, and of the phenomena of the night, were sufficiently interesting and exciting to me, who had lost entirely, in a continued sleep, the interest, beauty and wonder of the occasion.

It must be remembered that I had everything to learn from my first school, in managing and teaching children. I had attended school but little, and that under coercive and repressive plans; and not having ever thought of teaching as a temporary business, much less as a life-work, I had little idea how it was to be done, and no disposition to study the subject. But really every day to me, in my school experience, was a day of study, experiments, and of partial or complete success. Thus my first school was a series of continued excitements, and of triumphs over new and unexpected difficulties.

It had never been my purpose to be a teacher, for I had concluded, after finding it impossible to live in Boston and pursue my father's business, that my health would require open air employment; and thus I had decided that my life-work should be that of engineering. Nor did I abandon this idea for many years afterward, although defeated again and again in my efforts in this direction.

In carrying on my preparation for engineering, I formed a literary society, including the more advanced pupils and other young people of the town of Monroe. We met weekly for purposes of improvement in debate, reading and criticising essays, in elocutionary readings, and in the reading of a weekly paper edited by one of the members. We named our literary society "The Monroe Lyceum." Among the exercises were several scientific lectures, delivered by myself, accompanied by illustrations on the blackboard, and with such simple apparatus as I could construct in that village. I was encouraged to think, from the satisfaction which these efforts for gaining literary power seemed to give to all my audience, that I could, if I so desired, prepare myself for a public lecturer, and for the organization of lyceums, as my father was doing before me. I was, however, more intent upon pursuing my chosen life-work, or rather my preparation for it, and for this reason declined the offer of continuing the school through the summer at the same rate—$14 per month. This offer was the more acceptable, as it had been customary for a lady to teach the summer school at $4 per month.

It was the law at that time in Connecticut that in order that any district should draw its public money from the school fund, the Directors should certify to the Township Treasurer that they had visited the school twice during the term for which the money was drawn. My term of six months had nearly expired and the Directors had not yet made their appearance. I inquired of different members of the board, at different times, when they would be pleased to make me their legal and formal visit. "Oh," they said, "they would come in some time when they could get together, and could make it convenient." I waited rather anxiously the last week, expecting them every day; but the last day came and the Directors had not yet made even one visit. Then I supposed they would make one visit in the morning and the other in the afternoon, to comply with the law. But the forenoon passed, and yet no visitors. The time of closing school for the term arrived. I made my closing speech, not alluding in the least to the visitors, and dismissed my school. As the first pupils were passing out of the door, the Directors entered, and inquired very quietly if school was dismissed? I replied: "The school is dismissed for the term." "Never mind," said a Director, "call them back and we will visit the school as the law requires." It occurred to me, "How will you visit them twice?" The children were seated, and one of the visitors made a few remarks, complimenting the teacher and the pupils, and informed me that I could give the children a recess. So the children were excused for five minutes, being told to return at the usual signal. The visitors went out to a store near by. After the children had taken their seats again, the Directors made their second visit, bowing to the school and the teacher. Another member of the committee expressed his views of the school, stating his appreciation of the cheerful and happy condition of all concerned, and giving us his congratulations, and hoped that some one of those present might one day become President of the

United States. The Committee withdrawing, the school was dismissed again. The legal demands were answered, and my salary was secured from the school fund.

Soon after commencing my work in Monroe, there appeared a young Frenchman amongst the children one day, taking his seat with the other pupils. I found that he was a fresh arrival from Paris, and was sent by his uncle in New York to Monroe to learn English in a country school. At the time it appeared to me sufficiently absurd. He could say only "thank you," "if you please," and repeat the ordinary oaths which he had heard from the sailors, coming across the ocean. And that *he* should be sent to a school to learn English! But noticing the rapid progress of this young man from his contact with the children in the schoolroom and on the play-ground, day after day, I concluded that his uncle knew more about teaching language than I ever dreamed of. In less than five months, he could speak English more rapidly than any boy on the play-ground, but not, perhaps, as correctly. When he was sufficiently advanced, he told me his uncle had assured him he could learn English the most rapidly and correctly in a public school. He was being trained for a clerk in his uncle's jewelry shop, and he was thus placed among children to learn English in its simplest expressions and in its purest idiomatic forms. This was a lesson in the study of languages which has been of use to me in all succeeding years. In consequence, I have never furnished an American teacher for a foreign language, nor permitted my pupils to waste their time in such a hopeless manner.

After closing my career in Monroe, I made my arrangements to go to New York, and prosecute my preparations for the business of engineering.

CHAPTER VII.

MY EXPERIENCES IN NEW YORK CITY.

In the early summer of 1835, I went to New York City, without letters of introduction or recommendation, seeking for such business as would give me support and preparation for the profession of engineering. There were no engineering-schools, and had there been, I would not have been able to attend them as a pupil. It was necessary that I should make my own support. In looking about the city, for an establishment where engineering instruments were manufactured, the first that I came to of this kind, was Blunt's, corner of Water Street and Maiden Lane. I addressed one of the brothers, asking him if he wished to hire a hand. "What can you do, sir?" "I don't know, indeed, sir, until I am tried." "What wages do you expect?" "No more than I am worth, sir." "Who is to determine what you are worth?" "I will leave that to you, sir; but you will surely be willing to pay me my board?" "Have you ever worked with tools?" "Yes, sir." "Well, when do you wish to begin?" This was about the middle of the afternoon.

"Now, sir, if you please." He spoke to his foreman in the fourth story, through a speaking-tube, telling him that a new hand would be sent up to him. I passed up, and found myself in a shop with about a dozen workmen. The foreman placed me at a heavy lathe. The work he set me at was that of turning gimbals, about twelve inches in diameter, for mariners' compasses. Remembering that I was on trial, I did my very best, so much so, that I had very little sleep that night. I was on hand in good time the next morning, determined to push through my work, but after turning several of these brass rings, I told the foreman, who was an intelligent Yankee, that it was rather hard work for me to begin with, and if he would give me something lighter for a day or two, I should then be able to do this kind of work. He did so, and I was so successful in various kinds of work given me, that I had the exquisite satisfaction, at the end of the week, of receiving pay for my time at the rate of a dollar a day, in silver dollars. The foreman himself, only received $1.50, and the other hands, $1.25. The next week I was paid $7 for six days' work, which, to me, under the circumstances, was very encouraging. I had secured board at a respectable house in the Bowery, with a cousin, the managing editor of a daily paper. My fellow-boarders were two married gentlemen with their wives and children, two editors, four journeyman printers, four young ladies employed in a hat establishment, besides the niece of my landlady. . Our hostess was the wife of the brother of the partner of Horace Greely. She was an educated lady, yet of most excellent business ability. Her husband proving a wreck from intemperance, she was obliged to support herself and her children. The niece was taking music lessons in the city, and paid her board. With such a variety of minds and employments, my experiences in my New York home were full of incidents, and sufficiently novel and spicy. Our discussions on politics, science and religion were continuous, earnest, and in some cases, rather belligerent. Among our male boarders we had a Mr. Mitchell, who was an avowed skeptic; two Universalists; three Nothingarians, as they called themselves; and the little Presbyterian, myself. In all the discussions, whether in politics, or religion, or science, I stood by the standard, and read up for every discussion, which I thought it possible to provoke. Thus, my evenings were occupied, either in this running social converse and vivacious discussion, or in my room with my books, of which I had a very considerable collection. Notwithstanding that in my opinion, the other young men, being unmarried, were entirely my superiors in physique, and in knowledge of the world, and in familiarity with society usages, I was not a little flattered in being selected by Miss M——, the niece before spoken of, as the recipient of a free ticket of admission from her, to the rehearsals of the New York Society of Music, and their public concerts. This was my first experience in listening to any other music than that found in religious circles and societies. For, in Boston, I had never been present at concerts, and only once at the theater. There were a sufficient number of boarders in our house for all sorts of amusements and games and plays within our own parlor. It was proposed, however, one night, that we should visit a public ball, given on Broadway. Each gentleman selected his lady from the party, and I found myself, for the first time, in a promiscuous dance. Not, that I took any part in the dancing, for I never took a dancing step in my life, but it was a novel scene. My partner, Miss Householder, was kept upon the floor in every set of the evening. This gave me leisure to make my observations. It was the first and last "Public Assembly" that I ever attended. On returning from Broadway to the Bowery, I took the lead, and making a mistake in choosing the street for crossing the Bowery, I led my company into the very center of *Five Points.* Such sights, and such sounds, and such performances as were presented, and impossible to avoid, made, in my opinion, a good moral impression on most of the company. The dancing groups which we saw, were many grades lower than the one which we had left, but still, to my mind, a legitimate sequence in immoral descent. Occasionally, I visited the theater, but usually with a lady of whom I was proud, but I spent very little money on the theater compared with the other young men of our company. My observations upon city life and city associations, even with the respectable parties with which I was familiar, were sufficient, independent of any religious convictions, to insure my safety against all the seductions of city life.

My common evening employment, as I have before stated, was with my books, in pursuing my studies, and in reading such other volumes as I could borrow from the Mechanics' Institute Library. This association was designed to afford a respectable and safe place for evening entertainment. The membership fee was only $1, and a course of scientific lectures was furnished; competent and interesting lecturers were employed to give us a course of weekly lectures on chemistry. I had myself, in Boston, given considerable attention to this science, and had been engaged in the manufacture of chemical apparatus, with my father. I was sufficiently interested to attend these lectures regularly, and to invite a young lady to go with me. Almost every lecture was attended with some experience not laid down in the programme. On one occasion, while attending a lecture by Dr. Gale, on chemistry, he was manufacturing water, by passing an electric spark through a gallon measure of oxygen and hydrogen contained in a heavy glass globe. This globe was connected by means of a stopcock, with a larger vessel containing many gallons of those two gases mingled in suitable proportions. He managed the stopcock, and his assistant turned the electric machine which furnished the spark. In explaining the theory, he neglected, at a certain point, to turn the stopcock, while the attendant, as usual, turned his machine. The result was a terrible explosion of the gas in the larger vessel, as well as in the smaller one. The lights were extinguished, the glass globe was fractured, and the screams of the ladies added excitement to the disaster. The attendant hastened to light the gas, and found the Doctor badly wounded in his arm, and blood flowing freely. No other one in the room was injured, although I was conscious of a fragment of glass passing near my right ear. The Doctor quietly remarked that the demonstration of the force of the gases was rather more *striking*, so far as he was concerned, than he had intended. I said to my companion, it was a more interesting experiment, excepting the Doctor's wound, than I had paid for.

On another occasion, the Doctor exhibited the power of oxygen as a supporter of combustion, in connection with phosphorus. Whether he was aware of the quantity of phosphorus he had used, or not, I am not able to say, but another explosion followed as before. The lights were extinguished, and the ladies screamed. I heard a a lady in my rear groan as if badly wounded. When the lights were restored, it was found that this lady was very badly wounded in her cheek. The Doctor was called, she was taken to an adjoining room, and the lecture, for this time, was adjourned, all feeling that either the Doctor was too lavish of his materials, or too lacking in previous experience.

After the lectures on chemistry were concluded, Mr. Graham, of Graham-bread notoriety, was employed to give a course of lectures on diet. There was not enough of variety or interest in this to hold the attendance. As I now remember, these lectures closed my connection with the Mechanics' Institute. But the greatest advantage of this Institute was that it furnished me all the books I needed, in order to pursue my studies and reading. This course of study and reading in my evening hours, was then, as it ever has been, a leading feature of my life, and perhaps contributed more than any other human means to my moral safety. And it seems to me now, as far as I can observe, that the parent who does not furnish his family with home reading, or the young man or young woman who does not furnish himself with this kind of occupation and interest, is very derelict in his duty, and throws his family or himself into very unnecessary and dangerous temptation. My studies were frequently protracted until eleven or twelve o'clock at night, after working ten hours a day in the mathematical instrument shop, and no doubt, the lack of sleep and the want of muscular activity, for I was then furnished with the nice and delicate work which confined me to a seat, were causes of the sudden collapse of my health. My employers were very patient with me, and generally paid me full wages when I was detained on account of sickness, as I frequently was one or two days in a week. I became dissatisfied with this kind of life, and concluded I would seek a change in the country. It was at this time that I went to West Troy, and obtained employment with the Meneely's Mathematical Instrument Makers. My work was agreeable, and my wages were better than in the city, but my health was miserable. I returned again to the city, thinking that I would try to board myself, and pursue such a regimen as would relieve my dyspepsia. This experiment was only, a partial success. It was during this period of boarding myself, and working as well as my health would admit, that I received a visit from my father, who was then lecturing in Pennsylvania. In May of 1836, he came to attend the National Association of Education, which he had previously been instrumental in organizing in Boston. My father's dissatisfaction with the course pursued by the gentlemen who were leaders in this enterprise was very forcibly expressed, in language something like this: "There is nothing that can be acceptable to these gentlemen, that I have not tried and rejected in teaching, years ago, and anything new I may propose for the consideration of the Association is dismissed as impracticable and visionary. The time will come, however," said he, "when these gentlemen or their successors will say that the measures which I have proposed, are such as have been entertained and practiced by all educators from the time of Socrates, though now they declare them revolutionary and visionary." Not being then a teacher myself, or expecting to be, I took comparatively little interest in my father's work in education. Since then, and especially for the last twenty years, father's experience of fifty years ago has often recurred to me in my experience with leading educators and others of my time.

At our boarding-place in the Bowery, we had occasionally, as an invited guest, at our dinner-table on Sabbath, Horace Greeley. Mr. Greeley added but little to the interest of the occasion, for the reason that he was rather reticent, and not particularly attractive in person. He was even then conceived to be a kind of curiosity. The same method of wearing his hat, and the same old white overcoat in which he has been caricatured, made up a part of his personal appearance. I do not remember that he made a single brilliant or interesting observation during the several occasions when he was with us at the long Sunday dinners. His paper at that time was beginning to excite attention, and his robust and energetic thinking was making for itself its own channel through politics, agriculture, and social improvements. Little did I think at that time that Horace Greeley would afterward stand at the head of the profession of journalism, or that he would ever be a candidate for the Presidency, for any party whatever, and much less for the Democratic party.

Our hostess, one day, came in to dinner with a letter in her hand, remarking: "It is too good to keep; I must read you this letter. Mr. P—— has just left us, and I suppose not to return. He had put into my hands this letter from a lady of New Jersey, who is reputed to be immensely wealthy, having an income of $20,000 a year." Perhaps I ought to have mentioned that this gentleman was a refugee from Ireland. He had been apprehended and imprisoned by the British Government, as having been engaged in treasonable meetings in Ireland. He was well aware that the testimony was sufficient to hang him for treason. During the three days that he was incarcerated, expecting to be tried and convicted, his consternation and agony were of such an intense character, that, being released as he was, through bribing his jailer, he found that his hair had turned white, although he was only twenty-five years old. He was, otherwise than his hair, one of the finest specimens of physical manhood that I ever saw. The letter which the good lady read to us—and she said it was not a letter which she conceived to be of a confidential nature—was simply an offer of marriage from the wealthy New Jersey lady to our friend Mr. P——. She further remarked that he had consulted her in regard to the propriety of his accepting her overtures, and she had told him that she was utterly unable to decide; in fact, he had nothing to do but consult his own feelings and interest. As she described it, the poor man was utterly at a loss, and suffered intensely from anxiety. She smilingly remarked, that she hoped his anxiety would turn his hair black again, as it had previously turned it white. Whether he ever married the New Jersey lady or not, (we were informed she was over sixty) I never ascertained, and I never heard anything more of the handsome Irishman.

While I was employed in New York City in pursuing the preparation for my proposed profession—engineering—this circumstance occurred: A Catholic gentleman came to our boarding-place at the instance of the white-haired Irishman, who was also a Catholic, and made a pleasant impression. He claimed to be, and no doubt was, an Italian nobleman. After the loss of young Mr. P——, our Italian friend disappeared, and I heard no more from him for some weeks. The papers then had a long account of an affair in Baltimore, which I shall here condense:

It seems that, having adopted the vocation of priest in Italy, and having given up his estates to the Church, he had found himself so restless that he concluded to take orders as a missionary in foreign parts. The circumstances of his taking orders, as related in the papers, were these: He was a nobleman by birth, the heir to extensive estates in the Pope's dominions in Northern Italy. At Rome he met a princess, the heiress, also, to immense estates in Southern Italy. A mutual attachment sprung up, and they were engaged to be married at a not remote time in the future. A brisk correspondence was carried on, as is usual in such cases; but at length the correspondence waned; the letters were not immediately answered. The prince now and then received a letter, but at length the princess's letters ceased entirely, and he learned from a priest, the father confessor of the princess, that she was sick with a dangerous disease, and was furthermore informed that it would be fatal to her if she were subjected, in this condition, to the excitement of seeing him. Thus he was deterred from making further investigation, waiting most anxiously the result of this sickness. He was at length informed that she had died and was buried. Under such circumstances, in his despair, and in the consolations which were rendered by the Church, he was led to devote himself to the Church and to immure himself in a monastery as one of the brethren. He passed two or three years in this condition, secluding himself almost from human intercourse, and thus taking upon himself what he supposed to be voluntary punishment of his sins in addition to the loss of his beloved one. Recovering somewhat in course of time from his depression, he sought an opportunity from his superiors to obtain an appointment on a mission to foreign parts, not in the least abjuring his vows or claiming his estates. He passed through France and England

and America, all the while keeping himself in association with the brethren of his order, who were found in almost every Catholic community. After leaving New York, as I have before said, he visited the Catholic College of Baltimore. Now, with that college is connected a convent, the first, most extensive and wealthy of any of the convents in America. In one of his visits to the convent, and to the chapel where the nuns were accustomed to worship, he, from some accident or misdirection or misunderstanding of the course he should take to reach the chapel, passed through a hall designed exclusively for the use of the nuns. The nuns, not now being in public, had removed their veils, and were, no doubt, a little surprised to see a man in that unwonted locality. Our priest was also somewhat discomposed by the succession and array of beauties that passed under his unexpected observation. As he became interterested in their countenances, his eyes met those of his princess among the nuns. They, of course, recognized each other, but not a word, not a lisp, not a sign, passed between them; they understood their ground too well. Now the object was to get communication with each other. The servants around such establishments are not entirely beyond price, and the prince managed in some way or other to secure the friendship and confidence of the servant who was accustomed to give her attentions to the most beautiful of the daughters of the Church. Their correspondence was carried on through this means most industriously for a length of time. By some means the poor, impoverished priest, the prince that was, secured for the use of his princess a rope ladder, and she was enabled, under some holy pretense or other, to find herself in a cell which opened upon the outer grounds. Having this arrangement made, he appeared in the neighborhood with a covered carriage, and, finding himself under the appointed window of an outside cell, received her in his arms, as she descended by the rope ladder. They escaped; but what was the sequel of this romantic affair— whether they obtained their estates and their titles —I never learned. It will be inferred that a similar course of deceit had been practiced on the princess, and that her estates had been secured for the Church by similar means. But these circumstances were the wonder of the day, or of the week, in the newspapers of New York and other cities.

Speaking of the Catholics, I am reminded here of a circumstance related to me by my former partner, Dr. John Nichols, of Kirtland, now of Columbus. He was attending medical lectures at Transylvania University, Louisville, Ky. Being desirous of learning the French language, he accepted, as a room-mate, a French Catholic, who was attending the same course of lectures with himself. The conversation was held for the most part in French, and the frequent subject of discussion was the claims of the Catholic Church, ecclesiastically and historically considered. The Frenchman had received an academical education in a Catholic college in Paris, and was well versed in all the literature and technique of the Catholic Church and priesthood, having been educated with the priests, but himself not yet having taken orders. There was no end of discussion; in fact, all the time consistent with the claims of their professional study was given to this matter of common interest—the claims (*pretensions*, as Dr. Nichols termed it) of the Catholic Church, as the one and only successor and possessor of Christ's authority on earth. The history of the Catholic Church, as given by Dr. Nichols from Protestant writers, was treated with utter contempt by his room-mate, as utterly unworthy of credence or of respect. The doctor found that there was no historical statement made by any Protestant which militated in any way against the dignity and rectitude of the Church as a church, or against the Pope as a Pope, or the Cardinal as as a Cardinal, or priests as priests, in any of these special capacities, but there was a counterpart found in the Catholic books which the Frenchman had in his possession. No greater confidence or veneration or devotion could be possibly expressed or conceived than that which the gentleman gave to these authorities and to the Church at large. In his view, the Church was infallible and had never done wrong. Every form of persecution and assassination attributed to the Church, or any of its officials, was utterly denied, or so modified as to prove the extreme liberality, charity, truthfulness and faithfulness of the Church. These two gentlemen occupied adjoining rooms, one for study and the other as a sleeping-room, with two beds. Coming in from some business one day, the doctor overheard his chum talking earnestly and excitedly with a stranger in the bedroom, the stranger apparently attending meanwhile to his toilet. The doctor was a common occupant of the two rooms. The door was ajar, and the sum and substance of the conversation, as he gleaned it from the inquiries and protestations and exclamations of his room-mate, revealed to the doctor his utter disbelief and contempt of the Catholic Church and its assumptions; of its priestcraft and its subjugation of women, etc., etc. In speaking of this friend and that as having taken orders, of this young lady and that as having taken the veil, amazement was mingled with execrations of the priests and their managing to get possession of such remarkably intelligent men and beautiful and attractive women, and getting them under their priestly control. The doctor was, of course, interested in this line of revelation from his devoted Catholic friend; but, the doctor coughing, or making some other audible sign, his chum opened the door, found him there and saw at once the situation. "Oh," said the Frenchman, "you have caught me at last. Oh, well," said he, "you know well enough how it is; religion is necessary for society, to control women and weak-minded men; but so far as you and I and other intelligent men are concerned, in this country and France— bah! it's only so deep," making a gesture (by drawing his finger across his lips), supposed to signify "skin deep." "Now, doctor, confess— you have got to confess!—you have no more confidence in your Protestant fables than I have in the rigmaroles and stupidity and assumptions of our Church. Both are useful for women and children, to keep them in their places."

One of our boarders was the confidential clerk in the establishment of Arthur Tappan, the leading silk merchant of New York at that time. Now, several months previous to this, his house had been mobbed, his windows broken in, and much of his furniture ruined, while he escaped by a back passage. This frenzy of the mob was occasioned by the fact that he was an abolitionist. It was, perhaps, incited by his rivals in the silk trade, who had desired to secure that part of the Southern patronage which he controlled. His patronage was not diminished in any direction, but was very much increased in the North, by the mob which was set on by his rivals. His store was well guarded by private police, and was never attacked. The fire companies, however, refused to take risks on any of his property, either on his residence or on his silk establishment. On New Year's night, of 1836, commenced the great fire of New York, the first great fire on this Continent.

I ascended to the observatory of my boarding-place, and looking for the fire, discovered that it was in the direction of my place of business, and was an immense and rapidly extending conflagration. The fire continued all that night, and raged with uncontrolled fury. The bells were tolled in every direction, and there was little sleep in the city that night. There being no telegraph, word was sent as speedily as possible to Philadelphia and other places for help in the fire department. The firemen and citizens were utterly exhausted; water froze in the hose. It became impossible to obtain water, or when obtained, to throw it upon the fire. In the early part of the evening, "Old *Hayes*," High Sheriff of the city, ever on the alert, went to the post-office, and remarked to the postmaster that he had better commence packing the letters for removal. The fire at that time was more than a mile from the post-office. The postmaster pooh-poohed at the idea of the fire reaching that part of the city. Hayes went out to view the fire again. He returned and begged the postmaster to prepare at once for removing the postal matter. The postmaster refused, and said it was impossible for the fire to come that distance. Hayes declared it would be there before morning, and went out again, and was gone but a few minutes, when he returned, and declared: "I command you in the name of the commonwealth of New York, immediately to begin the removal of these letters, or I shall take charge of them myself."

The postmaster at once commenced to prepare for removal. The fire reached the post-office before they could remove all the letters, to say nothing of the papers and other mail matter. The Sheriff had taken possession of the city, and had ordered out military companies in addition to all the police force, and at a sufficient distance from the ever-increasing energy of the fire, he placed kegs of powder under the beams of houses, and destroyed a sufficient number to check the onward march of the raging element. In this way only was the city saved from utter destruction. Going down to my place of business on the next day but one after the fire had been checked, and in a measure brought under control, I found that it had come within one block of our building. Passing down into the fire-district, I found a man here and there standing upon the wrecks of his fortune. Especially do I remember the conversation of two men who were adjoining wholesale merchants. One said, "Did you save your books?" "Yes; did you save yours?" "No, everything is gone. It is the only night for ten years that I have not taken my books out, but it was so cold I thought I would not take them."

The insurance companies were all broken up, and paid from five to ten per cent. of all their insurance claims. Now, Arthur Tappan had not been able to effect any insurance in any of the companies in New York, on account of being threatened by mobs and incendiaries. For this reason he had obtained insurance, and full insurance too, in Boston companies. I was standing upon the debris of this immense establishment on Pearl Street, with the confidential clerk above mentioned, when he remarked to me that he had heard Mr. Tappan say a short time previous that he was worth more in consequence of the fire than if it had not occurred. While many other merchants had offered $10 an hour for draymen to take away their goods to a place of safety, the colored draymen had come without his solicitation, and charging no more than the usual rates, and had taken all his goods to a colored church, in a remote part of the city. More than that, in consequence of the straightening and widening of the street, and the erection of new stores, and the greater attractiveness of the location, for different forms of wholesale business, he was satisfied that the lots with the buildings burned upon them, for he owned a block, were worth more than they were before the fire. At the same time, of course, he recovered his insurance for whatever apparent loss he had been subjected to. So, in these ways, he was reimbursed for the hazards that his maintenance of a principle had brought upon him. Not long after this, Mr. Tappan, with perhaps one or two other capitalists, furnished the means for beginning the educational career of Oberlin, Ohio.

While in New York, I was accustomed to attend services on Sabbath wherever there was a prominent preacher or an eloquent speaker. Most frequently was I found at the Chatham Street Theater, then used by Mr. Finney as a place of his great revival work. It was in the immediate vicinity of Five Points. His labors there, his earnestness, his eloquence, and his great success, drew immense crowds, more than could ever enter the building. I had always had my religious convictions; for, trained as I was, it could not be otherwise, and I should have felt that religion was a positive, energizing power to save mankind, and bless our race; but in the natural course, as I conceive, of all original and earnest thinkers, there came a time to me, a time of doubt, while attending Mr. Finney's preaching. I don't remember that I read any infidel books. I had known of Tom Paine's cavilings, and I had been in conversation with many infidels, more or less, all my lifetime; and especially during the previous winter I had had many an argument with my fellow-boarder, Mr. Mitchell, on the authenticity of the Scriptures, and the validity of the Christian hope. It was not in consequence, so far as I can remember, of anything that Mr. Mitchell had presented, nor of my readings, as I have before said, that skepticism invaded my line of thought. But rather, as I now think, from my deductions, from the declarations and affirmations of Mr. Finney, and his what seemed to me unreasonable assertions of the power of the gospel in making man a new creature. I went through this terrible season of doubt. I don't know now that I ever should have recovered, if my health and youthful energies had not been impaired. The Lord knew better how to manage me than I knew how to manage myself. When my health had failed, my animal spirits were subsided, my hopes were shattered and my ambitions frustrated, I had time and disposition then to reflect, and feel the utter helplessness of man in himself. In sickness, and disappointment, and defeat, I found spiritual deliverance, and learned to rejoice in a kind Providence, in his watchful care, and in his abounding mercies. Such an experience I should never perhaps, so far as I can see, have known, had not I been the subject of this merciful line of training.

CHAPTER VIII.

MELISSA AND I.

WE were first cousins. I was two years older than she, but we were born in the same house, in the same room. It happened on this wise: After my Grandfather Holbrook's death, my father took charge of the home farm and occupied the house that had been built by his grandfather—an immense frame structure, with a chimney in the middle as large as most modern houses. During this time he was building a residence for himself on Sentinel Hill, about a quarter of a mile away. After my father moved, Aunt Irene Pierson, with her family, occupied the old homestead, while her husband was carrying on his business in the valley. The family nursery was, of course, occupied by each family. My grandfather and my thirteen uncles and aunts were also born in the same room.

After my mother died, I being two and a half years old, my brother Dwight was taken by his Grandmother Swift and I by Aunt Craft, the wife of Dr. Craft, the leading physician of Derby, and the oldest of my uncles or aunts. Melissa was named after this aunt, and was ever a child of special interest, as, of course, I was to this same aunt. As children we were both trained to self-denial; to active benevolence; to know that we were the children of many prayers; to feel that religion was a practical, living, working principle, and otherwise it was the worst of shams—hypocrisy.

As exemplifying my aunt's religion, I might state hundreds of facts, but two or three will suffice. While her income from her husband's estate—she having been left a widow about a year after she took me—was small, not more than three or four hundred dollars annually, her house was the home or refuge consecutively of several of my cousins who were, for the time, left homeless; also for several others beyond the kindred, who were needy.

For several years she added to her means of benevolence by dipping candles for the uptown store. It was my part to prepare the wood, the fire, the tallow, the candle-wicks and to trim the candles after they were dipped. I think she received a cent a pound for this work, the tallow and wicking being furnished.

There were two maiden ladies living near us, great aunts of Melissa's, who were in indigent circumstances. It was the business of Aunt Craft to see that these women were not wanting in either necessaries or comforts. For several years, through aunt's solicitations, not only was their winter's wood furnished them by farmers who had wood to sell, but her nephews and other boys were induced to make a chopping bee and cut up and split the big pile of wood thus furnished, and to carry it into the wood-house. The cake and pies for such occasions were given, in part, by my good aunt. The work done by us boys under such circumstances was reckoned as fun rather than as drudgery. While my aunt kept a comfortable table for those whom she sheltered, it was a common remark that she would use nothing for herself that she could give away. Besides Aunt Craft and Aunt Pierson, we, Melissa and I, had two other married aunts in Derby. At the home of each of these, the several sisters, with their children, were accustomed to meet from time to time. Melissa and I were among the youngest at these gatherings, and played together as a part of the group. Melissa was a frequent visitor at Aunt Craft's; but the most definite recollection I have of her in our childhood was that I was set down by her side as a punishment, in our pay-school, conducted by Miss Julia Ann Tomlinson, afterwards, Mrs. George Blakeman. Whether or not it had the desired effect of keeping me out of mischief, I do not remember. It was my aunt's special aim to find work to keep me out of the streets, and work that I would cheerfully do. She frequently gave me stints in cutting and splitting wood, with some money compensation when the work was done. She encouraged me to read, obtaining books by borrowing or purchasing. She put me in charge of her cow and garden, always working with me when practicable. The only penalty she ever inflicted, that I remember, was when I had disobeyed her and gone away with other boys to the river for bathing, much to the injury of my health, as she thought, to look at me very sorrowfully on my return and say, with tears, "I am so sorry, Alfred, that you will go with those boys, when you know that they are disobeying their parents as you are disobeying me." This was too much for me; I broke down completely, and promised her that I would do everything she wished.

When I was ten years of age and Melissa eight, Melissa's parents moved to Ohio. We were thus lost to each other for ten years, both developing under influences favorable for our future fitness for our united destinies and allotted work.

I have heard Melissa say that she never knew when she was converted, and she could not remember the time when she did not pray in secret and of her own accord. She was the leader in every good work, though modest and timid to the last degree, and continued so to the end, always placing everybody's interest and comfort before her own.

In her girlhood, in Kirtland, she would go a mile every night through the woods in the dark, over an almost impassable road, to attend a revival meeting or a singing-school. She was put on all committees for active benevolent work. While she was trained by her parents to habits of industry in the ordinary work of a country farmhouse, she always had a volume convenient to read in all odd moments. She made good use of Uncle Coe's library, containing all the works of the standard English writers, as Milton, Young, Cowper, Addison, Johnson, etc.

If she were only here I could get many more facts. I only give such as I came into the knowledge of from observation, or incidentally by narration from others. She attended Oberlin one year and worked for her board in the boarding-hall. She was put in control of certain duties, as she was found to be the most interested in seeing that the work was done.

When I came from the East, being then twenty-one years of age, I first became acquainted with her as a woman. She was the most intelligent, the best read, the most attractive of any of my Western cousins, and I soon found Melissa's society very agreeable and intellectually healthy. She was the leading soprano singer in the Kirtland Congregational Church and the leading Sabbath-school teacher; she could get up a celebration at the Kirtland Seminary; she could bring the singers together for a musicale at Uncle Coe's, with whom she was a great favorite. His conversations with her were as with his equal in mental force. No one could talk gossip in her presence; she would deftly turn the conversation. Nor could any one peaceably lavish compliments upon her, though she confessed she was extremely eager for the good opinion of all the good. She sometimes remarked that she was afraid that she appeared too forward in her endeavors to do good, and that she would gladly follow, as she frequently did, when any one else would lead.

Now, could a little sickly mortal, paralyzed with the dyspepsia, dependent upon relatives and friends for a subsistence; could such a victim of sickness, of poverty, with no prospect, in the estimation of his friends, look on such a personality with any other feelings or expectations than respect and admiration? Besides, she was a great favorite in Akron, Ohio, where she spent the most of two years. I heard, through her friends, that she had had several offers from the best young men of that thriving town. She has told me incidentally of these young men, of her growing attachment for one of them; but when he expressed in her presence, not a disavowal of religious belief, but a commonplace sneer at some church usage, which she considered scriptural and vital, she candidly informed him that her views and his of religion and religious sanctities were so utterly at variance that she could not get her own consent to any further association than that of the courtesies of members of the same young society. He made every necessary and possible apology and explanation, but she could not condone any disrespect for that which was of all things the most sacred to her.

Melissa found her patience and Christian charity most tried in the care of an aunt in Akron. For many months before this aunt's death Melissa took the place of a nurse. Her exactions in her low condition were often most trying, but Melissa waited upon her with the greatest sweetness and patience, notwithstanding the demands and complaints of the declining woman. After her aunt's death, she taught in Middleburg for a season, at the same time boarding in Akron at a cousin's. While there she was much sought after as a leading soprano singer in all the churches. I think the Episcopal Church offered her a salary, which she did not accept, but continued her services in the Congregational Church, of which she was a member. These circumstances occurred in the years 1838, '39 and '40.

When I returned from Boonville, Ind., where I had passed a year and a half, arriving at Akron on horseback on my way to Kirtland, and coming up the street toward our cousin's residence, the first person that I saw was Melissa, looking out of a chamber-window, for any other object than what she saw. Catherine Smith, another cousin, was with her; she was not expecting me, though she had recently come from Boonville. Their welcome was characteristic. Catherine: "Why, Alfred Holbrook, I should as soon have expected to see an angel from heaven as you. How did you get here?" Melissa ran down to meet me at the door, and with every proper demonstration led me into the house, and drew out my story. "Why did you leave Boonville? How long have you been on the road? How did you think you could ride so far in such poor health? Where are you going now? You will stay with us to recuperate? You are certainly a great deal better than when you left Kirtland. Catherine has told me how miserable you were in Boonville, how hard you tried to do something to support yourself; how many times you broke down, seemingly worse than ever." To all these interrogations and exclamations, I made, of course, fitting replies. But when I told her of a conversation that I overheard between Catherine and Aunt Mary, whose guest I was, and had been for three years, she burst out, "What a plucky fellow." The conversation that I overheard, and which I related in the presence of Cousin Catherine, was substantially as follows:

I had been out surveying for Mr. Spelman, a couple of days. The line between his farm and that of Mr. Clutter, an original settler, had become obliterated. Mr. Spelman, one of our Yankee colonists, was convinced that the dividing fence was far within and upon his land, as originally laid out by the United States surveyors. Mr. Clutter would listen to nothing of the kind. At last, however, he agreed to have the line run, and said, if it was not where the fence was, he would pay the expense, but if it were, Mr. Spelman should foot the bill. It was necessary to go back some five miles to find a reliable corner. From this corner we all started, a company of a dozen men, as several others were interested in this boundary line. Pursuing my way carefully with my compass, it was soon discovered that Mr. Clutter was badly mistaken in the location of the fence. As we entered his farm, the line that I was following with the compass, was several rods within Clutter's field, as bounded by the fence. Mr. Clutter was very much excited, and swore that he would not give up five or ten acres of his best land, even though he had agreed to abide by my work as surveyor. I had previously gone to the county records, and obtained a copy of the plat of the line, and a description of the corner. It was originally marked by three trees, a black walnut, two feet in diameter, a sassafras, twelve inches, and a red oak, eighteen inches in diameter. On reaching the corner with my chain, and taking out my notes for the description of the corner, only one tree was within many feet of my corner, as determined by the survey, that was a red oak, in the right direction, and at the right distance, but more than three feet in diameter. I asked Mr. Spelman to cut into this tree. Mr. Clutter was wild with rage, declaring he would prosecute us for trespass, etc. Mr. Spelman very calmly cut away for a while, then handed the axe to another man interested as he was in this line. At length, after cutting nearly to the heart of the tree, the original blaze was found, and the marks agreeing with the record. A general hurrah was raised, especially by those on the winning side. Mr. Clutter and others who were the losers, were glum enough, but gave up the fight. I had come out within four inches of the corner, as laid down in the record. He paid me for my work as he had agreed; Mr. Spelman gave me double the amount. It was after such a two-days' work, walking through woods and underbrush, that I found myself prostrated, and glad to lie abed. And now the conversation that I overheard as I lay in an adjoining room, with the door ajar:

Catherine.—"Alfred is down again worse than ever. I am afraid he will not live long."

Aunt Mary.—"It is such a pity, he is so smart and so ambitious. This is the twentieth time, I believe, he has overworked and made himself sick."

Catherine.—"I should think he would learn to hold himself, and not break himself down so often."

Aunt Mary.—Why, he seems to be so anxious to earn something to support himself, and not be a burden on anybody. He needn't feel that he is a burden to us; we would rather have him with us than not. His influence with the children is worth a great deal; I should hate to have him leave us, but I am afraid he will not live long; every time he breaks down, he is worse, and it takes him longer to get up again." This was as much as I could stand. I rose from the bed, opened the door, and said: "Aunt Mary, I am much obliged for your sympathy. I've heard all you and

Cousin Catherine have said, and I am thankful for all your patience and kindness; but I am not going to be gotten rid of so easily as you seem to imagine; I expect to live a long time yet, and I hope some time or other to be able to repay you or your children for all you are doing for me. Why, I may have the privilege of supporting you in your old age, who knows?

Aunt Mary.—"Why, Alfred, that is just like you, I am sorry you overheard us, but you are the most hopeful being I ever saw."

Alfred.—"Well, Aunt, faith, hope and charity are sisters; I have the faith and hope, and you have the charity, the greatest of them all. You are to me the very personification and incarnation of patience, fortitude and goodness." Years after, when Aunt Mary had become a widow, had lost all her property, and was dependent on a son-in-law, I had the privilege of contributing for several years to her support, though I never assumed it entirely. Thus, in a small measure, my my faith and hope, dominant in all my helplessness, brought compensation for Aunt Mary's charity, and I enjoyed the privilege thankfully. Melissa took it on herself to convey to Aunt Mary, from time to time, our united offering. She did it in her own sweet way.

Remaining a few days in Akron, I proceeded to Kirtland, and was welcomed again by Uncle and Aunt Coe—she was my father's sister. Melissa being released from her duties in Akron, returned also to her home in Kirtland. Melissa and I were much together that summer, talking, reading, riding, visiting. Whether she ever thought I would be anybody's husband, or not, I do not know; I never asked her. One thing I do know, that our cousinly intercourse contributed much to the improvement of my health and spirits. There were few days that we were not together most of the time. In my growing acquaintance with her, she revealed a wide intelligence, a true Christian culture, a familiarity with all the standard literature of the time, an ambition to do something and be something far beyond the plodding of other good and amiable women. Her highly cultivated musical taste, and her exquisite execution of sacred music, added much to her personal attractions and her sweet and winning ways. In all these respects, and in every other, she came nearer to my ideal than any one that I had known before. But what was I? A little, hopeless and helpless invalid. She afterward quoted a reply to one of her letters, in which, according to her, I said: "Your kind words and cousinly affection, so sweetly expressed, brought up all the blood in my body, to make, if possible, a blush, in revealing to myself how dear you are to me."

During the summer, I had visited Berea, expecting to meet my father there. He was in New York, engaged in introducing the new Berea grindstones to the national market, and selling stock of the proposed Lyceum village.

I found John Baldwin deeply engaged in constructing lathes, and adapting them to his water-power on Rocky River and on Mill Creek. He narrated the means by which father had discovered the value of the Berea grit, and the prospect thus of paying off debts contracted in the support of the religious community which they had succeeded in drawing together, a large part of whom, according to Baldwin, were "too religious for any earthly use, and continued so as long as bread and butter were furnished to their faith and devotion, by his works and credit."

A few only of these remained—those too sick or too worthless to get away. They obtained very meager supplies from Baldwin, and erelong, they had all disappeared, finding it just as easy to work for a living elsewhere as at Berea.

I was much interested in Baldwin, and in his peculiar personal appearance and habits, his sacrifices to what he considered a scriptural plan for a Christian living; and I never discovered that he changed his views, of having all things in common, though he did confess that they ought to have had more vigorous tests in examining those whom they admitted to the privileges and immunities of the community. At Baldwin's solicitation, I took up my residence in Berea, still expecting father to join me. Not feeling able to teach six hours per day, I agreed to commence a school for the children of Berea, at $15.00 per month, teaching three hours daily.

My school began with two pupils in the forenoon, with an increase of one in the afternoon. In the course of two weeks, the attendance was fifteen, all the children of Methodist families.

The school-room was in a rickety, unfinished, cheerless building. It had been used for the offices and meetings of the community, now disbanded. Soon the influx of laborers and families, drawn by the new industry, made it necessary to put up a new building for the school. It was of two stories, the lower being used for a store. The upper story was properly furnished with seats, desks and apparatus, at Mr. Baldwin's expense. I began my second term in the new building with thirty-five pupils. As yet, I dared teach but three hours per day. Of course, help was needed, and brother Baldwin agreed to pay an assistant $25 a month, leaving the selection to me.

I wrote to Melissa, requesting her to join me in the Berea School, stating the conditions. I was receiving $15 a month for half time, she would be paid $25 per month for full time.

The school filled up rapidly. We organized classes in the higher branches, including the higher mathematics and Latin.

In order to receive Melissa as a pupil in Latin, I taught the fourth hour, the recitation being before breakfast. She had studied Latin somewhat before, but encouraged me by affirming, after a few recitations, that all the time and effort she had spent on Latin were worse than wasted, adding, "It was the only study that I ever attempted that I did not enjoy; I had only learned to hate Latin; but the way you manage the subject and the pupils is a revelation to me. There is no study that I ever enjoyed so much." In fact, she rose at four o'clock to get out her Latin lessons. It is hardly necessary to say that I studied in the same room with her. I was reading Bourdon's Algebra (a new book to me), and keeping ahead of my class in that subject.

Now my readers will naturally incline to the opinion that I was in love with this splendid cousin. Well, perhaps so; but my health was so precarious, my animal vigor so low, my blood so thin, that love must have been of an ethereal mold—a spiritual afflatus, far removed from what ordinarily passes under that name. Melissa had, from the first renewal of my acquaintance with her in Ohio, been an object of deep interest, of increasing affection; but no idea of marriage had ever intervened as desirable or possible with me, and I am equally sure not with her.

But, as we lived in so close relations in our daily work, in our studies, in our mutual confidences, she became, as it were, a part of my daily life, and the greater part of my enjoyment.

In the course of my work, in trying to meet the necessary demands of my pupils, who had commenced coming from abroad, I had begun teaching six hours a day. My health was miserable; dyspepsia, with all its train, preyed upon my energies and embittered my physical existence. Melissa was accustomed to prepare my food. For a considerable time it was no more than a thin piece of corn bread, about three inches square, at each meal.

Under such circumstances, it is now unaccountable to me how I could have worked as well as I did, and have brought a continually increasing attendance from parts near and remote; for animal vigor, as well as a cheerful spirit, is essential, ordinarily, to any successful teaching.

Among those who came from abroad were several Quaker students from Marlboro, Ohio: the Wilemans, Abram and Hannah; Amos Walton, Eugene Pierce, Augusta Pratt and others. They were all earnest students, devoted friends, and are all remembered for their thousand kindnesses, both in Berea and afterward in Marlboro, with the warmest feelings of gratitude and affection. I secured the aid of these friends at different times in managing my classes, or other exercises, when I was too much exhausted to go on with my work. (It was through the solicitation of these same friends that I subsequently went to Marlboro). Keeping myself in an exhausted condition, by trying to do the full work of a teacher, with not one-fifth the strength that health would have given, it is a marvel now how it was done. Undoubtedly Melissa's sympathy, care and encouragement may account for it in some measure; but divine aid was daily, hourly sought, and, as I have sufficient reason to know, were vouchsafed. At length I was seized with a severe form of dysentery. For a day or two the disease continued and seemed to grow worse; whatever little blood I had in me was fast flowing away. A physician was called by my anxious friends. He prescribed rhubarb powders, as he called them; what else I do not know; but they had little effect, unless to increase the malady. I was lifted frequently off and on the bed; but, as I was placed back, perhaps for the fiftieth time, I found that I had no vitality left; I could hardly move a limb or bend a finger. I concluded death was near. I refused the medicine I had been taking every fifteen minutes when awake. Abram Wileman was watching with me. When I refused to take the powders, he urged them as my only hope; I still refused; I could not talk. He left the room in alarm—it was near midnight—and aroused the inmates of the house. They all came in and thought I was delirious; the doctor was sent for in great haste. He soon came, and feeling my pulse, assured me that, unless I took the powders, gangrene would speedily commence in my bowels, and that would be fatal. I whispered, "Let me die in peace." He gave me up, and told my friends that I could hardly hold out till morning.

When thus I ceased to be disturbed externally by the watchers and internally by the medicine, I became easier and fell asleep. Nothing passed my lips for three days; then I took a glass of water, then another. On the fifth day I walked across the room and ate a little rice which Melissa had prepared for me. In another five days I was in charge of my classes—a wonder to my friends and an astonishment to myself. In my work I recovered speedily, and found myself gaining flesh, in consequence of restored digestion; and if there was ever anything in me besides will-power and a good purpose, it was when I discovered that I weighed 120 pounds—a phenomenon never occurring before or since in my career. Now psychical devotion for my cousin was doubtless reinforced by physical energy. I was another being in my feelings, in my work, in my conversation, and especially in my interest in my cousin. Could it be supposed that such a man as I would have dared to think of—well, of addressing such a woman as I well knew Melissa to be! The venture was made with many a doubt and more fear. I was accepted. I hardly believed that she could *love* me. I had thought she had watched over me and taken care of me in my long good-for-nothingness, as I had known her to do for others, out of the natural goodness of heart, or from pure Christian benevolence; but that she loved me was more than I dared to hope. In talking over the matter, when we had come to an understanding, she assured me that she had long before made up her mind that, if she could not marry her cousin Alfred, she would never marry anybody else; she would live for him, and for him alone. My protestations were, doubtless, none the less sincere and fervent.

Our engagement being known, we were the subjects of much more interest than before, perhaps. Melissa was a great favorite with all the good people of Berea, as she had been everywhere else. She was a devoted church and Sabbath-school worker; she was ready in every case of sickness and bereavement; she was a kind of omnipresence, as she always was wherever sorrow called for sympathy, sickness for watching, or distress for relief.

We were ill-prepared for married life, in any other sense than that I needed a helpmeet, just such a good angel as Melissa had proven herself to be. I had saved nothing from my meager income, always giving to the Church and other benevolences more than I had earned. In looking over my finances, I found that, if my debts were paid, I should then be $20 in debt; but, however, Melissa was not exactly in the same condition, for she had, in her own right and at her control, about $12 the day that we were married. In fact, I had to take four dollars from her funds to pay our marriage fee. The minister, Uncle Coe, handed the money back immediately to her, though he had come forty miles to marry us at his own expense.

Melissa, at this time about twenty-four years of age, was to me a most lovely woman. Her height was just about the same as mine (she had a way of making herself shorter when we stood together); her figure was lithe and graceful; her motions were light, easy and rapid; her features were regular and classic; her eyes were blue, gentle and winning; her expression was ordinarily sedate and self-possessed: when interested or excited, glowing with such emotion or fancy as possessed her at the moment. In her conversational ability she was far superior to most intelligent society women; her powers of description, narrative and mimicry were seldom equaled; her vocabulary was extensive and always equal to the occasion; her selection of words was spontaneously refined and exquisite; her sympathy with all who came near her, and her interest in their well-being, were an unbounded and perpetual flow, always engaging and winning by their sincerity and sweetness. Though never aggressive in society, she was always accepted as a leading spirit in every good enterprise; her counsel was always sought and her administrative ability always recognized. In after life her efforts in public speaking, especially in addressing our large body of students, were impressive, sometimes affecting, and were always sought for; and when her person graced our rostrum, were always spoken of with appreciation and admiration. Her work in private with students, whether sick or well, was always kindly, thankfully received. Her ministrations to the sick, bereaved and desolate, especially of the poor, can but be remembered by hundreds with benedictions on her memory.

But her full power to yield blessings and happiness are only known to her servants, her children and her husband. No devotion could be more unselfish; no sacrifice more exhausting; no influence more pure; no affection could be more sweet, warm, charming, than that bestowed, as an ever-flowing stream, upon the special objects—her home-ties and duties. She always declared if there were any excellencies in her character and conduct, they were all of grace, and all the result of her trust in the love and mercy of her Redeemer. "I feel that I ought to do what little I can for him in his creatures, who has done so much for me," was her not infrequent expression.

I have said that, being cousins, there was, or seemed to be, a very general disposition among our friends to question the propriety of our marriage. We, of course, talked the matter over, and each came to the conclusion that we were designed for each other, and that this one match had been made in heaven; at any rate neither of us would be worth much without the other. This was surely true so far as I was concerned.

While I do not by any means advise cousins to marry, I never regretted the transaction; but, on the other hand, feel now as I always felt, that Melissa was the one woman of all others that the good Lord had made, trained and fully endowed with all the necessary forces and graces to compensate for my deficiencies—to stimulate, beautify and sanctify my life. I have never felt otherwise.

After boarding a week or two, we set up housekeeping in the rooms that we had occupied before marriage, save that they were one less in number. We were adding three rooms to the house Brother Baldwin had given us. Our outfit for housekeeping was, as nearly as I can remember, an air-tight stove, three chairs (one a rocker), a deal table, washstand, bowl and ewer, a bedstead and bedding, a looking-glass, all borrowed; also three plates, two bowls, three knives and forks, three spoons, three larger dishes, two pitchers, a tin pan, two tin cups, obtained on credit from the store under our schoolroom. We were married on Sabbath, so we lost no time from our regular school work. Of one thing I am confident, that never young couple began life more thankfully; with less anxiety as to the future, or with more entire confidence in each other. We had tried each other, and each had seen the other tried as no others had been, at least, within our knowledge.

When in after years Melissa was alluding to one of several offers she had refused, and stating the reason why, I asked: "Then why didn't you refuse me? I wasn't the hundredth part as good a catch as any of those fellows. They are all now rich and getting richer." She replied: "Well, now, wouldn't you like to know? I won't tell you; but I will say that I never found a man before whom I dared to trust with my destiny and happiness." We commenced family worship, alternating daily in leading the worship—a practice which we continued as long as I felt it prudent to ask her: "Mother, will you pray with us?" Her prayers were always an inspiration to me, as her presence was joy and peace. It is chiefly through her gentle, kindly, motherly influence that my children are a great help and comfort to me, and, as I can thankfully and truly feel, a blessing to the world.

When Brother Clayton came among us as pastor of our M. E. Church, and became acquainted with our school work in all its variety, extent and "power for good," as he expressed it, he said to me one day, "This is all a mystery, how such an institution could have grown up here, with no support from any Church; with no endowment or appropriation from the State; but when I became acquainted with your praying wife, and discovered her power with the Source of all power, the mystery was explained." The life of every mother is one of continued sacrifice at the best, but that of Melissa, above all others, in that in the infancy and childhood of all our children, she spared no effort or self-denial to leave me free for my school work. She felt that my sleep must be disturbed as little as possible, in order that I could be at my best with my classes; and so of all other family cares and labors—they were assumed and carried with a devotion and martyrdom that few, even of mothers, can measure or understand.

But not in her family only—for her husband and for her children—were her powers of endurance and of charity taxed; until the last five years of her life she was the matron of the institution, having a motherly care over all the young ladies in attendance, and personally watching with the sick or providing them with nurses and every attention possible for their well-being. Indeed her husband and children feel that it was this extraordinary exertion, and these continued and exhausting efforts for sick students, that brought her to her grave many years sooner than would otherwise have been the case.

Her sympathy for the sick was not confined to the school, but had become a proverb in Lebanon: "The only way to have a call from Mrs. Holbrook is for some one in the house to get sick, then she will come without being invited or sent for."

In many a financial extremity, when she would, as it were, instinctively divine the difficulty, the consolation and support offered was, "Well, husband, I can do nothing but pray for you; but if I am weak, my Lord is mighty, and he will deliver you; I know he will."

It was Melissa that suggested and initiated the daily students' prayer-meeting. It was a matter of unceasing interest to her, and she not infrequently gave it her presence and her counsels, which the students were ever most eager to receive and to follow.

It was her suggestion that a contribution be taken up semi-weekly for missionary purposes. The prayer-meeting made her the almoner of these funds so raised. Seldom less than fifty dollars a year passed through her hands, for which she always presented her vouchers to the committee appointed by the prayer-meeting to record them.

Melissa was a stern patriot. She sent her two oldest boys into the army at the first call for 75,000, the oldest then only seventeen. The third was sent two years afterward, he being then only fifteen. She kept up constant communication with her boys, her daily and constant prayers following them. While she felt her country's need, she had, more than most mothers, a confidence that her sons would act a brave and honorable part in every time of danger and of trial. She treasured to her death their letters from all parts of the South where their country's emergencies took them. There was scarcely an important battle, East or West, in which one of them was not present and engaged.

They all returned in due time, without a wound or a scratch, though the oldest had a ball-hole through his coat. The youngest, John, went round with Sherman in his march to the sea. In his first experience he was taken prisoner at Harper's Ferry, but immediately paroled; so that none of the three suffered the terrible fate of the thousands who were starved in the Southern prisons.

On one occasion during the war, when a Northern man had come from the rebel army, in which he had enlisted, and had been received by his relatives in Lebanon, though the general opinion was that he was really a spy, or a Southern emissary of some kind, Melissa declared that she would not have such a man in her house. "But," said I, "be careful, wife; perhaps your brothers (she had two brothers in Tennessee, extensive land and slave-owners) will come to see us, and you don't know but that they are both rebels." "They are no rebels; but if they are, they needn't come here; I don't want to see them." The Northern lines having soon after passed Ripley, Tenn., where these brothers were living, one of them knocked at our door one day. Melissa went to the door. "Why, Josiah, is that you? Are you a Union man?" not offering her hand. He demurred somewhat at such an unexpected reception from his gentle sister, and replied: "Well, what if I'm not?" "Then I don't want any Northern rebels in my house—not even my brother." "Well, I'm all right, sister. I have escaped the Southern service only at the risk of my life a hundred times." "Come in. I am so glad to see you. I knew you and John would both prove true men."

Her personal animosity to rebels was confined to Northern men, however. We had, all during the war, more or less Southern students in school, many of whom were outspoken rebels. They received just as much care and sympathy in sickness, and, perhaps, more consideration, generally, than Northern students. She sometimes remarked: "If I had been born and educated in the South, doubtless I should have been among the bitterest of the rebels."

One of our teachers, Mrs. Roberts, was a Southern lady. She had three brothers in the Southern army and four brothers, or brothers-in-law, in the Federal ranks.

When the war closed, or rather, when Richmond was taken, one of her brothers, who had been a body-guard to Jeff. Davis, made his appearance at our house, where she was boarding. She did not hesitate to inform us who he was, where he had come from and all other particulars. We received him, but felt it prudent to conceal him, or at least, not to let it be known who he was. He remained with us three days, and was safely housed and hospitably entertained.

I relate this circumstance to show that Melissa's charity was of no narrow quality. It was, on the other hand, of the most considerate and far-reaching character, winning the confidence of her country's foes even.

She did not go as far as one mother that I heard make a short speech during the war. Said she: "I have sent seven sons into the army; my only regret is that I haven't seven more to send with them."

But Melissa gave her sons prayerfully and thankfully, saying, as one after another left us, "I may never see this boy again; he is a free gift to my country. No sacrifice is too dear for my country's liberties."

Her boys all returned, and not one of them was charged with dishonorable conduct, that she or I ever heard of, during the war, though they, one or the other, were in all the great battles of the Rebellion, and altogether they were in the service nine years. Were their mother's prayers their panoply?

Melissa's correspondence was extensive, and continued to within a few weeks of her death. It was chiefly, beyond that with her own immediate relatives, confined to letters of sympathy and condolence, or to special cases when she thought a word of counsel and encouragement would be well received and do good. No case was so hard and hopeless among the young men of Lebanon but that she would venture a letter of kindness, admonition and encouragement; and often I have read letters from such "hard cases"—replies to hers—which evidenced the fact that no man can be so debased but that there is humanity in him that can be reached.

Letters from the leading thinkers of the times are found in her desk in reply to something from her, though it was her practice in all such cases to state that she did not expect a reply; she only wished to give her word of approval "to the manly course," "the outspoken sentiment so needed by the times." The most of such letters were written without the knowledge of her husband, but the returns always came to my knowledge and appreciation. Truly, "she did what she could." Her last words to her husband were,

"Husband, I shall be at home before to-morrow." Her earthly home had been made, by her gentle presence, her sweet influence, unswerving integrity, her loving counsel, her affectionate ministrations, her superhuman devotion to the comfort and happiness of her husband, children and servants, as near a heaven as is ever enjoyed on earth. Her heavenly home, doubtless, will be the theater of larger and sweeter activities.

The words of King Lemuel were never more fitting: "Her children arise up and call her blessed; her husband also, and he praiseth her. Many daughters have done virtuously, but thou excellest them all."

CHAPTER IX.

A REMINISCENCE IN BEREA.

In 1847, as near as I can remember, the first Institutes were held in Ohio. One was conducted by Marcellus Cowdry and Horace Benton in Norwalk; another by Thomas W. Harvey in Chardon, and a third in Berea by myself. All were held in the month of August. The new brick building having just been completed, with a chapel to hold 300, it was a fitting opportunity, as I conceived, to initiate these new accommodations with a Teachers' Institute. I expected to conduct most of the exercises myself, but had also engaged Professor Hamilton L. Smith, of Cleveland, and my uncle, Truman Coe, of Kirtland, to assist me in lecturing on natural sciences.

Professor Smith had already acquired a reputation by lecturing, and also by having written a volume, and was, as I supposed, the very man I needed to carry through a course of lectures on electricity and mechanics. He commenced his course in due time, and such was the profundity and erudition displayed in his first lecture, that nobody but Uncle Coe and myself were able to understand or be interested in his remarks. The rest of his audience were teachers who were yet scarcely familiar with the most simple and fundamental principles of these departments of science. At the close of the lecture, I congratulated the professor upon the originality and profundity of his presentation of his subject, but tried to apprize him, as well as I was able, of the fact that such a course of lectures would be utterly useless to those whom he was employed to instruct. He seemed to realize the fact as I presented it; but, as his entire line of procedure had been prepared for a body of learned and practical scientists, his second lecture was not unlike his first, but rather more recondite and far-reaching. I found I had an elephant on my hands, and was much relieved when he received word of sickness in his family and begged to be excused from the remaining lectures of his course. This procedure only illustrated to me the better a fact which I had long dwelt upon, that erudition is very likely to stand in the way of successful elementary teaching. The presentation of rare and peculiar phenomena, with their explanations, and illustrations, is but a waste of time for those who are not familiar with first principles. By this I do not intend to say that a man or woman can ever know too much to teach any class of pupils on any subject, even A, B, C; but it is rather difficult for those who have been engaged for years after they have passed the fundamental principles, and have spent time, money and labor in original investigation, to come back again to the simple and general principles of a science; in other words, adaptation to the class of pupils and to the circumstances is one of the essential characteristics of a wide-awake and successful teacher.

Uncle Coe and I followed the plan of instruction I had laid out and advertised. Our Institute was a great success, and aided very much in bringing the school into repute and filling up our accommodations next year.

While Uncle Coe was with me, spending these two or three weeks, his brother, Daniel Coe, came from New England—from the old homestead which Truman, the younger brother, had sold to him when he left Derby—to visit his brother in Kirtland. Not finding him in Kirtland, he came to Berea, where we, Melissa and I, made arrangements to entertain him, as well as we were able, in our own family. Before I go further with my story, it will be necessary to go back three or four years and narrate a circumstance connected with the Coe family. Uncle Truman's oldest son, Milton, had, after pursuing a college course, gone to Derby, expecting to spend the winter in his uncle's family, and, if possible, to obtain business. He had hoped that, if he could do nothing better, he could obtain a school and teach in Derby, or its vicinity, six months or more; but he had no other expectation than of making his headquarters at his uncle's home—the place which had formerly been his home. He arrived there Saturday, remaining with them over Sabbath. On Monday morning his uncle informed him that he had secured a very comfortable and cheap boarding-place for him in the town, about half a mile distant. Milton hardly knew what to say or how to manage the matter. He had no means of paying his board for any length of time, and from what his uncle said he found that he did not expect to pay it for him, so that he was compelled to go to other relatives until he could secure an income of some kind. His uncle, however, very kindly told him that whenever he felt disposed he would like to have him call and see him. It is hardly necessary to say that Milton never called at his uncle's after that. It was a different kind of hospitality from that which had always been exhibited in his Kirtland home toward all his father's and mother's relatives, and, indeed, to almost everybody else.

Now, when Daniel Coe, who was a Methodist local preacher, found that he was to be entertained at my house for two or three weeks, he expressed his extreme reluctance to accept of such hospitality, and urged me very seriously and earnestly to accept of pay for his board, all of which, under the circumstances, was somewhat trying and somewhat amusing. After he had spent the night with me, however, he was invited by three different families to come and spend the entire time with them. He hardly knew what to do, or how to explain it, or what interpretation to put upon it. It was so entirely different from anything that he had ever seen or experienced, or had ever practiced himself. There was no end to his varied expressions of appreciation and amazement, that a perfect stranger should be made the object of such unbounded and unrecompensed hospitality. I relate this circumstance to illustrate the difference between Eastern and Western hospitality, as I have witnessed and experienced both in different times and places, East and West. By this I do not intend to imply that all my friends and relatives in the East are of the character of Daniel Coe. On the other hand, they are as boundless and unremitting in their attentions to their Western cousins as could possibly be desired, and are most thoroughly appreciated; nor do I intend to say that all Western people are lavish, by any means, in their gifts and graces, in entertaining either friends or strangers. So far, however, as Melissa and I were concerned, we had both of us from childhood and youth been too often the recipients of this kind of unpaid kindness, not to feel it a privilege at all times to entertain friends and strangers as best we were able. Melissa had a "Prophet's Chamber" in her house, always in readiness to entertain the preacher, the missionary, or the agent in any good cause.

CHAPTER X.

SOME EXPERIENCES WITH JOHN BALDWIN.

Mr. John Baldwin in 1839 had freed himself from a Methodist religious community in Berea, O. He had disengaged himself from his partners by assuming the financial responsibility of the community. In this community there had been a collection of several hundred people of deep religious convictions, but of utter incapacity for business. Mr. Baldwin had become convinced that, whatever were his religious views in regard to having all things in common, it was impracticable with such a class of men and women as had collected there. Hundreds of acres of valuable land, which he had devoted to the use of the community, had proved insufficient to furnish food even, and in order to save the company from bankruptcy, he had found it necessary to assume all the debts and liabilities of those who had been looking to him for support.

About this time, through H. O. Sheldon, he became acquainted with my father's plan of a Lyceum village, and invited him to Berea to establish his Lyceum village in that place. Burdened with debt as he was, Mr. Baldwin, still feeling that he should use himself and his property for a higher end than the mere accumulation of wealth, thought my father's plan of a Lyceum village would be feasible and desirable. On the arrival of my father at Berea, from New York City, the first work in hand was to lay out the proposed Lyceum village, in streets and squares, on the property Mr. Baldwin had used for the community. After a forenoon had been spent in running lines with the compass, and the party had partaken of dinner, father suggested to Mr. Baldwin, since they had been delayed in their work by a dull axe, in sharpening the corner stakes, that they should go out and grind the axe. Mr. Baldwin proposed to turn the grindstone while father held the axe. Grinding and talking for some little time father failed to look at the axe. In turning it over to examine it, he was astonished to find what an amount of steel had been ground away. Said he: "Brother Baldwin, where did you get this grindstone?" "Down in the creek below here." "In the creek below here?" "Yes, the whole country is based on this kind of grit." "Is that so? You have a fortune more substantial than the Bank of England underlying your possessions." This was the discovery of the famous Berea grindstone grit. Mr. Baldwin immediately proceeded to rig lathes, apply water-power, and turned out grindstones by the hundred. My father had always been accustomed to the blue-grit of Nova Scotia for grindstones. He affirmed that this grit was as much sharper than the blue-grit of Nova Scotia, as that was sharper than any common bowlder by the roadside. A market was at once opened in New York for the Berea grindstones. They displaced all others, and I suppose millions have been realized from that quarry, a large proportion of which Mr. Baldwin gave the institution of which he was the founder.

After paying off the debts of the community, Mr. Baldwin went into various expenditures for the benefit of education, among which was the erection of a large three-story building for the accommodation of the school which I had begun with two pupils, and of which I was still in charge. It had by this time increased to one hundred and fifty pupils.

Mr. Baldwin persistently held to the theory that young men and women could support themselves at the same time that they were pursuing an education. Notwithstanding every pupil he tried to educate in this way cost him more or less out of pocket, yet he never gave up the idea that there might yet be found some who could support themselves in this way. He furnished me every desired facility in building up a school. For example, on my wedding day he presented me with a deed to a house and lot for my immediate occupancy. Being himself a devoted Christian, and earnest Methodist, he concluded to make the school a Methodist Institution, and place it under Conference management. He had some difficulty in obtaining acceptance of the property, which has since proved to be worth not less than half a million of dollars. The Conference consented, at last, to receive the property, provided Brother Baldwin would raise two thousand dollars for apparatus and other facilities for the Conference School. He complied with the condition and paid the money himself.

When this school, which I had originated and built up, with Brother Baldwin's financial help, had passed into the hands of the Methodist Conference, I was urged to become a preacher, from the usage of having preachers at the head of Methodist institutions. I declined, saying that I was not a preacher, nor had the Lord called me to serve him in that manner. I was a teacher, and would serve the Conference in that capacity and in that only. The result was, that several preachers were placed over this Institution, among whom was Dr. Warner, afterward chaplain of the Ohio Penitentiary. He was a most eloquent preacher, an earnest Christian, a splendid worker, but no teacher. The students, in a measure, lost their respect for him in that capacity. He was perhaps incited by his friends to think that I was a party to his failure as Principal of the Institution. At the end of the year he resigned, and the Conference sent Rev. Wm. L. Harris to take the position.

The circumstances of my re-election that year are interesting at least to me. Brother Baldwin took a very earnest part in it. It was said by the friends of Dr. Warner that all the trouble between the School and Dr. Warner originated with me; hence there was considerable effort, on the part of the preachers especially, to dislodge me. Adam Poe, who was our Presiding Elder, had been posted on all the difficulties in the school, and at the election by the Board of Trustees, eight of whom were preachers, and seven, laymen, it was thought that there could not be a majority secured for my re-election. Knowing the prejudices in the case, I went to Brother Baldwin and told him I was not a candidate for re-election. He wished me to permit my name to be submitted as a candidate. I told him I could only consent on two conditions. The one was, that I should have my salary secured, with an advance of one hundred dollars; the other, that I should have the unanimous vote of the Board. "The first condition I will take care of myself," said he; "the second condition is too hard, but I will see." Not being a member of the Conference, or of the Board, I was not present at the election of the several teachers, but as soon as the election had transpired, Brother Baldwin came to me somewhat elated, saying: "You are trapped, your conditions are met." "How can that be?" said I. "I understood the preachers were all going to vote against me. He said: "I don't know how that was, but there are fifteen members of the Board, and there were fourteen white beans, and one black one, and we know the President voted. He was not authorized to do so except in case of a tie. So there is no doubt of your conditions being met, you have received a unanimous vote." I replied: "That being the case, I shall continue in the Baldwin Institute" (the name which was adopted). Brother Harris came on in September, and assumed the responsibility of the Principalship. I had heretofore, although nominally assistant, been Principal of the school, and had taken the chief responsibility in maintaining the order and discipline of the Institution. Brother Harris insisted, although he was Principal, and received double the salary, that I should still continue in charge of the general study-room, thus burdening me with the responsibility of the government and order of the Institution. Brother Baldwin was absent in New York at the time Brother Harris assumed his position, and I had not him to appeal to. I soon gave in my resignation and withdrew, having previously received a call to establish a school at Chardon.

I went immediately there to complete arrangements for my removal. On my return, I met Brother Baldwin in Cleveland, on his way home from New York. Of course, I was compelled to inform him of the reason why I was not in school. I had made arrangements to move to Chardon to open a school there. He seemed very much affected, very much chagrined, and asked if it were not possible for me to remain in Berea. I told him it was impossible for me to work in slavery; that Brother Harris had come there prejudiced against me, and that he and I could never work together. So I moved to Chardon and commenced my work there.

I soon had an application for the purchase of one or both of my houses in Berea. I returned to Berea to complete the negotiations for the sale of my property. Now this property had been virtually given me by Brother Baldwin, in addition to the regular salary which I felt to be satisfactory. In view of this fact, I offered to give the property to Brother Baldwin for anything he chose to pay for it. He refused to purchase it for anything less than its full value, and assured me I should feel free to dispose of it as well as I could and he would aid me in making the sales.

I have not related the manner in which I came into possession of the second house and lot. My labor in the management of the school in the new brick building before it came into possession of Conference, was severe and exciting, and Brother Baldwin suggested that I build a new home on the lot near the school-grounds. I told him I had nothing to build with. He said it made no difference. "You need a home here, and it will be my business to see that you get one. Now," said he, "will you come with me and select a lot? You may have any lot which you select, and I will make you a deed for it." I selected one overlooking the water. He didn't know whether it would be healthy, as we had suffered considerably from malaria of the same pond. "Well," said I,

"I will select another lot more remote." He objected to that, because, he said, the land was marshy and would cost too much to drain it. "Brother Holbrook," said he, "let me select you a lot, won't you?" "Yes," said I. He took me to his orchard, and, looking upon the village plan (which didn't include his orchard), he said, "I think the southern part of the orchard will make you a good lot." "Sir," said I, "do you mean to say that you intend to give me a lot including one-third of your splendid orchard?" "Does it suit you?" said he. "I am satisfied, if you are." That settled the matter. He proceeded at once to furnish me building materials for a new house, a two-story brick, 36x18. In digging the cellar I struck a vein of soft water, all the water in that region being specially impregnated with various salts from the clay soil, and too hard for many domestic uses. This is the way I obtained my two houses in Berea.

On another visit to Berea I met Brother Baldwin going home from Cleveland. After inquiring as to my condition, and the health of my family, he began to give me the news from Berea, during the few weeks in which I had been absent. Among other things of interest that he mentioned, he said that he had been engaged in building a new railroad to his quarries in Berea, and the railroad would be completed in a few days, for the transportation of his produce, grindstones, and other such wares. "Oh," said he, "I want to tell you a little experience I had the other day in going to Cleveland. You know I am not very particular in my dress, and I started from my quarries with several thousand dollars in my pockets to pay for the iron which I had purchased from the Cleveland and Columbus Railroad Company. When the conductor came along to collect the fare, he addressed me rather roughly, saying: 'You old cuss, what are you doing here?' I told him I was on my way to Cleveland to attend to some business. 'Well,' said he, 'come here with me.' I did not move quite as fast as I do sometimes, and he found it necessary to assist me, by taking hold of my collar and leading me out into the baggage car, where he set me upon a pile of mail bags. After collecting the fare of the rest of the passengers, he returned to me with the inquiry, 'Well, old chap, have you got your fare ready?' I told him I would get it ready as soon as I could. Said he, 'Hurry up, hurry up,' I took out my old pocket-book, which happened to have about $10,000 in it, and turned over the bills one after another, apparently to see if I could find a small bill to pay my fare. As I was turning over the $100 bills, I looked up to the fellow to see how he was taking it. He was beginning to sweat and look rather wild. I told him for his encouragement that I thought I could pay my fare, if he would only give me a little more time. I didn't find the bill I was looking for, in fact, I had a pass, but I knew it was not there. In the meantime he broke out: 'Who in h—l are you any how?' 'Oh, that doesn't make any special difference, does it, if you get your fare all right? Now, come to think of it, I have a pass over this road, if I have not left it at home.' Not waiting for my pass, he shot out of the car. I continued sitting on the mail-bags until I got to Cleveland, as I had not obtained permission to occupy any other place. The authorities, however, heard of the occurrence through the passengers, or some of the employes, and assured me that I should never be troubled with him again. He was discharged, I suppose, as I never saw him afterward."

Another piece of news he related on our way to Berea. I will try to relate it in his own words as nearly as I can. "You remember Sister C——, Brother Holbrook?" "Yes, sir." "Well, you know that she is a devoted Christian, but has her moods. She came into our house one morning in a special mood of exultation, and addressed me with, 'Brother Baldwin, don't you think there was a special interposition of Providence in Brother Holbrook's leaving here and Brother H—— taking his place as Principal of our school?' 'How so?' said I, 'Why, don't you see, *that* little man could never have controlled these bad young men that have been here this year. It takes Brother H—— to crush them and keep things in order.' I replied, 'Why Sister C——, Brother Holbrook was here nine years and the school grew continually under his management, and I never knew of his having any bad students to manage. It is my opinion if he had remained here nine years longer that there would have been no bad boys in the school to manage.'"

After he had completed the large brick building which I have mentioned before, his wife, having exerted herself to board the hands, was prostrated with a low, nervous fever, brought on by overwork and exhaustion. He left all his business to other people and gave his entire attention to nursing his wife, with such other help as he deemed necessary. He employed no physician. He heard that some of the neighbors were circulating the scandal that he was too stingy or too crotchety to employ a physician. Now, no man thought more of his wife than Brother Baldwin, nor had reason to. This report, therefore, was more than he could stand. He did not wish to trust his wife in the hands of a physician, fearing the result might be very uncertain, but felt that his own constant care and affection were necessary to her recovery. The plan which he adopted to quell these scandalous remarks was to me exceedingly interesting and like the man himself. He made me his confident from the first. The plan was this: He first sent for Dr. H——, the leading physician of ———, about twenty miles from Berea. He came, spent about twelve hours in examining Mrs. Baldwin's case, and decided, after this long, serious and faithful examination, that if there was any local trouble it was in her lungs, prescribed for her and said that the most she needed was good nursing. He left the case in Bro. B.'s hands. The next day Brother Baldwin sent for Dr. W——, an old physician about four miles south of Berea, in Strongsville. He came and spent a day examining her symptoms, for Brother Baldwin was considered the most important patron in that part of the State, perhaps. Not being informed as to the decision of Dr. H——, he concluded that the difficulty of Mrs. B. — if there was any local disease — was in her kidneys, saying also, that her sickness was principally from overwork, and the most that she needed was rest and careful nursing. Next day Dr. L——, a young physician, was sent for. He came, and examining the case about five minutes, without hesitation said the only difficulty was in her stomach, and that her digestion was impaired. The next day these three physicians were called to hold a consultation. Each found that the others had been called before. They were previously committed on these diagnoses. After they had wrangled about two hours and had come to no agreement, Brother Baldwin dismissed them, saying perhaps he had better take the case again himself. He paid their fees and they departed, not suspecting the trick that had been played upon them. The fun of the thing was the intelligence, penetration and confidence of the young doctor, who had been practicing only a few weeks, while it took all day for the old physicians to find out what he ascertained in five minutes, and prescribed for accordingly.

I left Berea in 1849. In 1880, Brother Baldwin, on his annual visit from Bayou Teche, La., where he had purchased a plantation, gave me a call at my residence in Lebanon, O. It was on this wise. The whole country, for some two or three years, had been terribly afflicted with tramps. Almost daily one or more called at my house. No doubt they had learned from each other that my wife never permitted a person to go away hungry from our door. Being seated with my family at dinner one day, we noticed a disagreeable-looking man going toward the kitchen where the tramps generally called. Josiah remarked, looking at his mother, "There, ma, is one of your friends." Mrs. Holbrook started to the kitchen, to meet him at the door. Looking at him kindly and earnestly, she said: "What do you want, sir?" He looked at her intently and said: "Why, Sister Holbrook, don't you know me?" "Why, Brother Baldwin, is that you?" My wife, in relating the circumstance afterward, vindicated her practice of feeding tramps by quoting the Scripture. "Be careful to entertain strangers," etc.

CHAPTER VIII.

MY EXPERIENCES IN CHARDON, O.

Having received an invitation from the citizens of Chardon to commence a school in that place, I removed there with my family in the fall of 1849. My school opened pleasantly, with a larger patronage than I had expected, or than had been promised. I took with me for an assistant, Miss Edna Whipple, a former pupil. We were thoroughly occupied with the work of the school. The patronage was at first entirely from the village and from the immediate surrounding country, and the study, for the most part, accomplished in the schoolroom. As the school progressed, students came in from abroad and secured rooms, some of whom only recited in the schoolrooms, studying in their own rooms. The children of the village, however, continued to do their school-work in the schoolrooms, both recitation and study. I took charge of the principal room, which was the study-room, hearing my recitations in the same room. Miss Whipple occupied a similar room and heard recitations, her classes studying under my charge. I introduced here the self-reporting plan of sustaining order, the same as I had previously used in Berea. There is no form of school management which has been the theme of so much bitter discussion as this method. It is charged against it that it is an infallible method of training to lie; that it never, in any instance, can have any other effect upon the character and morals of its victims; that even the best of pupils will be demoralized by its inevitable influence. Where I first received my idea of the advantage of self-reporting, I am unable now to determine; but the result in my practice and with my pupils, while it did not make a perfectly truthful individual of every pupil under its influence at once, was such that I was satisfied it was the best plan I had ever employed to train pupils to truthfulness and to respect those who told the truth. In reflecting upon this matter and endeavoring to account for the sad differences of opinion with regard to its influence upon the moral character of the students under its control, I have made this generalization: That in all cases where it has trained pupils to falsehood, deceit or treachery, it was from the utter mismanagement of the system, or from the unreliable character of him or her who attempted to apply it. For a moody or exacting person to adopt this plan would, as I apprehend, result in a failure. For an untruthful person, or one in whom the students had not the most implicit confidence, trusting to his honesty, and, I may say, his honor, the results would be sad indeed—infallibly so.

Much is said upon moral instruction, and many books are written for the purpose of aiding teachers in reclaiming their pupils from the immorality of untruthfulness, and, doubtless, there are few teachers who have not made the strongest effort to aid their pupils in overcoming this disastrous habit; but these efforts, so far as I have noticed, have been, for the most part, hortatory rather than practical. And if any measures have been used in this direction, they were nothing more nor less than punitive, and understood by the student to be vindictive. The hortatory plan, in other words, preaching, does very little good, so far as I have noticed, unless sustained by a consistent and kindly administration of thorough-going and practical love for the truth and forbearance with those who have little regard for it.

Now, training in any direction, as I understand it, requires that the trained have opportunity for practice under the possibility of failure in the lines of the desired improvement. The only practical plan in training for truthfulness—that is, such a plan as will give the student an opportunity to help himself, for training is nothing unless the trained takes hold of his own case—and the only really successful plan of training the pupil in overcoming this bad habit, that I have ever seen recommended or experimented upon, is that of self-reporting in some form or other. For, how can there be any training, in the true sense, other than that the pupil shall accept of the fact of his being trained, and make an effort to help the trainer to overcome the difficulty involved? Self-reporting, involving proper precaution, consistent, kindly administration, a hopeful purpose on the part of the trainer, a charitable construction for the partial failure of the trained, involves just the elements which constitute a successful course of training in any and every other line of human experience; none the less so in the matter of truthfulness, as the first object to be gained in moral improvement in an ordinary school of ordinary children. My experience in this direction was, on the whole, in every case wherever I used it, the gradual improvement of all who came under its influence. It did not prevent lying and deceit the first day entirely, nor the first month, nor the first term, nor the first year, with a good many children. What plan ever did, that did not involve self-reporting? But it never failed to reach a large majority of untruthful students, and to make them more watchful of themselves and more respectful to those whom they had reason to know were truthful, and better prepared to accept the conditions of religious influences in the church and Sabbath-school. To those who have tried it and failed, I would simply state, that there were some conditions mentioned above, which were lacking, as causes of the failure. The causes were not in the system itself; and if any teacher has any other system more practical or practicable, of training children out of this form of wickedness into a reliable and truthful character, I have never heard of anything of the kind. I am still waiting and watching for a more practical plan of training in this direction.

In its geological character Chardon was an interesting study for me. It is situated on a knob of higher elevation than any other point, perhaps, in Northern Ohio. Near the summit of this knob was a never-failing spring. The town seems to have been laid out about this spring, as "The Green," so-called, being in the center of the town, incloses the spring. It mattered little whether it was wet or dry, cold or hot, the overflow from this spring was not affected. A considerable brook flowed from it. Other springs on different sides of the knob also shed their smaller streams in various directions. It was a query with me, whence the source of all this supply of water, pure, clear and soft? In examining the outcroppings, I discovered that the formation was conglomerate, constituted almost entirely of quartz pebbles of all sizes, from the most minute to the size of a man's head. These were held together by sufficiently fine cement, and not having analyzed it myself, or having known of others analyzing it, I could hardly think the cement was limestone cement, as the water which flowed from it was entirely soft. The supply was found over the entire extent of the village—not that there were overflowing springs in every village lot, but that the well of nearly every house, so far as I knew, was made by boring an orifice about four inches in diameter to a sufficient depth, varying from six to twelve feet. A long, cylindrical bucket of tin, with a valve at the bottom, was used for taking water from these wells. The question arises, Whence the supply of water? since no land any higher was found anywhere within fifty miles, if within a hundred miles. The only solution suggesting itself to me was, that the water came up from beneath—from the conglomerate formation by capillary attraction, as it finds its way through the bottom of a sugar loaf to its top.

At the close of my first year Miss Whipple left me and entered into a marriage arrangement to emigrate to Walla Walla, Washington Territory. There were then no roads, and her company was, so far as I know, the first company that went through the wilderness to that coast. I presume she and her descendants can be found in that locality at the present day.

In those days St. Paul was far enough out of the world, and any educational efforts in that direction were certainly of a missionary character. It was my good fortune to meet, in one of my trips to Cleveland, a Miss Bishop, educated by Governor Slade, of Vermont, for the purpose of aiding the West in her educational progress. It was somewhat on this wise: I was buying books at the Cleveland Bookstore. It seems that the ladies of Cleveland had formed a temporary association, with very liberal contributions, for the purpose of furnishing Miss Bishop an outfit with which to commence her school work at St. Paul, among the half-breeds and other children inhabiting that locality. Miss Bishop was selecting the requisite books, school apparatus and stationery for her enterprise. While conversing with her her brother came in upon us, a reputable lawyer of Cleveland at that time. As there were no public conveyances further West than Chicago, I inquired of her how she ever expected to get to St. Paul. "Why," said she, "my brother, here, intends to go with me as far as the public stages go; then I expect to go alone." "What!" said I, "all alone?" She said: "Yes; he is going with me as far as he dare. I am going the rest of the way by myself." The lawyer brother accepted the statement with a smile, and, I suppose, at least, there was the semblance of truth in the statement, though not so much, perhaps, as there was of humor and bravado. It was characteristic, however, of Miss Bishop, as an educator, as a missionary and as a lady. For many months afterward her communications from St. Paul appeared in the *Independent*, and were exceedingly instructive, interesting and racy. They at length ceased. It was some years afterward that I learned the cause of the discontinuance of her communications to the *Independent*. It was the old story. She fell in love with a reckless fellow out there and threw herself away. And I must always think that this, and other like results, of Governor Slade's missionary efforts in behalf of the West, deterred him from continuing what seemed to me a very laudable enterprise.

It was while living at Chardon, in 1850, that I first heard Governor Corwin as a public speaker. I had seen him in New York City and heard him in friendly conversation, but only knew of his oratorical powers as a current, historical fact. I made the journey of forty miles from Chardon to Cleveland for the express purpose of listening to Governor Corwin. He was canvassing the State in behalf of Henry Clay, the Whig candidate for the Presidency. Cassius M. Clay made the first speech. It was logical and commanding; about an hour in length. Governor Corwin followed, and, according to my judgment, Mr. Corwin's effort transcended anything and everything I had ever heard from the leading orators of the nation, among whom I could enumerate Daniel Webster, John Quincy Adams and Henry Clay. In any *rôle* in which any one of these gentlemen excelled all others, whether that of senatorial dignity, of fiery declamation, or of winning and irresistible persuasion, Corwin was, according to my estimate, superior to any of the gentlemen above named. But in humor, in wit, in buffoonery, in ridicule, in travesty, in burlesque and in every line of the comic and grotesque, Governor Corwin was transcendent over everything that I ever witnessed.

My journey, the time and expense involved, and the fact of standing three hours, without any possibility of securing a seat, as one in a crowd of ten thousand, were a thousandfold compensated by the wonderful gifts of the inimitable orator; inimitable, as I think, in all these directions.

On returning from Berea after the sale of my property, and being delayed beyond expectation, and feeling it necessary that I should be at home on Sabbath morning, I started from Berea to Cleveland late in the afternoon. Passing through Cleveland, I took supper, it being already dark, at a public house, several miles east of Cleveland. Calling for my horse immediately after supper, I went out to find the most unmitigated density of darkness that I had ever experienced. It was my purpose to travel as far as Kirtland, at least, that night. It was utterly impossible for me to distinguish the road. I left the guidance of the horse to his own better sight. Before I had traveled very far—a half a mile or so—it gradually became lighter, so that I could distinguish the road. The clouds seemed to be as heavy and as dense, and the atmosphere as thick with fog as before, but all around the eastern horizon was a beautiful ribbon of light shining through the darkness. I had never witnessed such a phenomenon before, and have never since. What would have been the result of my night's venture in the darkness without this providential interposition in my favor, I am unable to opine. As it was, however, I traveled with the usual rapidity over the muddy road until I reached my destination for the night, about nine o'clock. The next morning, starting early for Chardon, I found my family in good condition, as I had hoped, the doctor in attendance, and one of my children born soon after my arrival.

My experience with county examiners in the different counties where I have taught has been somewhat varied and considerably interesting. In every county I have found one of the examiners in a rival school. In Geauga County, as in other counties, it was the practice for the examiner to drill his pupils previous to the examination for days or weeks upon the very questions on which they were to be examined. Of course there was sufficient reason for objection to this plan. Every such examiner, for a temporary advantage, was working against the interest and honesty of the schools, his pupils and the community. Every such examiner has worked himself out of the confidence of his patrons and out of his position, sooner or later. Still, this is a grievous evil found in many parts of this State and in many others. The laws which have been enacted to correct the evil are, in most cases, by the conniving of the Probate Judge, whose duty it is to enforce them, ignored. The dishonesty thus practiced on pupil teachers becomes a working element in the schools thus obtained, and thus the malign influence extends itself through the working forces of the counties and States. It is one of the unsolved mysteries to me, how respectable and religious people can trust their children or wards, or others in whom they are interested, to that kind of demoralizing teachers. Why do not the people of the county, or of the township, or of the town, execute the laws, exterminate such dishonesty and save their children from its terrible influence? Our laws are sufficiently explicit, but the community lack the necessary thoughtfulness and moral firmness to execute them.

Using the means obtained from the sale of my property in Berea, I went through Philadelphia and New York to Boston, with the purpose of selecting such apparatus as I might need for the illustration of the physical sciences. I expended $2,500 in making this outfit. The manufacturer of whom I bought the apparatus had been trained in the manufactory of my father, and had been a shop-mate of mine in Boston. He was afterward Mayor of that city. As I had been raised in a manufactory of apparatus, and had been trained in all its scientific uses, I felt it impossible to teach these sciences without apparatus and such aid as it would afford in the way of illustration and practical work. Much of the same apparatus I retain at the present time; some, however, was destroyed in the burning of our university building in Lebanon, Ohio, in January, 1883. It consisted of a thorough outfit in pneumatics, mechanics' and chemistry. This was, perhaps, one reason why my school grew so rapidly in Chardon and more than filled the accommodations of the town. During the first half of my second school year, from overwork, my health began to fail, and I thought it best on the whole to retire for awhile from the business. I closed my school, refunded tuition and concluded to travel. Meanwhile, Dr. Nicholls, of the Western Reserve Seminary, offered me an equal partnership in the institution of which he was Principal. I accepted the proposition, and after a few weeks' rest moved to Kirtland and took my position as Associate Principal in Western Reserve Teachers' Seminary.

CHAPTER XII.

EXPERIENCES IN KIRTLAND.

HAVING sold my property in Chardon, and closed up my business, I accepted the invitation of Rev. Truman Coe, to occupy his house in Kirtland with my family. "Uncle Coe," as both wife and I called him, had been intimately connected with our childhood and youth, as he was in partnership with my father in the Derby Academy, and afterward in a private school which both wife and I had attended as children. Truman Coe's father was a tanner; Truman himself was a shoemaker. On the shoemaker's bench he acquired his education, at the time my father was at Yale. I have heard Uncle Coe allude to his studies upon the shoemaker's bench in words something like these: "For years, while working and mending my neighbors' shoes, I was mending my own wits from such authors as Cicero, Sallust, and Virgil." In fact, his familiarity with the Greek and Latin was more thorough and longer continued than that of most college graduates. I have heard my father allude to Uncle Coe in words like these: "*I* could always accomplish anything I undertook, if I had good tools; Brother Coe can do equally as well without any tools." Truman Coe had married my aunt, Anne Holbrook; hence we called him Uncle Coe. His education was extended and thorough. The dons of Yale thought his success in self-education demanded recognition. The honorary degree of M. A. was conferred upon him before my memory. I remember him always as a man of very kindly disposition, of equable temperament, and especially fond, as I supposed, of his cousins, as he used to call my wife and me. He had always been, from my earliest recollection, a praying man, and maintained family prayer and prayer in his school; but it was not until an extensive revival swept over the country that Uncle Coe united with the church. He then took a decided stand as a working, efficient, aggressive Christian. He was ordained as a minister, and occasionally preached in Derby, and supplied vacant pulpits in the neighboring towns. About this time he was called to fill the pulpit at Kirtland, Ohio, where three of my Holbrook aunts had moved with their husbands and families, to take possession of their respective farms, which had come to each as her patrimony. When I came to Ohio, I made Uncle David Holbrook's and Uncle Coe's equally my homes, but Melissa Pierson (my cousin) was at Uncle Coe's with her cousins, more, perhaps, than at her own home. Here we renewed our acquaintance; she having left Derby at eight years of age. Uncle Coe was a cogent writer, and an interesting preacher, and reckoned one of the strong men of Western Reserve. Exceedingly modest and reserved, he always waited to be called and urged before he acted, but when thus urged and roused, he exhibited powers which always commanded respect. In Kirtland, after concentrating the activities of the religious people in the Congregational Church to which he was called, and erecting a church building, he put up a very comfortable home for himself. It was this home that Melissa and I frequented before we were married, and now occupied after we had been married seven years. Apropos, Uncle Coe traveled from Kirtland to Berea, a distance of forty miles or so, to marry "his children," as he then called us. When he was presented with the meager fee for the ceremony, by the newly-made husband, he turned to my wife and said: "Mrs. Holbrook, this is yours." It was the first time she was addressed by that name. As an instance of Uncle Coe's temperament and self-forgetfulness, I will relate a circumstance which I had from my father: Once on a time, while he was paying addresses to Anne Holbrook, she being engaged in domestic affairs, just at that time having taken a batch of bread from the oven and distributed it upon the table to cool, Truman, thinking it time to depart, and being interested in Aunt Anne, more than in any other sublunary affair, seized a loaf of bread, and departed with it under his arm, leaving his hat upon a table. Whether Anne called after him, and corrected his mistake, or whether he put the newly-baked loaf on his head, and discovered his mistake in that way, I was not informed, but he returned after a while, and dumping the bread on the table, seized his hat and escaped.

Before entering upon my duties in Western Reserve Seminary with Dr. Nichols, feeling that, as yet, my health was not sufficiently restored for the confinement of the school-room, I made a journey to Cincinnati and New Orleans, for the purpose of introducing Holbrook's apparatus into the public schools in these two cities. I succeeded in selling about twenty sets to the Cincinnati schools, and about fifty sets to the New Orleans public schools. I had no letters of introduction; in fact, knew no one, to whom I could address myself. This was in 1850. I found Mr. Gilford, Superintendent of Public Schools in Cincinnati, and Mr. Barney, afterward State Commissioner, Principal of the High School. Mr. Knowlton was Assistant in the High School. I was treated with all desirable consideration by all these gentlemen, and my visit to Cincinnati was to me agreeable and profitable in every sense.

I will go back a little and give an incident in Columbus, where I stopped to visit an old friend, Dr. Asa D. Lord. The Democrats were then in possession of the old State House. As a joke, I suppose, more perhaps than for any other reason, they had granted the use of the Representatives' Hall for a course of lectures to Mrs. Cole, of Michigan. She was the first female lecturer that I ever listened to. I had attended two lectures of her course, and was about to depart for Cincinnati, when I learned, incidentally, that her last lecture was to be delivered on Woman Suffrage. I was informed at the hotel, where I was stopping, by those who seemed to know, that arrangements had been made by those worthy legislators to get the cream of their joke in giving Mrs. Cole the use of their hall, out of the lady, by turning her into ridicule in her last lecture, which was on Woman Suffrage. The most witty Democratic speaker was selected for this purpose. He prepared himself for the occasion. The hall was crowded; the front seats were occupied by the most fashionable ladies of Columbus and Cincinnati. They came to see their sister, Mrs. Cole, made a laughing-stock for their amusement. For aught I know there were as many Republican ladies present as there were Democratic. From Mrs. Cole's appearance, when she ascended the Speaker's desk, she had evidently been informed of the fate which had been planned for her. Though her lectures were written, she had, in delivering them, given her notes little attention, speaking very fluently and forcibly from memory or from the excitement of the occasion. This evening, as she commenced reading her notes very closely, she made several errors in enunciation, miscalling her words and exhibiting other signs of embarrassment and distress. Standing as I did, where I could see the countenances of all those ladies upon the front seats, it was very apparent to me that they enjoyed her discomfiture. A smile and a mutual recognition of her stumbling went along the whole line. But she proceeded and it was some minutes before she recovered herself. Leaving her notes, even throwing them aside, she commenced her address in earnest, talking to the Legislature, and not to those ladies who she discovered expected her defeat and annihilation. It is impossible for me at this day, having read and heard a hundred such lines of argument since, to reproduce her able address, but this I remember, that after she had recovered herself she soon made some very happy points, in answering objections to woman's use of the ballot, and as she made these points, one after another, the aforesaid ladies looked glum and in a measure subdued. Proceeding, however, giving little or no attention to the ladies, she took up one objection after another, making to each in succession a reply more able, more crushing and more unanswerable, until, at some happy turn of her discussion, she brought down the house. I looked along the row of ladies to see how they took it. They began to smile in spite of themselves. Another happy hit accomplished the demolition, if you please, of all opposition from these same ladies who had gone there to enjoy her crushing, but who now seemed rejoice in her triumph, and several of her last replies to the oft-repeated and stupid objections won these ladies to clap as loud as their little hands and their fans would admit. I looked for the Senator who had taken a prominent place, sitting on one of the window-sills, and who had expected to leave not even a shadow of her or her argument, but a vacant window-sill only was all there was left of him. The replicant was missing. She closed amid the uproarious and continued applause of all present.

It was also my good fortune, while in Columbus at that date, to listen to John B. Gough for the first time, in the First Presbyterian Church of that city. I had heard much of Gough, but had never seen him. As it happened, two legislators took their seats near me, and as the speaker was delayed an hour beyond the time appointed for his appearance, by an accident to the train, these worthy legislators took up Mr. Gough as a theme for discussion. Each seemed to vie with the other in denouncing, traducing and abusing him as a shallow-pated "jack in the pulpit," who put on theatrical airs and spoke something he had borrowed or stolen from some writer or orator. At length Gough entered the church. There was no particular demonstration for or against him as a speaker. He took his place in the pulpit, but had only spoken a few sentences when he said he could not speak in that place, in that box. Turning to the committee he suggested that they bring two or three dry-goods boxes and make a platform. The boxes being brought, and a temporary platform erected, he again took his place as speaker. From the very commencement of his speech he carried his audience with him His humor, his wit, his scathing denunciation of liquor-sellers, his terrible pictures of the drunkard, the calamities of his home, were terribly thrilling and vivid. In one of his remarkable climaxes, in which, as I thought, his first sentence was as powerful an enunciation of his position as could be made, he went on for six progressive, accumulative steps in his climax, until the house, carried by spontaneous energy, *rose*, *rose*, *rose* to their feet—many standing on the benches—stretching their necks to the uttermost, ascending, if possible, by the same ladder of argument with his climax. It occurred to me, "How about my legislative friends who had called him 'jackanapes' and 'jack in the pulpit,' and all that?" I found both of them stretching themselves upon the benches and throwing their hats toward the ceiling, in common sympathy with the general appreciation of the wonderfully eloquent flight of the speaker. The special theme for this climax was the feelings of a mother when she first found that her only son was a drunkard.

After I had spent a week or two in Cincinnati, and had become somewhat familiar with the workings of their school systems and with some of their prominent teachers, Mr. Gifford proposed to take me to Mount Adams and introduce me to Prof. O. M. Mitchell, who, he had been informed, had just returned from his first lecture tour through New

England. The Professor was in a very happy mood. I was especially interested in his narrative of his triumph over the Harvard professors, Pierce and Bond. It seems he had met these gentlemen at some scientific association previous to this, in New York or elsewhere, and knew them at sight. When lecturing in New Haven to the highly intelligent people of that city, with increasing audiences, he had sent his agent to Boston to advertise his course of lectures. He had heard from this agent that the professors there had said that his claims were preposterous, especially his claim in which he stated that he could measure the tenth part of a second of circular distance in the heavens with his new apparatus. By the way, I ought to say here, to make the matter more intelligible, that Dr. Locke, of Cincinnati, and Professor Mitchell were each claimants for the invention of a machine by which wonderful accuracy was obtained both in measuring time and circular distance. I had already visited Dr. Locke and found him very communicative, very intelligent and very interesting, and not at all sparing in his denunciations of his rival in his "absurd" claims for originality in this invention. The apparatus in both cases was connected with an astronomical clock carried by electricity. But I will go on with my story. Under the influence of some men of leading social position in Boston, who had been reached by letters from Prof. Silliman, who had previously lectured in Boston, and through communications to the daily newspapers, Prof. Mitchell found, when he reached his audience hall, an immense assemblage; seats full and almost every standing place filled. The aforesaid Professors were not present. Mitchell felt very much disappointed. He, however, proceeded with his lecture as usual. He had not occupied many minutes before he noticed the entrance of these two gentlemen to whom he had sent a polite note of invitation. They stood in a very remote part of the room and as far in the shade as possible. Prof. Mitchell proceeded with his lecture, and, I am sure, if his lecture was as interesting and as fascinating as his description of it, he must have brought down the house over and over. "All the time," said he, "I was making my advances and winning the acknowledgments of my audience and their appreciation of my points, I was slyly viewing the place to see what influence it would have upon the Harvard gentlemen." He took his hat, as he was talking to me, and commenced his explanation that he had then given to his audience, coming by degrees to the final irrefragable demonstration of the point, that he could measure, instead of the one-tenth, the one-hundreth part of a second with entire accuracy. He continued: "As I was approaching the climax I noticed the people were beginning to rise and reach forward, as if to catch more clearly and distinctly my line of argument. But as I reached my final declaration, which 'left not a loop to hang a lingering doubt upon,' a general storm of applause burst from the audience. Where were the Professors? They had, unconsciously to me, been supplied with chairs. Each of them stood on his chair, reaching and stretching his neck, and clapping for his life. It was the supreme moment of my existence. The Professors very kindly came up afterward and offered me their hands, making all sorts of apologies for raising a question as to my claim to a new advance in astronomical precision."

In New Orleans I presented myself without letters of introduction to Mr. Shaw, Superintendent of Public Schools of that city. He had been acquainted with my father in Boston, and I was very cordially received, and my plans for introducing apparatus into the public school system furthered by his representations in my behalf. I was assigned a very pleasant room in the City Hall for the exhibition of my apparatus, and was visited by several members of the board, and had an opportunity to explain the uses of different articles of apparatus to these gentlemen. When the subject came before the board for action, thirty sets were purchased. While the matter was pending, I had an opportunity to visit the different institutions and different points of interest in New Orleans. I found Dr. Olmstead, a former pupil, who was practicing medicine in the suburbs. His acquaintance in the city rendered my visit more satisfactory by far than it would otherwise have been. With him I visited the slave market and attended a slave auction. With him I also visited the cotton market and witnessed the operations in that arena. Through his influence I was invited to the homes of several Southern men, both in the city and in the suburbs. All represented New Orleans as a good place in which to make money, but not a place where any one would desire to raise a family. After moving my boarding place several times, from one hotel to another, for the purpose of becoming better acquainted with Southern people and Southern usages, I secured board at last with a Mrs. Drake on Tchoupitoulas Street. She occupied three or four buildings, arranged in continuity, and, perhaps, had the most fashionable business boarding-house in the city. Her boarders were chiefly from Boston, and, so far as my acquaintance extended among them, they were courteous and communicative.

Being, for the time, the last arrival, I was seated at the table in the place of honor, next to our hostess. As is true of the great majority of Southern ladies, Mrs. Drake was an excellent conversationalist, and while ready at replying to my objections to Southern life and Southern usages, and especially to that of the Southern institution, *slavery*, she was equally ready on stating objections to all Northern usages, and especially to our position on the aforesaid Southern institution. She represented that her servants were the most happy and contented class of people — and she employed a dozen or more — that could be found, and that she had recently made a fine wedding for one of her servant girls with the head butler of her establishment, whom she had hired of a neighbor. I don't remember how much she said the wedding cost her, but it was a considerable amount more than is often spent by respectable families in the North for a daughter's wedding. She had been the wife of a physician of South Carolina, who owned a plantation adjoining that of John C. Calhoun. He had, however, sold his plantation and invested the avails in banking in New Orleans. Here he had been unsuccessful, had failed and died, leaving her with little or nothing, to take care of herself and educate her children. She expressed the warmest admiration for John C. Calhoun as a citizen, slave-holder and Christian. "And," said she, "Mr. Calhoun sacrificed more for his thirty or more servants than any Northern man—I might say, than all Northern men—have sacrificed to benefit the colored population of the South. For instance, he built a continuous line of brick tenements, sufficient to accommodate all the families of his plantation, at an expense of $25,000 or more, and furnished them in a manner more comfortable, I apprehend, than the majority of the tenements and homes of laborers at the North. Unfortunately, however, the negroes, fearing the depredations of each other, or of negroes in the adjacent plantations, shut themselves at night so closely as to bring upon themselves a contagious disease, by which a number of them were swept off. Again, to save the remainder, he erected other cabins and permitted his line of brick tenements to go to wreck. He thus proved that, beyond a certain limit, it is worse than useless to expend money on the negro. But whatever can be spent, and whatever advantages can safely be bestowed upon the slave population, I believe for the most part — I admit there are exceptions — are bestowed upon negroes for their health, for their religious enlightenment and for their prosperity. In fact, if there can be found a corresponding population in the North — I do not think there can be, in regard to content, and industry and satisfaction with their state, it is my opinion, having traveled in the North very considerably, that the slaves are better provided for, more are converted and saved, than in the corresponding laboring population of the North."

Her denunciations of the Abolitionists were bitter and endless. But especially did she declare that if she could get that black-hearted Abolitionist, Giddings, under her power, she would show him as little mercy as he was exhibiting toward the slave-holding population in the South. "Why," said she, "I really believe that if he could have his own way, he would incite the negroes to rise and murder every one of us." "But," said I, "Madam, it may be my misfortune that I live in the vicinity of Joshua R. Giddings. Though I have only known him as a public speaker, having no personal acquaintance, from all I do know of him as a citizen, he is a public-spirited gentleman, and enjoys the confidence and respect of all his neighbors. He secures the largest majority in his Congressional district of almost any man in the North, and except among the lowest class of our population, the saloon men and their abettors, he enjoys an enviable and unimpeachable reputation."

This Mrs. Drake was a lady, and there was a bitter contest going on in her mind between her desire to annihilate the Abolitionist and to treat me with the respect which she always gave to strangers, and, I suppose, to friends. I hardly ventured so far as to say that I was one of Joshua R. Giddings' constituents, and had given my vote to send him to Congress. A circumstance which occurred, however, in Painesville, O., with which I was conversant, I made use of in such a way as I thought would interest rather than offend her.

My story ran thus: "We had an interesting Abolitionist lecturer passing through Northern Ohio. I had the pleasure of hearing him twice. He was, however, of Southern birth, the natural son of Governor Mason, of Virginia; he called himself by the name of his father and former master. He secured crowded audiences wherever he went; his natural oratory carried conviction even to those most opposed to his views, and his representations of his own disabilities and sufferings from the '*sacred institution*' enlisted the sympathies of the most obdurate. I will not give his history, but will only narrate an incident in his

Northern life. Making Painesville his headquarters with his family, which he had redeemed from slavery, he joined the Congregational Church of the town. He was accustomed to attend the Thursday evening prayer-meeting. A noted slave-catcher of Virginia, having heard of his whereabouts, and having come to Painesville with a gang of six men, was tracking Mason, to find a favorable opportunity in which to seize and manacle him and to restore him to his legal owner, one of the heirs of Gov. Mason, for which, of course, he expected a large reward. The time selected for the seizure of his victim was on his return home from prayer-meeting, as it was discovered that he went through an unfrequented and unlighted street. Armed to the teeth the gang surrounded and rushed upon Mason; three or four of them seized him and attempted to throttle him in order to handcuff him, bind him and take him in the vehicle already provided, beyond reach of any hope of release and relief. Mason, being a powerful man, and his liberty being at stake — which he declared he valued more than life — he was enabled to hurl the ruffians in all directions and to jump upon the man whom he at once recognized as the chief kidnapper. He then ran and escaped, not going to his home at all, but rushing away in the dark; he found the lake shore as speedily as possible, went aboard of a sloop and went to Canada. The kidnapper upon which this man, weighing two hundred and fifty pouuds, had jumped, found himself disabled with fractured ribs. He was taken to the hotel and left there. The other ruffians at once made their escape for fear of arrest for kidnapping, leaving him with little money and no friends, and liable to arrest, for the onslaught had been observed by several witnesses. Now, Madam, who do you think ministered to the wants of this crushed and miserable wretch? Who do you think carried him supplies and food? Who do you think employed a physician to set his bones, and assured the hotel-keeper that the bills would be paid? In short, who do you think took care of this desperado in his extremity? Was it your friends, so called, in the North?" Said she: "I suppose you wish me to understand that it was the Republicans?" "Most assuredly," said I, "It was the wives of these same '*black-hearted* Abolitionists' who cared for him, and when the kidnapper was sufficiently recovered to leave, the bills were paid and he was furnished money enough to return to Virginia by these same women." Said I, "Madam, the South are truly mistaken in their views with regard to the intentions and purposes of the Abolitionists. If you will permit me to say, and will not be offended, I will state that I have been an Abolitionist and voted the Abolition ticket, and voted for James G. Burney. My position in regard to slavery is this, not that I have any special admiration for the colored population, either North or South. It, is true, I would have them have their rights and opportunities to be prepared for citizenship, but my chief interest and aim in all Abolition movements is to save the white population of the South from the degradation which slavery inflicts. For, through all my acquaintance with Southern men — and I have known a great many — the evils of slavery fall immensely more heavily upon the white families, their sons, and I may say, the daughters, of the South, than upon the negroes, in the fact, the idleness imposed upon the young men, in consequence of the *disgrace of labor*, brings upon the South and upon all its families the inevitable evils which would be removed by a necessity for industry." This was as far in discussing this subject as I wished to go with this highly accomplished, intelligent, and, as I believe, most worthy Christian woman. I must conclude my narration in regard to her, however, by saying that my confession that I was one of those "black-hearted Abolitionists" did not seem to diminish her kindness and attention to me personally.

I was informed by Superintendent Shaw that the Catholics of New Orleans had a distinct set of schools for Catholic children, and that the parents in confession were required to tell where their children attended school. But in passing through the various school buildings, I discovered in nearly every room more or less Irish children. Remarking to Superintendent Shaw that I thought that the control of the priests over the parents was not very stringent, he replied that undoubtedly the mothers, in giving their confessions, stated that their children attended Catholic schools. In a sense this was true, as the children were absent generally about two half days each week from the public schools, and this was condoned by the teachers under the direction of the board. Thus, while the mothers were able, in their confessions, to state that their children were attending the parochial schools of the Catholic Church, they were, in fact, regular attendants, with these exceptions, in the public schools almost universally throughout the city. This may be taken as a sample of the truthfulness of the Catholic confessional, and really of the lax control of the priests over their parishioners.

The most able Methodist preacher that I heard while in New Orleans, was Dr. C——, from Vermont, who had been there some months. His history and the occasion of his being in New Orleans seem worth relating. Being a presiding elder in the North, a man of first-class ability, he wielded a widespread influence in every department of the Methodist denomination. His wife was a devout and earnest Christian; she conceived that she was the recipient of direct communications from the spirit world. Among other impressions that she received from these heavenly messengers was, that on a certain day, at twelve o'clock at night, she was to die and be translated at once. The impression was so decided, and her conviction so positive, that she communicated it to her husband, persuading and convincing him of the truthfulness of this spiritual revelation. She entreated her husband to make all necessary arrangements for her departure, and begged of him to place their three children in charge of a niece who had lived with them some length of time. The plan was opened up to the niece and gained her assent, and even went so far, under the expressed wish of the wife, as to have it understood, that, in due time, she should take the position of mother to their children. Through the young lady and her confidences with her lady friends, the matter leaked out and became subject of general gossip. It did not seem to excite any inimical remark, nor to impair the influence of the worthy presiding elder, but all seemed to be convinced that the impression of the good wife and mother was really of heavenly origin. The time approached. The wife was in her usual health. She was of the opinion that she was to be taken at the appointed time. The time arrived—but she didn't die and she couldn't die. And the disappointment of all parties, of the good Methodist people, of the presiding elder, and of the young lady whose prospects were thus blighted, were intense and immense. The result was that the reverend doctor was compelled to abandon his work and seek another home. He found it with his wife, and was preaching with great power, satisfaction and success in New Orleans. The story I obtained from one of my pupils afterward, who was familiar with all the circumstances in the North.

While in New Orleans, I suffered severely with cholera. This was in 1851. While walking on Canal Street, one morning about ten o'clock, I was attacked as if by an instantaneous shock. I had had one siege of cholera in Canada, three years before, and had just escaped with my life, but I had learned to manage myself. I staggered into a bath-house just near me, and called for a hot bath and a glass of brandy, and with all speed, with the little strength I had left, I let the hot water in upon me, sipping every few moments from the brandy. I continued, perhaps, half an hour, perhaps longer, in the hot bath, just as hot as I could bear it without scalding, until I felt the perspiration running down my forehead. I then knew that I was safe from that attack, but felt it imperatively necessary for me to leave New Orleans at once. Advertisements were out for two boats to leave that day for St. Louis. I visited the boats and found the "Grand Turk" about to start at one o'clock in the afternoon. The passage was $12. The boat seemed to me to be a very desirable one, and I was assured that the passengers were of the most respectable character and that all the berths had been engaged except one or two. It occurred to me that it would be better, before paying for a berth, to visit the other boat, the "Alex. Scott." I found an equally respectable boat, the charge $20, and few berths engaged. I concluded it would be the best for me, under the circumstances, to take the boat which was least crowded and pay a higher price. The boat started at six o'clock in the evening. In the course of the trip up the river we passed the "Grand Turk," as it stopped at intervening ports much more frequently than the "Alex. Scott." Being hailed, it was reported that all was well. On the day after we arrived at St. Louis, however, it was reported that the "Grand Turk" had gone into quarantine with fourteen cases of cholera on board, having had twenty-one deaths on the way up. I then thought that I had been providentially guided in taking passage upon the "Alex Scott."

On the trip I met with Mr. Chouteau, of St. Louis, with whom I formed a very agreeable acquaintance. The ground of our acquaintance was our sympathy in mineralogy. I had collected, at New Orleans, from the wharves and other sources, a very considerable little cabinet of minerals, and exhibiting them to one of the passengers, and explaining how I had obtained one and another, and another, and where each of these minerals was found, *in situ*, Mr. Chouteau happened to overhear our conversation, and immediately formed one of our party. I found him a very ready conversationalist and an intelligent mineralogist. I will give some of his statements which were at the time to me very interesting. On a tract of land in Missouri, which he had received as part of his patrimony, he had discovered a lead mine, and had excavated and reduced a large quantity of ore, producing many tons of lead.

Now, one of the chief uses of lead is in making glass. He sold several tons of his lead thus obtained to a glass firm in Louisville. They informed him that the lead he had furnished was useless, as it colored all the glass purple. He at once employed an assayist to determine what was the ingredient in the lead ore which rendered his lead unsalable. The assayist found a considerable proportion of oxide of cobalt. Now, this oxide was found in the mineral in such proportions that it was more valuable than the lead itself, when separated. It was used extensively in the potteries of England for coloring the enamel blue. Having learned by his correspondence the value of this mineral in London, as furnished to various potteries, he chartered a ship at New Orleans, and, by means of steamboats, loaded the ship with ore of lead and cobalt. He went on the same ship to Liverpool and opened a correspondence with the principal potteries of England, informing them of the material he had and of its proportions of both lead and cobalt, the lead more than paying for the reduction. Before, however, he had received any definite reply or orders from any of these establishments, he found that they had been corresponding with each other, and agreed to give him half a cent a pound, instead of two cents, as he had proposed. After having visited them separately, and finding that there was no breaking the league, he went aboard the ship and departed to New Orleans, taking his ore with him. Before he reached New Orleans, however, orders had been sent to St. Louis to his address, calling for many times as much of the material as he had exported to England and back again, and at his own price.

While I was in New Orleans there was a Wm. McKinney there in business, who afterward marriee my cousin, Miss Catherine Coe. The same year he closed business in that city, and in coming up the river, the boat was burned on which he had taken passage. Not being able to reach a landing place, the passengers were obliged to jump overboard. Among the rest was a German who had a considerable amount of gold. He tied his gold in a handkerchief, and with another handkerchief around his neck. McKinney assured him that he could not swim with that gold; he would certainly go to the bottom. "No matter," said the German, "if my gold is gone I may as well go myself." So over he went into the water, and was never seen more. Whether his handkerchief of gold was ever fished up, I am not able to say. Mr. McKinney himself jumped over, with his drafts for $5,000 in his pocket; as he rose to the surface he was seized by another passenger, who said he could not swim. Feeling that it was a matter of life and death for both of them, he was compelled to beat the individual off by striking him in the face. Being a good swimmer, he reached land, but it was a very narrow escape. With many doubts and some compunctions, I have heard him narrate the fact to several private audiences. I ought here to say that Mr. McKinney was one of the most considerate and humane of men.

On reaching St. Louis, I thought it advisable to visit several cousins who lived at Marine Settlement, about 30 miles east of St. Louis in Illinois. This was on the line of the Ohio and Mississippi Railway, which was not then sufficiently completed for the conveyance of passengers. Consequently I made my journey in a stage coach, over the seven-mile bottom of the Mississippi River. In conversation with some passengers, about the overflow of the Mississippi, it was remarked that there had been no overflow for several years, but that on an average, the entire bottom was placed under water, from two to five feet deep, once in seven years. I completed my trip; the rain was falling steadily all the way. I thought it necessary to return and make business arrangements in St. Louis. I reached Illinoistown just in time to take the last boat that went to St. Louis that night; the whole country, at this time, being submerged by the rising flood. Next morning, going to the observatory of the hotel, I saw the entire bottom, as far as eye could reach, up and down the river, covered with the swelling flood. It was a fearful sight, considering the immense damage done to houses, stock and other property.

I made, while visiting in St. Louis, acquaintance with many of the city teachers in the public schools, and with Mr. Edward Wyman, who was in charge of a very popular private institution for boys. He was preparing for a grand exhibition and procession, and semi-military display of his school. It came off while I was there. Being an invited guest, I went with the procession to a suburban garden, and enjoyed the occasion with its festivities and demonstrations, as an observer rather than as a participator in the various sports and games in which the boys delighted themselves in the garden.

The Principal of one of the public schools gave me an interesting account of his listening to Jenny Lind, who had been in the city just before I arrived. My friend was enjoying a salary of $1,500 a year, which was a meager income for himself and wife. Said he, "I made up my mind before Jenny Lind came here, that it would be beyond my means to purchase tickets at the crazy prices at which they were selling, but as all my friends and everybody else of any respectability were buying tickets, I concluded it would be better and safer for me to go. But it cost me $14 to hear Jenny Lind the first night she was in St. Louis, and this extravagance was really against my judgment and my preference. Tickets for the second night had much increased in price, but I went the second night and paid my $20, not because I had to, but because I wanted to."

Being in New Orleans during the last week of April, strawberries were upon the table, but for the last time of the season. Before I left the city they had disappeared. Arriving in St. Louis, the first thing that was presented to me as a guest, was a plate of most luscious strawberries. The week after, when spending a few days in Cincinnati, the common dessert at the hotel was strawberries. When I arrived at Kirtland, the following week, strawberries were scarcely yet in bloom. So that I had my turn of strawberries at home in due time, but my family thought, that as I had my rations of strawberries previously to that, I could well afford to let them have whatever came, to themselves—to which I readily assented.

In commencing work in the Western Reserve Teachers' Seminary, I took the department of mathematics. All this work was, so far as practicable, assigned to me, in making up the general programme. Other teachers took literature and language. It was amusing to me to learn, perhaps by overhearing, and perhaps by direct statement, that, "while Holbrook was considered first-rate in mathematics, it was thought he didn't amount to much in any other line of study and instruction." This was the more amusing as I had heard the same remark made with regard to Holbrook in Berea, in reference to his skill as a teacher of languages. "Holbrook is first-rate in languages, but I don't believe he knows much in any other department." On coming to Lebanon, the same line of remark was not uncommon, but was varied thus: "That Holbrook was really very good in natural sciences, but no one supposed that he was very well versed in any other branch." The truth being, that whatever Holbrook undertook, he tried to make so much more emphatic, impressive and successful than anything else that was done in any other direction, that it seemed to him and to others, for the time being, that there was nothing else in any direction of equal importance with the work in which he was then engaged.

A young man by the name of Giddings, who had been formerly a pupil of mine in Berea, and had left me, and had come to Kirtland for the reason, as he said, that he could not learn arithmetic under my instruction, but had succeeded admirably under the instruction of Dr. Lord, was now in attendance at Kirtland. Being somewhat curious to know in what Dr. Lord had excelled me, in reaching Giddings' case, and inquiring of Giddings as to why he preferred Dr. Lord, and succeeded with him and made no progress with me, he told me, he could understand the subject with Dr. Lord, but could not with me. Whether Dr. Lord had informed him before or afterward of his own difficulty in comprehending mathematics, I do not know, but this is the statement I received from Dr. Lord in regard to his own aptitude in mathematics. Said he: "I was dull enough in all branches, but especially in arithmetic and algebra. My teachers gave me up almost as impracticable, but by dint of continued effort in having most of the examples wrought for me by other pupils, or by taking them down in recitation, I had recorded in a proper note-book the solution of every question in every text-book which I had ever studied during my course of instruction. And even with my classes, as teacher, it is necessary to resolve every question in arithmetic and algebra, before trusting myself in giving instruction to ordinary classes of young people."

My inference was, at the time, that my failure with Giddings and many others, was from the fact of my own celerity in grasping mathematical calculations, and my consequent impatience with pupils. It taught me a valuable lesson, not only in teaching mathematics, but in every other line of my work, that a quick thinker needs to be constantly on his guard against impatience in energizing those of slower mold. Giddings came again into my algebra class, and under the influence of my new conception of my inefficiency and incompetency to teach mathematics to slow minds, and my determination to reach even the slowest cases, Giddings acknowledged that he found me a very satisfactory teacher. In this, I was very much encouraged, and not a little elated.

In one of the recitations of my teachers' arithmetic class, I exhibited three methods of dividing one fraction by another, and, presenting them to the class, I desired them to bring in the demonstration the next day. Mr. Edson, a gentleman older than myself, and a popular teacher of the public schools, in the country round about, arose, and securing an opportunity to speak, said, "Mr. Holbrook, are these the only methods that you know of, of dividing one fraction by another?" It was more in the tone in which the question was asked, than, perhaps, the question itself, that roused me somewhat to indignation; and yet, knowing Mr. Edson to be one of the most loyal and earnest of my pupils, there was no sufficient cause for resentment. I held myself as well as I was able under the circumstances, and thinking a moment replied : "Mr. Edson, I will give you from this to next Monday (it was then Friday) to master all the methods that you can discover or invent, for dividing one fraction by another, and will give you the first opportunity, on Monday, of presenting them to the class. After you have exhausted all your methods, I will present as many more different methods of dividing one fraction by another, as you may be able to give and demonstrate. Not only so," I added, "but I will give you the use of my library, and I think, doubtless, Dr. Nicholls will give you the use of his. I am willing you should get all the help you can from Dr. Nicholls himself, and from any other quarter, and still I will give as many more different methods of dividing one fraction by another as you may be able to give in any amount of study you may give outside, or from any amount of help you may obtain."

The class, consisting of eighty or so, of course, were much excited, and no doubt sympathized with Mr. Edson. He was a popular student. They thought I had involved myself in a losing game.

On Monday, at the usual hour, the class assembled, and as many others as could find space, in the recitation-room, to witness the result of the contest between pupil and teacher. Mr. Edson presented six new methods, in addition to those which I had presented, with satisfactory demonstration. At the close of his effort, I asked the pupils if they were satisfied that he had given new and different demonstrations, different from each other, and different from those which I had presented. They all expressed their assent; I took my place at the board, and presented at once six other methods, and gave my demonstrations. I asked Mr. Edson if these were different, and clearly demonstrated. He said, "Entirely so." "Are you satisfied, Mr. Edson?" "Yes, sir." "But, Mr. Edson, I have six more; would you like to see them?" "Yes, sir." I immediately proceeded to present six more methods with their demonstrations, asking the class each time if the method was satisfactory and different from anything that had been given before. Each of these was so received. At last I said, "Mr. Edson, *are* you satisfied?" He replied, "I am more than satisfied; I give up. I don't want any more." "But, Mr. Edson," said I, "I have twelve more to present." "But," said he, "I don't want any more, I have enough." "Very well," said I, "if you are satisfied we will not have any more; we will proceed with the recitation."

Mr. Edson came to me and apologized for his

abruptness, and we are to-day, as we were ever afterward, the best of friends. Not long since, a pupil, who had gone to Michigan on an agency, had the same story to tell, as he obtained it from Mr. Edson, who is now in Michigan in business.

During my connection with the Teachers' Seminary, the school increased rapidly, there being about 250 in actual attendance at our last session. I had previously had a call to go to Marlborough, and take the Principalship of the public schools of that town. Two, of the six Trustees of the Union School District had been pupils of mine at Berea— Mr. Abram Wileman and Mr. Amos Walton. Feeling that there was one part of the work of training teachers with which I was not sufficiently familiar by actual practice, namely, that of superintendency, I accepted the invitation, and quietly made my arrangements to leave Kirtland at the close of the school year. At the request of Dr. Nicholls, I permitted none of the pupils to know my intentions. The first that was known by any pupil, or in fact, by any citizen, beyond "Uncle Coe," was my closing speech at our Reunion Exercises, at the close of the year. My determination was given as unalterable, and I had already contracted for a house in Marlborough, and for teams to move my family. Nevertheless, a considerable effort was made by the citizens, and a special demonstration by the students, to change my determination. Finding, however, that my separation from the school was inevitable, the students, in the course of the evening, collected a very considerable purse, as a parting present, and appointed a committee to make the presentation. I believe, if I could have possibly or honorably put aside my contracts, I should have been induced to remain. I have in my possession the subscription paper, with the names of the donors and the amounts contributed. This, with many other such mementoes of the kindness and appreciation of my pupils at different times and places are treasured with fond and lasting appreciation; especially, as many of my former pupils, who, were engaged in such acts of kindness and liberality, are now occupying honorable and distinguished places in their various lines of business.

When I first arrived at Kirtland, O., from the East, in 1837, the Mormons had collected there in large numbers under the leadership of Joe Smith. They were coming in rapidly from various directions, many of them having sold their farms, homesteads and other property in order to reach the "promised land." The fact that Joe Smith had a revelation soon after a convert arrived, by which any property he might have brought with him was to be loaned to the Church, and he thrown upon himself for his support, did not seem to diminish his confidence in Smith's prophetical claims. Some very well-to-do and intelligent gentlemen had already moved into Kirtland, and thus had thrown in their property and their destinies with the Mormons. Among these was Dr.

Cowdrey, a very intelligent and worthy gentleman, formerly an elder of a Presbyterian Church in New York State. He was the father of Marcellus Cowdrey, a most estimable teacher, for many years Superintendent of Schools at Sandusky. Sidney Rigdon, formerly a Baptist minister of Hamilton, O., had recently joined Joe Smith, and was a leading force in the Mormon Church. The history of Rigdon is somewhat interesting. From being a Regular Baptist, and no doubt honest in his convictions that immersion was the only baptism and the true way of following Christ, he had, in due time, in urging this tenet, carried it so far that he made it, with Alex. Campbell, an essential to salvation. He left the Baptists, therefore, and became a follower of Alex. Campbell; in other words, he became a Disciple, or Bible Christian. In this capacity he appeared in Geauga County, and carried several Baptist Churches almost bodily over to the Disciples' doctrines, among which were the Baptist Churches of Kirtland and Chardon. The next step in the line of baptism, he now having become an adherent of Joe Smith, was to baptize for the dead, that being one of the Mormon doctrines. It seemed to me and others that this was running baptism into the ground. Be this as it may, Mr. Rigdon was an able man, a powerful preacher and a ready controversialist. It was through his labors that large accessions were made to the Mormon Church. I do not think, however, that Mr. Rigdon ever favored the idea of polygamy. In fact, so far as I know, this matter of polygamy made a division in the Mormon Church. Those who opposed it followed Rigdon, and those who favored it, Joe Smith. The doctrine was first broached in Kirtland by the revelation of Joe Smith, with reference to the daughter of one of the old inhabitants of Kirtland, who was sealed to Joe as his spiritual wife. It was not the prevalent doctrine, nor generally received as binding upon other persons than those who were called by a distinct revelation, the first of whom was Joe Smith himself. This tenet has gained strength from that time down to the present, when it is now made an essential belief of those in good standing in the Mormon Church.

Before Rigdon separated himself from Smith, the Church had established a bank, issued considerable amounts of paper money and purchased a number of farms in the immediate neighborhood of the temple, among which was my uncle David Holbrook's farm, of about two hundred acres, purchased at the rate of $400 per acre. The Mormons paid my uncle about $10,000 down, in merchandise, and took possession of the farm.

Many other members of the Congregational Church, besides uncle David, sold their farms to the Mormons. The result was a very general breaking up of Kirtland society. A committee was sent out by the Kirtland people, consisting of the Rev. John L. Tomlinson, my cousin George Smith, and myself, to prospect for a good site for a new settlement. We started on horseback and traveled through the southern part of the State for some four or five weeks, but found no location that we thought would meet all the demands of the friends in making a new settlement. We were best pleased with the Mad River Valley, in the vicinity of Urbana, and concluded to report favorably of that section of country. It was admitted by the citizens that milk sickness prevailed there to some extent. When our report was received, the price of lands and the possibility of sickness deterred the Kirtland people from making further investigation in that direction; but other parties were sent out into Indiana, and it was found that Booneville, Ind., offered stronger inducements, considering the nature of the soil, the abundance of water, the price of land, and the facilities for market, than any other locality.

My uncle, without investigating for himself, concluded to move to Booneville. I was sent, in charge of his family, his wife and four young children, overland, with horse and wagon, while he, in possession of the goods, should go down the Ohio River and meet us at Booneville.

My experiences in this overland journey from Kirtland, O., to Booneville, Ind., were quite novel and sufficiently varied. We carried our provisions, bedding and cooking utensils in our wagon with us, stopping by the wayside at noon, or in such farmhouses at night as we could get accommodations in. Being from Kirtland, the place of the Mormons, it was assumed, since that was all that was known of Kirtland in most places, that we were recreant Mormons, having had enough of them, and were making our escape. After a few days, in consequence of these suspicions, which seemed to be everywhere excited, we concluded to say what was true, that we had come from Geauga County, when inquired of. The expenses of our journey were very trivial, while the incidents were in some cases rather amusing and exciting. On approaching Mt. Vernon, through a road winding about among the hills, we met a burly Irishman in a buggy. We turned up on the right side of the road to give him room to pass us. My cousin, who was driving, seems to have turned too far and the wagon went over, scattering cooking utensils, edibles and ourselves in a promiscuous *mélange* down the hill. As we were gathering ourselves up, the five children of Mr. Chase came around the hill and the man saw them. Their family wagon, however, had not yet come in sight. The burly stranger, lifting his hands and eyes in wonderment, burst forth with: "My God! are these all the children of one couple?" There were about ten of the younger members of both families, counting myself. We made no satisfactory reply, being busy in gathering up our utensils and setting our wagon upright. He crowded by and left the family of ten children to take care of themselves.

The last day before we reached our destination,

we came into a settlement, some ten or fifteen miles north of Booneville, late in the afternoon. Making inquiries as to where we could get accommodations for the night, we were told that there was a vacant cabin, that had been used for a school-house, about two miles further on. We were denied any accommodations in the place, and our only alternative was to proceed on our way, and find, if possible, a covering for the night. We found no school-house nor cabin. After proceeding several miles we concluded that it would be well for us to stop and do the best we could under the circumstances. There was a drizzling rain, and it was sufficiently chilly, but we made ready for the night, taking the horses from the wagon; the elder boys and myself, wrapping ourselves as well as we could, slept under the wagon. The rest of the family were lodged in the wagon, under cover. During the night we imagined we heard the barking of wolves in the distance, but it did not materially disturb our slumbers. But as morning approached we heard the crowing of roosters in the neighborhood and concluded that we must be near some human habitation. As soon as day dawned I started out in the direction of the indications of humanity, and, passing through a narrow portion of wood, soon found myself in a large open space, within which stood a very comfortable double cabin. The good people were astir and received me very cordially, and said that they felt that there was something unusual in the neighborhood, as the dog in the house was quite restless, but thinking it was not possible that any one would be out in such a night as that, they gave no further attention to the matter and passed the night as usual, but assured us if they had known of our being there they would have gone out and given us all the accommodations that their cabin could offer. Securing whatever we needed for our morning repast, I returned and found my friends. After making our breakfast in the wagon, we started on, arriving at Booneville about ten o'clock Sabbath morning.

TORNADO IN KIRTLAND.

The Congregational Church in Kirtland had been raised from its foundations, and turned perhaps five degrees, and set down again, thus wrenching the frame badly, and shattering the walls to a considerable extent, and making it necessary to rebuild the foundations, and replaster the walls. This tornado took place when I was living in Berea. The first observation that I had of its effect, was in coming up over the hills of South Kirtland, crossing the Chagrin River, where was a mill. It was a wonderful sight; the contents of the milldam, including much of the dam itself, were carried from their location, in the course of the stream, up to the top of a neighboring hill, about 100 feet in height. As I passed on up the hill, over the road, the devastation of the tornado was evident in the prostration of fences, but more fiercely in an immense swath through an extended tract of forest. Apparently, a mighty giant had swung his scythe, passing through the forest, and cutting the trees about twenty feet from the ground over a breadth of about four rods and nearly a mile in length. The trees were cut off at this height, and in a very well-defined breadth, through this tract of wooded country. Not going near enough to see what became of the trees thus severed by the mighty scythe, it was impossible to form any very definite idea of the character and extent of the destruction, other than could be seen in the distance. But it was a wonderful demonstration, as I conceived, of the irresistible power of air in motion. This northern branch of the tornado passed over the church, lifting it from its foundation, and placing it as before described. On the opposite side of the street, leading to Kirtland Flats, stood a log cabin, consisting of the ordinary two rooms and a new addition of frame and clapboards. This addition had been used as a spare sleeping-room. In it was stored the outfit of the daughter of Mr. Stannard, and all the wedding paraphernalia, waiting for the nuptials to take place, a day or two after the tornado visited them. The heavy log cabin seemed to have resisted the power of the wind, but the frame addition was taken as if in a mighty fist, and whirled through the air in the direction of the tornado, sending its clapboards, shingles, and the wedding outfit over the country some rods in width and miles in continued extent. Some of these wedding ribbons and other habiliments were picked up along the line of the tornado, through a distance of five to nine miles. No one happened to be in that part of the house at the time of the disaster, so that the young lady was on time for the ceremony, but whether she ever recovered any part of her outfit, or whether she purchased another, I never learned. The southern branch of this tornado, separating from this northern branch at the mill-pond and hill before spoken of, proceeded in a southeastern direction, over the township of Chester. It there accomplished no special destruction, but played some merry freaks with fences, plows, wagons, and a couple of damsels, who, being in the loft of the cabin, and noticing the destructive energy of the approaching storm, had thrown themselves upon a feather-bed, with the idea that the lightning would not strike them when protected by the non-conductor, feathers. They *were* protected from *lightning*, but I was shown the cabin unroofed, and the neighboring apple-tree into which the young ladies were carried with their protecting apparatus, the feather-bed, and lodged both of them bodily among its branches. I was shown a long furrow, made by a plow, which had been taken up by the wind and carried, as if drawn by horses at full galop, the clods having been thrown, twisted and rolled several rods from the place where the plow had lifted them from the soil. It was not my fortune to witness this tornado in either of its branches. I have only described what I saw as the results of its tremendous work.

This road over the Chagrin River, up over the hills, led me by Mr. Harvey Morse's. On a visit there one day, he took me out upon the brow of the hill, and, pointing to the valley, distant from the house fifty rods or more, showed a small stream where his father, as an early settler, had shot a couple of wolves. Being in the house one moonlight night, and the doors being open, they were annoyed by hearing moans of distress coming from this valley. As it continued some length of time, their curiosity was sufficiently excited to go out and see what was the trouble with the cattle pasturing in the valley. As they approached the brow of the hill they saw at once the cause of the distress. A yearling heifer was being driven across the valley, from hill to hill, through the water and mud of the stream, backward and forward, by a couple of wolves, that were biting and worrying her, attacking her at the rear, and then, turning about, biting her nose, driving her back and forth, until, when they discovered them, the heifer was so nearly exhausted that the wolves were ready to fall upon her as their prey. A rifle being secured, a good aim brought one of the wolves to the ground; the other escaped for the time being, but the heifer was so far exhausted and so badly wounded that she died before morning. The other wolf was captured before many days. These were the last of the wolves in that neighborhood.

CHAPTER XIII.

EXPERIENCES WHILE IN MARLBOROUGH, OHIO.

BEFORE narrating my experiences in Marlborough, I will give a few points in the character of the worthy people of that place. The country had been originally settled almost exclusively by Quakers. But in the commotion which came from the preaching of Elias Hicks, a large majority abandoned the orthodox usages and beliefs, and became much more liberal in their views and practices. From being Unitarians or Universalists, they passed to still more liberal views and became what were generally called "Comeouters," separating themselves from all religious associations and restraints. Thus, nearly all my patrons and friends in Marlborough were "Freethinkers," many of them avowed Atheists. A few of the less educated and intelligent were Methodists. "The Comeouters," as a class, were intelligent, well read, and, otherwise than in their religious beliefs, most excellent people. My two pupils, members of the board that called me to Marlborough, expressed no religious beliefs of any kind. They were virtually Agnostics, although that term had not been invented at that time. The young people who were my pupils had grown up with little or no religious training, but with excellent home culture otherwise. The Sabbath was only regarded as a day of amusement, of social enjoyment, or of labor. These explanations are perhaps necessary, in order that my experiences may be the better understood.

My object in taking this public school was, not that I might obtain a larger salary, but that I might prepare myself the better to train teachers for their work in public schools, either as subordinates or superintendents. I conceived that theory in this direction, without actual previous service in the work, would be of comparatively little value in training teachers. My contract with the Directors of the Marlborough School was merely a verbal one, of a very loose character. The only item mentioned in the contract was that I was to receive $800 for nine months' service. All else was left undetermined. The Board of Directors consisted of six members, all Freethinkers excepting one, and he the husband of a Methodist lady. He generally attended church with her. When I arrived in town, I was met very cordially by the deputation, which had secured a comfortable tenement for our occupancy. After two or three days occupied in getting settled, I found myself in charge of a school of three departments, in a new house, tolerably well arranged, with comfortable furniture and pleasant surroundings. I met the entire body of the pupils in the one large room and proceeded at once to organize, making use of whatever information I could derive from my pupils for this purpose. Before, however, commencing my work, I read from my pocket Bible a short passage from the Sermon on the Mount, and offered a brief prayer. On passing from the school through the town at noon, I was met by one of the Directors, who told me that there was an intense excitement in town from the fact that one of the pupils had gone immediately after I had offered the prayer and reported at the center store that the new teacher had read the Bible and prayed in the new school-house. This was a little too much for the good people, who had cast off all such superstitions, and they were very much humiliated in the fact that their new building, their school-house, should be so degraded by (to them) cast-off superstition and bygone ignorance and darkness, as to have that old Hebrew mythology brought into their advanced mode of thinking and living. The excitement was tremendous. One man, more frenzied than the rest, tore off his coat and rolled up his sleeves, and rushed around town, declaring, amongst other things, that he would rather Holbrook, or any other teacher, would swear by the hour in the new building than to "pray"—"pray" five minutes. The prayer did not occupy two minutes. My two friends, Wileman and Walton, came to advise with me about it. They did not seem to be very much alarmed, but were rather anxious to know what I was going to do about it. I gave them no definite answer, but told them I thought it would come out all right; we would call a meeting of the Board, and I would see what arrangement we could make that would be satisfactory to all parties. I believed they were reasonable men, and I told them they would find me a reasonable man, and I thought there would be no further trouble about it. "But," they said, "there was a tremendous opposition to prayer in the new building; I could have it in the old building, but not the new." "All right," said I, "we will see about it." They smiled and left me, knowing that I would not give up the prayers. The meeting was called; six members were present. The president, Mr. Wm. Morgan, a very earnest Freethinker and a most excellent and worthy citizen, was called to the chair. He hardly knew how to open the meeting, or to state its object, but requested that I would state, if I was willing, my views with regard to the religious exercises. I had previously thought the matter all out and knew precisely what ground I should take. It was simply this: That I would hold religious exercises for ten or fifteen minutes in the general school-room before the regular six hours of school duty, in my own time. That I would invite the students of the different departments to attend, but would not hold any one as derelict in any sense, if he did not attend. That I would provide a comfortable room during the religious exercises, which those pupils who chose not to attend, or whose parents preferred that they should not, might occupy and be comfortable. In stating these views to the Board, as I did very briefly, I reiterated that I held no pupil in any sense constrained to attend the religious exercises who did not wish to; in fact, I should exclude any one from religious exercises if I received word from the parents that he or she wished the child not to attend. With these remarks I sat down. Mr. Morgan remarked that he saw no objections to my claims as a religionist, as there was no coercion, no stigma, no penalty, in any sense, attached to any one for being absent from religious exercises. If he understood the new teacher, in everything there was perfect liberty, and it was just the doctrine he was living up to. He thought the position I took was very reasonable, and if any member of the Board was not satisfied, and felt it his duty to contravene the exercises thus expressed and thus managed, he thought such an individual, instead of charging Mr. Holbrook with bigotry or narrow-mindedness, would feel that he himself was chargeable with the same state of feeling and judgment. Nothing more was ever said upon the subject in any meeting of the Board, but it was, I have no doubt, the subject of very general conversation throughout the families of the town. But the plan worked very pleasantly, as there was a most universal and prompt attendance of all the children from all the families, even from that of the man who was so tremendously excited, and, so far as I could see, all seemed to approve and acknowledge the good moral influence of the religious exercises. This position, with regard to the claims and duties of the religious teacher in his relations to his pupils, I have ever since maintained and inculcated. In fact, I believe it is now very generally adopted in all our public schools. The teacher takes his own course in religious exercises, but it must be without restraint or penalty, and in the teacher's own time, and not in the regular six hours of school time.

After the close of Mr. Morgan's remarks, I inquired if there was any provision made for fuel or janitor. The secretary of the Board remarked that fuel had generally been provided by the Board in the form of cord-wood, and, so far as he knew, Mr. Henry Cocke had either cut the wood, or had given the students time to cut it for the stove, and that Mr. Cocke had also taken upon himself to sweep and dust the house, although he believed that the older girls sometimes dusted the house after Mr. C. swept. Mr. Cocke, being present, assented to the statement. I replied that I supposed I was hired for six hours a day, as was the usage in all schools, and that if, in the opinion of the Board, I could use the time to better advantage in sweeping and dusting, and in chopping wood — and I was a poor hand at all these operations — if, however, I could serve the Board better in this capacity than in attending to my classes, which sorely needed all my strength and efforts, I would do the best I could in either or both these capacities. This statement seemed to strike them humorously, and they at once voted to furnish me a janitor and coal for the stoves in the several rooms. So that matter was settled very amicably and satisfactorily. The point made by the secretary was, that Mr. Cocke had received only $40 per month and had performed this extra service; I received more than double that amount, it was no more than reasonable that I should perform this, as he thought, necessary work.

Before school on the second day, an orthodox Quaker, Mr. Watson, came to my house saying that he hardly supposed that I would grant his request, and yet he felt it necessary to give his testimony against the use of music in schools. I told him that I should not introduce music into the school until the Directors required it. His two little girls being in attendance, he said he had felt it his duty to express his preference, although it was more than he had expected, that I should comply with his request, and he was accordingly much gratified.

Being about to leave, he remarked that his nephew, Highland Watson, had come home very much excited from school the night before. He had been a great friend of Mr. Cocke and thought Mr. C. an extraordinary mathemetician, and that hardly any man, especially the new teacher, would be able, in any sense, to fill the place of Mr. Cocke, especially as a teacher of mathematics. But Highland had gone home more than gratified, stating that they had a much better mathematician than Mr. C. in the new teacher. "Why," said he, "that little teacher, Holbrook, has more mathematics in his little finger than Cocke in his whole body." I found the Watsons, with several other orthodox Quaker families, always firm supporters, and very helpful and reliable friends. I never afterward found, among all the contending religious views of the people of Marlborough, any objections, expressed or implied, to my course in carrying out my religious convictions in school or in society. I presented my letter to the Methodist Church and tried to do my duty as a member of that organization always, so far as I could without being offensive in maintaining my ground. The change that came over the externals of the young people, in their regard for the Sabbath, in their (at least, outward) respect for religion and religionists, was very marked, and, I believe, was felt to be a decided improvement in all their social gatherings and in their general conduct.

At one time, being called to "Father Wileman's" to participate in a party gotten up in honor of an old teacher of theirs, Joseph Gilbert, a decided "Comeouter," and an outspoken infidel, I was accosted by him, while sitting in the parlor in the midst of a company of twenty or thirty persons, with the remark: "Alfred Holbrook, it is one of the most mysterious things, that a man of your intelligence, of your extensive reading, and your knowledge of the world and of the evils which have sprung from religious beliefs and credulity, that you can have any patience or belief in that miserable old Hebrew book called the Bible." Mr. Gilbert, after these words, awaited my reply. All were interested, to say the least, in what he said, and were waiting anxiously no doubt for my defense; all being in sympathy with him rather than me. Waiting until I could control my feelings a little before I made a reply, I turned to the venerable mother of these young people, my pupils and friends, saying: "Mrs. Wileman, I have known these children of yours for many years, as pupils and friends, and I have respected and loved them as sincere and truthful and worthy of all confidence; and, now, may I be permitted to ask you if they have not received these qualities from the training in the Bible given them by their mother?" "It is true, Alfred Holbrook, that these children have received their ideas of truth, and honor and virtue from the blessed old book." I was congratulated by the smiles and plaudits of all present. Mr. Gilbert never afterward troubled me with his aspersions or his doubts.

My first difficulty with my pupils was in the matter of dancing. These young Quaker people, when they had broken loose from Quaker restraints, went to the other extreme of almost recklessness in their amusements. Sabbath days and evenings and other evenings were frequently given to dancing and rollicking. After the first novelty of the school had, in a measure subsided, I found that one or two days a week the older students came to school tired, little inclined to study, irresponsive and cross. Inquiring into the recurrence of this state of affairs, on the part of the leading and best pupils in the school, I obtained from their own confession that, in every such case, it resulted from their dancing nearly all night. Several times I made serious appeals to their sense of duty, their self-respect, and their very earnest previous endeavors for the improvement of their privileges, and to their kindly feeling toward me, which had ever exhibited itself. But in spite of their promises of refraining from the practice, new occasions would call for breaking down their resolutions, and dancing became more and more an evil. In reflecting upon this state of things, and finding that the resolutions of the young people were not sufficient to hold them, and, in fact, that they were training themselves to make resolutions and break them, and thus, to immorality and untruthfulness, I concluded I could no longer be a party to this line of moral degradation. One morning at general exercises, after I had dismissed the pupils of the other departments to their rooms respectively, I told those who were present in the high school that I had something to say, and I wished to hold their attention for a few minutes before they commenced their regular work. My remarks were these: "Now, young ladies and gentlemen, you are well aware that I respect you, and that I like you all; there is not an exception; there is no one among you who has treated me otherwise than with the kindest feelings and attention; for all of which, as a stranger, I have ever felt, and do now feel, most grateful. For the first few weeks I enjoyed my position here as teacher, and felt that I was doing, or helping you to do yourselves, a great and good work, and I can not but feel that you have enjoyed your school work under my administration. Of late, however, my work and your efforts have been so frequently marred and defeated, in a large measure, by your lack of sustained interest, and by frequent breaks in your progress of study by the practice of dancing, that I have concluded that it is not safe nor right for me to remain longer a party to this wrong, which you, in spite of me, are inflicting upon your physical, intellectual and moral being. I have therefore concluded to resign, and shall offer my resignation to-day, to take place at the end of the term. I don't think I ought to hazard my reputation under such circumstances, and impair my future usefulness by a failure which I see is impending in our relations to each other." I sat down. Mr. James Morgan, the eldest, perhaps, and most respected of the pupils, presently rose and said something like this: "Mr. Holbrook, I don't want you to leave us, and I know that it is not the wish of any of your pupils that you should leave us. We are very sorry that we have brought you to this resolution; we have no one to blame but ourselves. Our attendance on dances has been very wrong, and we freely acknowledge it has been a great drawback upon our interest in school and upon our lives. We have never intended to go counter to your wishes, or in any way to bring reproach upon your character or our own success. But more recently circumstances have turned up that we did not foresee, where we felt that the social claim must be attended to, and one claim has led to another and another, till this matter has come to be the evil that it is. And I, for one, will do anything you want me to do, and I think every pupil here will say the same, for we don't want this thing to go on. We mean to do better." One young lady arose and expressed herself in the same manner, and that seemed to be the feeling of all who were in attendance that morning. "Well," said I, "I will draw up a very simple pledge, and if you are willing to sign it, I shall be willing to remain. But a pledge, as I have found, is of very little force unless attended with a sufficient penalty to make the violation of the pledge somewhat of an annoyance and disgrace. I will propose this penalty; whether it will meet your views, I do not know: That, in case any one feels it necessary to engage in dancing, or to be present at a dance, he will voluntarily absent himself from school the next two school days." One young lady suggested one day would be sufficient. "No," said I, "I do not think that would be any penalty at all, for you are good for nothing one whole day anyhow." So it was unanimously agreed to sign their names to the pledge and the penalty. Good order and diligence were restored and the classes went on as vigorously as could be desired.

In the course of time, however, one young gentleman in attendance, who had been visiting cousins in the country, found it necessary to join a dance which was gotten up especially for his entertainment. He reported the fact, stating that he could hardly courteously decline to be present at the dance, or to engage with the young folks of the neighborhood, since the party was given for him. He, however, left it for me to decide whether, under the circumstances, he was not excusable for violation of the rules. Sympathizing most heartily with the young man, and approving his honest manly report, I took it into consideration whether, under the circumstances, it would be safe to set aside the rule. Finally, however, I concluded that it would be best for the school, even for the young man himself, to let the law take its course. After two days of absence he returned and thanked me for my integrity, and said he believed I had taken the best course, and that he fully approved of my decision. Dancing in term time never afterward troubled us. I ought, perhaps, to relate here, that Prof. T. C. Mendenhall, a boy then about nine years of age, was one of my most promising pupils. He advanced rapidly, taking his place with pupils much older than himself. He was especially interested in practical scientific work. It was during the second year, I think, of my superintendency in Marlborough, that I introduced analytical chemistry, having obtained from New York a complete set of analytical apparatus and tests. With this advanced class of scholars I organized also an engineering class, having obtained the requisite instruments for that purpose; also a theodolite, a transit and a level, all in one instrument, together with other necessary apparatus for exact and practical work. The school rapidly increased with students from abroad. The old town hall, that had become dilapidated and was neglected for years, was repaired and utilized for a general school-room; in fact, for chapel purposes. These accommodations being filled, the M. E. Church was rented and brought into use during the third year. All the accommodations were crowded, and, perhaps, I felt more encouraged in the fact that the tuition in our school was $5 for a term of eleven weeks, while at Mt. Union College, eight miles distant, the tuition was only $3 a term.

It was during the third year, in the summer vacation, that I organized a Scientific Institute and had the satisfaction of a large and respectable attendance of the leading teachers of that part of the State. The brief services of Hon. Thomas

Harvey and President Loren Andrews were secured, but the rest of the work, the instruction, I performed myself. The work of the Scientific Institute was chiefly of a practical, scientific character, involving the construction and use of apparatus in the different sciences, and training in lecturing with apparatus in hand. Charles S. Royce was in attendance, also David Parsons, since Deputy State Superintendent of Michigan. Also other teachers of considerable note and reputation, among them Hon. John A. Norris, afterward State Commissioner of Schools in Ohio. Dr. Thomas, a physician of the town, organized a class in anatomy, physiology and hygiene. The class consisted of some eight persons, of whom Abram Wileman, his wife and sister, were pupils, also Mrs. Holbrook and Mrs. Markham. Mrs. Markham was a granddaughter of Rev. Dr. Coles, formerly pastor of the Congregational Church at Austinburg, Ohio, and a widow of remarkably fine physical development, of excellent education, of vigorous mental ability and of winning address. She was preparing herself here to lecture to ladies on physiology and hygiene, was a most diligent and successful student, and gave promise of being an efficient and popular lecturer. Soon after she came to Marlborough, there were spiritual demonstrations in connection with her as medium, which continued as long as she was in Marlborough, with endless variations and with remarkable and inexplicable phenomena.

It must be remembered in this connection that Abram Wileman believed in no spirit, devil, god, or anything of the kind. Now the first cadaver used in the course of their anatomical studies was reported to be the body of a frail girl from Cincinnati. The demonstrations of her spirit, according to all those who witnessed them or were disturbed by them, were always of a humorous character, and were related to my wife and me as interesting and funny. For instance, when the demonstrations had become frequent and somewhat annoying, Dr. Thomas called Dr. Whiting, from Canton, also Dr. Ackley, from Cleveland, to hold a consultation upon the spiritual manifestations. They were met in their applications in this case, in every instance, with some evasive answer, the answer always being in raps, given by calling the letters of the alphabet in order. After many such evasions and humorous rejoinders, Dr. Thomas said: "Now, Ann, you have been fooling us enough; give us something sensible, won't you?" She rapped affirmatively, then commenced rapping again in compliance with her promise. As they called the alphabet down they came to these letters successively in answer to her raps, "s-o-m-e-t-h-i-n-g-s-e-n-s-i-b-l-e."

While these three gentlemen were sitting around a table, a pebble came flying through the back window, which was open, and, indirectly in its course, lodged upon the snuffer tray. This was about all the satisfaction that the three learned gentlemen derived from the spirit of Ann.

Several times my wife and I tried to be present when these manifestations were going on, but were never successful in witnessing them in any of their varied forms. One evening, having been invited by Hannah Wileman and Mrs. Markham to call, we spent the evening very quietly and pleasantly in the usual conversation for such occasions. At nine o'clock we withdrew and went home. The next morning, while we were at breakfast, Hannah Wileman came to our house very much excited, stating that before we had come into their room, the night before, things were flying about in every direction; brushes, candlesticks and various other articles passing around the room, always missing them. But from the time they had heard us at the gate, to the time we left and shut the gate of the front yard, there were no manifestations, but the moment the gate was closed disturbances began and continued all night. They retired at a late hour. The sittting room was also their bedroom. The lights being extinguished, their bedclothes were suddenly jerked off, and a small riding-whip, which they thought was hanging in the hall, was applied rather lightly to their unprotected persons. Springing out of bed and lighting the candle, they found the riding-whip lying on the carpet. With very considerable trepidation they again placed themselves in position for repose, but scarcely had they reclined when the clothes were snatched off again and a ewer of water seemed to be suspended over them, and the water thrown quite all over them and the bed. Mrs. Markham being, as she claimed, the cause of all this trouble, concluded she would retire to another room, leaving Hannah to quiet rest for the night. She declared that no sooner had she placed herself under the bedclothes in the chamber above, than she was suddenly taken up bodily and set down on the floor and a large basket of about five bushels capacity was thrown over her head. She screamed for help. The doctor, coming in about this time from visiting a patient, released her, and no more spirits troubled them that night. The spirits seemed to stand somewhat in awe of him.

These last performances were from the spirit of Sallie, the second subject for dissection. She was a spiteful thing. The dissection had proceeded as far as taking the brain out of the skull, and examination of the muscles of the right arm, which had been previously removed from the body. Mrs. Markham and Hannah occupied the doctor's sitting room at night as a bedroom, the doctor spending most of his time in his office, and sleeping in a room contiguous. About twelve o'clock one night Hannah was wakened by a feeling of chilliness over her face. Opening her eyes, she discovered a phosphorescent hand extending over her. This hand and arm were attached to the phosphorescent body of the recently-arrived cadaver—the figure as it was left in the dissecting-room the evening before. The frightened Hannah roused Mrs. Markham, who witnessed the same phenomenon. Both jumped out of the window upon the adjoining porch, and waded through the snow, barefooted and in their nightclothes, along the streets to the other part of town, to Abram Wileman's house. Awakening them with considerable difficulty from sound sleep, they were admitted and spent the rest of the night in peace. The next morning, the body, mutilated as before described, was found in its place as if nothing had happened. This last subject, Sallie, appeared of a very different disposition from Ann, the first one. All of Sallie's manifestations were annoying, vicious, and many of them malicious. Mrs. Markham herself always professed that she had no control over these spirits; that she did not desire their presence, and they annoyed her a thousand-fold more than they could anybody else. She, however, used them occasionally for mediums in communicating with her deceased husband. These communications, so far as she revealed them, were always of a pleasant and consoling character.

In connection with Mrs. Markham, Miss Betsy Coles, her aunt, had communications with her father, Dr. Coles. She was induced one day, she said, to take her pencil in hand, holding it over the paper, and leaving her hand to be guided by spiritual influences that claimed to be those of her father. His communication resulted in his reiterating all his orthodox views as preached for years, and exhorting his daughter to pursue the even tenor of her way in her religious views, assuring her that the best that any mortal could experience in this world, of knowledge of spiritual things and the joy of acceptance with God, was but as the faintest dawn of the coming day, when compared with his condition in his heavenly abode. I saw and read this communication. Miss Betsy assured me that the handwriting, although loose and uncertain, very much resembled that of her father when living. Now, all these friends, the two Wilemans, Mrs. Markham and Miss Betsy Coles were persons whom I would believe on any other subject whatever. The Wilemans especially, I had known for years as worthy, reliable young people. But so far as these spiritual manifestations are concerned, they were truly mysterious, unaccountable, and to me, unreasonable, on any other theory than that they were the real work of evil spirits.

After leaving Marlborough and making a short and successful tour of lecturing, Mrs. Markham was married again, and so far as I know, was not further disturbed by spirit communications.

It was while my Scientific Institute was going on at Marlborough, and Hon. T. W. Harvey and Loren Andrews were taking dinner with me, that Mrs. Dr. Speer, of Massillon, was also an invited guest. The dinner being nearly concluded, Mr. Harvey withdrew somewhat from the table. Mr.

Andrews said: "Well, Tom, now for a cigar!" Mrs. Speer then addressed Mr. Harvey: "Mr. Harvey, are you aware that my son Henry is smoking again?" "No, madam, I have not noticed it." "Well, he is, and it is in spite of everything that his father and mother can do or say to prevent it. What do you suppose was his last argument, after he had promised me faithfully that he would smoke no more?" "I don't know, indeed, madam." "Well, it was simply this: If Mr. Harvey smokes and it does not hurt *him*, I don't see why it should hurt *me*. And the boy is so nervous and irritable, and has become so unmanageable, that we feel that we need your influence to aid us in saving our son." "Well, Mrs. Speer, I will think about it," Mr. Harvey said, turning away laughing. When he had left the room, Mrs. Speer said that her son Henry, being naturally very nervous and excitable, had become a perfect slave to tobacco, that his health had been very much impaired, and his feeble constitution seemed to have been almost wrecked, and that both father and mother had used every influence, by way of penalties and rewards, of exhortation and tears, and every endeavor and inducement which could be brought to bear upon the boy to save him. This last stroke seemed to be a little more than she could bear. The equanimity with which Mr. Harvey seemed to take her statement of the case did not in the least relieve her mind. What the result was, with the boy, I am not able to say, but all who know Mr. Harvey, know that it did not induce him to set a better example afterward.

One night, just as we were about to retire, there came a knock at our door. I found a stranger seeking admittance, a boy about eighteen years old, quite haggard and wan, and, as I judged, terribly homesick. He told us his name was John Norris. My wife inquired if he had had supper. He had not; so she prepared him some supper, and we offered him a bed, expecting to see him in better plight in the morning. The young man entered school, remained with us two terms, was very diligent, made excellent progress, supporting himself partly by doing chores and odd jobs for one and another. At the end of this time, he was prepared for county examination, and engaged a school in the neighborhood of Marlborough. He taught a year or more. Under the influence of Mr. Andrews, who had formed an acquaintance with him at Marlborough, he was induced to go to Kenyon, of which institution Mr. Andrews was then President. Proceeding to Kenyon immediately on the close of his school, he had six months left in which to prepare himself to enter the Freshman Class of '54.

After the war was over, in '65, Mr. Norris was candidate for the Commissionership of Schools in Ohio. He visited us in Lebanon. Sitting at our table, and addressing himself to Mrs. Holbrook, he said: "Madam, you are but little aware of what you did for me, that saddest night of my life, when I went with so much timidity to your door, not knowing what to do, or where else to go. I had run away from home, my mother being cognizant of the fact, and my father opposing my desire and purpose to acquire an education. I had heard of the Marlborough school, and thought perhaps I might be able to support myself in attending school there; and hence, with but little money in my pocket which my mother furnished me, and with a determined purpose, my small fund being exhausted, I reached your door. The sympathy, encouragement and kindness of your reception, and the interest you at once took in my case, was really my first start in life." Turning to me he said: "I want to tell you, Mr. Holbrook, how the impetus I received in the twenty-two weeks that I was with you in Marlborough enabled me to obtain my education in Kenyon, in one-half the usual time.

"When I went to Kenyon, I was very cordially received by President Andrews, who informed me that I had only six months in which to complete the course, which, in the curriculum, required two years. Being determined to accomplish this within the given time, I set myself at work to do it. At the examination for admission, I presented myself as a candidate. Passing tolerably well, I was informed that I could not be admitted, since I had not spent the requisite time in the preparatory school, one year being the least possible time for admission; Mr. Andrews, however, took up my case and argued with the faculty. He being the only member of the faculty who was not a college graduate, thought it would be bad economy to send off a likely young man who could be admitted to any other college on examination without reference to the time he had spent in preparing; the very fact that I had prepared myself in six months, being, he thought, sufficient evidence of my ability to sustain myself in the course. He stated also that he would give me a letter of introduction to any college which I might wish to enter, and that, according to his views, I would be an ornament to any institution that I chose to select. These arguments, with others, induced the faculty at last to vote to receive me as a Freshman. During that year, besides keeping up with the Freshman Class, I took the studies of the Sophomore year, hiring a Senior student to hear my recitations. At the end of the Freshman year, I presented myself as a candidate for the Junior year, and went through the examinations creditably, as the faculty admitted, but was refused admission to the Junior Class, some members of the faculty stating that such an irregularity would derogate very much from the integrity of their college curriculum. Mr. Andrews again came to my relief, saying as before, that he would send me with a letter of recommendation to Hudson, the institution that I had selected, provided I could not be retained here, and he knew that I would be received there on his recommendation, as well as on examination, if they chose to exact it. I was again permitted to break in upon the regular college routine, and was received as a student the second year into the Junior class. During the Junior year, I took not only the studies in the curriculum for that year, but all the studies of the Senior year, and in the final examinations found my grades rather above the average of those who had been engaged six years in the ordinary course at Kenyon. The faculty, except the President, were fully determined that they would not graduate me. No expostulations or arguments offered by the President could move the worthy faculty from their position. President Andrews, however, was not to be overcome by the faculty in their what seemed to him unreasonable course. He brought the matter before the Board of Trustees, in the presence of the faculty. The case was fully argued, and I had the satisfaction of learning from President Andrews, that there was a unanimous vote on the part of the Board to confer upon me the degree of Bachelor of Arts. Thus, Mr. Holbrook, through the methods of study which I derived from your instruction in Marlborough, during twenty-two weeks, I was able to accomplish my course of six years in two years and a half. My application proved none too severe for my health, and I am satisfied that any industrious boy in college can accomplish more than twice as much as he ordinarily does, and greatly to the advantage of his health and morals."

It was this statement of Mr. Norris that led me to establish a full college course in the Normal School, occupying two years and a half, rather than five or six years, according to the ordinary curriculum of colleges.

Bartley Gilbert was an intelligent and well-to-do farmer, in the neighborhood of Marlborough, connected with many of the leading Quaker or "Comeouter" families in the township. He had long previously taken a leading position in opposition to all claims of religion, and yet, so far as I know, was otherwise a good citizen, a kind neighbor and an active philanthropist. It happened, one dark, drizzly evening, as he was passing to the stable, looking after his stock, that he noticed a stranger leaning over the gate of the lane leading to the house. As he passed back from the barn, the stranger still continued standing there, and Gilbert, going down to the gate, a distance of some rods, found a man, with one of his feet wrapped up in cloth, and otherwise somewhat dilapidated. When addressed, he said he was on his way to Cleveland from Pittsburg. His money giving out at Limaville, he had been compelled to take to his feet, and now, not being able to walk further, he had stopped where he was, not knowing where to go nor what to do. Gilbert kindly invited the tramp to his house, furnishing him comfortable entertainment. In the morning, the man was found to be sick and somewhat delirious.

In his wandering talks, he seemed to be addressing now one friend, and now another, making frequent allusions to "Lord" this, and "Lady" that, and divers other persons of the nobility of England. Mr. and Mrs. Gilbert attended carefully to his wants, provided medical advice, and nursed the stranger through two or three weeks of sickness. On recovering, in answer to their questions, he said that he was a younger son of a noble father in England, and that he had been sent to America to enlarge and improve his education by travel. He had stopped in Reading, Pa., for some days, and while witnessing the pouring of iron in the iron-works of that place, one of the vessels containing molten metal had fallen, and the iron had been thrown upon his boot, burning his foot terribly. His funds, he said, were in Cleveland, and under such conditions that it was necessary that he should go there in person in order to obtain them. The Gilberts assured him that he could remain with them until he was able to travel, and that they would furnish him the necessary means when he chose to leave for Cleveland. They introduced him to their friends in the neighborhood, and at length he was brought to visit the public schools. I treated the gentleman with all possible courtesy, but from the first was led to believe that he was an impostor, and that he was receiving the kindness of these —the comeouter friends—under false pretenses. My suspicions were met with kindly but determined opposition by those who were entertaining the stranger. Under one pretext and another, he remained in the neighborhood several weeks, being entertained by one and another of these worthy families, and being supplied with money for various purposes. Some pretexts at last being found to be inconsistent with his first representations, excited the suspicion of Mrs. Gilbert. When he was absent one day, she took occasion to examine his satchel, the only baggage he brought with him. Whether she found it locked or not, I do not know, but the only contents she found were an old pair of pants; a bill for the pair, as it seemed, which he had on, and a very meager set of cobbler's tools. When he returned, she questioned him very rigorously with regard to his statements, which had seemed inconsistent with each other, and inconsistent with his baggage. He still maintained that his representations were in the main correct, and that he had learned from his correspondence that the money which should have been forwarded to Cleveland, was sent to Buffalo. The Gilberts being unwilling to furnish him more, for they had already lent him between $200 and $300, Dr. Brooks, my next neighbor, furnished him $50 with which to reach Buffalo, there to find funds to liquidate his indebtedness to his friends in Marlborough. But no money was received as he had promised, and when Dr. Brooks wrote him at Buffalo, he received in reply a very impudent, insulting and provoking attack upon

Dr. Brooks and all the other comeouter friends for their greenness in being thus imposed upon in the manner they had been, by a man of so little education and such meager powers as himself. The result of this misapplication of benevolent feeling from these worthy families was such, that Mrs. Gilbert declared that she didn't know that she would be able ever again to trust any human being who appealed to her good feelings for aid.

During my third year in Marlborough, my salary having been advanced from $800 to $1,000, I received an invitation to take the Superintendency of the public schools in Salem, Ohio, with an offer of $1,200 salary. Feeling still that superintendency was not my calling, and a more extensive experience in this work was needed, in order that I might be able to experiment in this field and carry my various theories into practice for future use in training teachers, I accepted, in spite of the many remonstrances and entreaties of my Marlborough friends. Another reason, perhaps, for my preferring to go to Salem was, that the accommodations for students in Marlborough were all filled to their extreme capacity, and there was no further opportunity for the school to grow from home or foreign patronage. With much reluctance, therefore, I concluded to leave my many friends and very agreeable and successful work in Marlborough.

During my last winter in Marlborough I attended, in company with my wife, the State

Teachers' Convention, in Columbus, Ohio. Such worthies as Dr. A. D. Lord, Mr. Andrews and Marcellus Cowdrey, were then the admitted leaders of educational affairs in Ohio, and it must certainly have been a satisfaction to bring together by their personal influence such a gathering of teachers, in midwinter, as assembled at that time and place. The questions under discussion were such as tended to the positive advantage of the school system, rather than to the personal advantage of the leaders and those confederated with them. The State Association then had the respect and confidence of legislators as well as of educators, being controlled by such philanthropic spirits. After an interesting series of meetings, the Association adjourned Friday night. We, that is, my wife and I, had been very hospitably entertained by Mr. and Mrs. Ayres, citizens of Columbus, and had made our arrangements to leave on Friday afternoon, in order to avoid traveling on the Sabbath. Having packed our trunks and removed them to the hall of our hospitable mansion, we sat waiting for the omnibus to take us to the depot, Mrs. and Mr. Ayres conversing with us as we waited. As the conversation proceeded and adieus were about to be said, I told my wife that I should not start for home that night. "Why not?" said she, "we are all ready; what is the necessity for our staying?" "Well, I don't think it best for us to go." "Why, husband, we shall not get home before

Sunday, and we don't like to travel on Sunday." "Well, wife, I don't think I shall go." "Why, husband, are you crazy? We have made all our arrangements to go, and we must go; the children at home will be expecting us." "Wife, I am not going, neither will you with my consent." Mrs. Ayres seconded my motion and begged us to remain; she would be very glad to have us remain until next morning, at nine o'clock. But wife still insisted, and, using as much authority as I ever did or could, I told wife that she could not go; if she did, she would have to go alone. "Well," said she, "if you are going to stay in this condition, you need somebody to stay with and take care of you." "I guess, Mrs. Ayres, we have concluded to stay."

The next morning we started on the first through train about nine o'clock, and had gone but a few miles when we learned by telegraph that the train which had left the previous night, on which we had designed to go home, had been thrown off the track about ten o'clock at night, and fourteen cars had been thrown alternately, one on one side, and another on the other side, of a high embankment, and all on board were terribly shaken, many seriously hurt, and some crippled for life, while two or three were supposed to be fatally injured. It is hardly necessary to say that wife and I could now understand why we could not embark the night before. After waiting some hours for the clearing of the track, we proceeded on our way, arriving home safely on Sabbath morning, and found all at home in comfortable circumstances. It is unnecessary to add, we were very thankful for our providential escape.

CHAPTER XIV.

REMINISCENCES IN SALEM.

IN entering upon my work in Salem, I studied the ground carefully before the school commenced. Knowing that my predecessor was an able and popular man, and had his stanch friends among my teachers, students and patrons, I conceived it necessary I should first establish my reputation as a teacher. I therefore took the position which my predecessor had left, as Principal of the High School, letting the other departments run as they had before, without any special superintendency. My experience with the classes of the High School was, to me, very satisfactory, and, so far as I could judge, popular both with the pupils and citizens. Near the close of the first term of twelve weeks, having now become familiar with the work to be done, and having determined that changes were necessary in order to place myself fully in charge of all the subordinate departments, I proposed to the Directors, in the first place, to give an extra hour to the school, provided they would allow me three hours a day for the distinct work of superintendency. I proposed, also, to change the entire order, as for occupancy, of the rooms of the different departments, and to put in the exclusive charge of every subordinate teacher about thirty pupils. The previous arrangement being that prevalent in most graded schools at that time, viz.: having an older teacher in charge of the large study room, with one hundred pupils, more or less, in the room, the teaching being performed partly by the teacher in charge of the room, but mostly by assistant teachers in other and smaller rooms. I found by careful attention to this arrangement that this plan had worked badly. The pupils made use of the fact of studying in one room with one teacher, and reciting in another room to another teacher, for shirking study and excusing themselves to both teachers. First, with the teacher in charge of the study room, that they had learned their lessons, and hence had time for amusement and idleness; then to the teacher to whom the recitation was made, that the lesson was so hard that they could not get it; and as there was no special arrangement made for preventing this deception, the pupils were difficult to manage in the study room and imperfect in their recitations. The plan was nothing more nor less than a training in deceit, idleness and wickedness generally.

The first thing, then, that I proposed to do in my new arrangement was to put each subordinate teacher in charge of one room, with as many students as that one room could accommodate, and to arrange the grades so that each teacher should have two or three grades to manage, as the case might be. Thus every teacher could be held exclusively responsible for all under her charge. This new arrangement of rooms and teachers required an entirely new organization and new grading. I found, however, that the rooms already in use, by proper management, could be so appropriated as to meet the demand. The high school could be placed in the large study room and all the smaller rooms could be utilized for the subordinate grades. My next proposition to the Directors was that they should furnish me with an assistant in the high school, who should have charge of the order of the high school; and my classes, whichever I might select for my four hours a day, should be attended to in the adjoining room. So far as I was concerned, I was willing to trust the good order and diligence of the classes which I taught, to the care and charge of my assistant teacher, although I would hardly have been willing to put her in my position, being myself in charge, and having the classes recite to her in another room.

These several propositions were accepted by the Board of Directors, and the new organization was accomplished, and I then entered upon my second term as superintendent. Before making my reorganization, I called the Directors together, and, with their aid and such as I could obtain from the teachers—they not being especially favorable to the new organization—I succeeded in making a new grading of the school of about 550 scholars, quite to my satisfaction, placing each subordinate teacher in charge of those grades which she had somewhat irregularly taught under the previous arrangement.

I then made a careful calculation as to how often I could visit each class in the entire system. I found that I could spend half an hour, by very economical arrangement of my time, with each class, once in two weeks in all the departments, excepting the high school. In my first round of visits I asked each teacher to assign about as much in extent in the subject matter to each class as she thought they could well and thoroughly learn in two weeks, leaving this matter almost entirely to the teacher herself, informing her that in just two weeks from that time I would be present and spend half an hour in examining that class, saying also that I should expect her to be present at the examination and to aid me in pursuing a course which would be fair and equitable for the pupils and satisfactory to herself. Now, I had known that such examinations had generally been carried on by Superintendents with the teacher not present, and I had found that it worked badly: the teacher was not properly represented by her pupils, and her plans under such circumstances were very likely to be misunderstood; hence her work was not properly appreciated. One most important object that I had in view by this arrangement was to secure the entire confidence and good will of my teachers. Not only so, I called the teachers together Saturday morning and heard reports from them of the progress of their departments and of the especial difficulties which they met in governing, and, especially, of all pupils who were wayward, or absent, or tardy, or lazy, and of any other matters that were of common interest, where I could, in any sense, be of help to any teacher or pupil.

When my second round of supervising commenced, having made a record of the precise extent of the work to be done in every subject on which each class was to be examined, and prepared for the examination of almost every class ten questions, I took my seat at the desk, the class being on the recitation seats some distance away from me, and the teacher being seated also at the desk at my side, acting as my secretary. I called each pupil to the desk separately, and examined him by propounding any one of the ten questions which I thought the most difficult, as involving a more perfect knowledge of the subject. My questions were given almost in a whisper, so that it was almost impossible for the other pupils on the recitation seat to hear either the question or the answer. The same ten questions, with the possibility of varying them, if I thought it necessary, answered the purpose for the examination of the whole class. In fact, I had showed my list of questions to the teacher just before I commenced the examination, and requested her to make any changes or modifications which she thought desirable. Suggestions were sometimes made by the teachers, and were invariably adopted by me. If the first question was answered correctly and promptly, I frequently dismissed the pupil, and requested the teachers to grade that pupil in this examination 100 per cent. If, however, the answer was incorrect, I gave the pupil another chance with another question, and if still not satisfactory, the pupil was tested with another question, all within the hearing of the teacher. Thus, those who were least prepared might be asked ten questions or even more. Those who were found to be well prepared were dismissed to their seats, with possibly only one or two questions, thus economizing my time, and giving such as seemed least prepared the best opportunity to vindicate themselves in the examination. My grading was in every instance to be rectified by the opinion of the teacher, as she certainly knew the standing and merit of the pupil by her line of instruction for two weeks much better than I could in so brief a trial. It might be asked then, Why not take the opinion of the teacher at once, and take the grades of the pupils from her opinions and further knowledge of the pupils' diligence and power? The reply is, that my work as Superintendent was designed as much to show the teacher that I appreciated her faithfulness and skill in training her pupils, by what I should ascertain by this comparatively independent examination in her presence, as to grade the pupils properly in their thoroughness and advancement. When the examination was closed, I requested the teacher to assign according to her judgment, the additional matter which could well and thoroughly be mastered within the next two weeks. This decision of the teacher, accepted always by myself, was made known at the time also to the class. Hence, in the second and third consecutive examinations more and more work was continually given, and better and better results obtained, very frequently by the urgency of the pupils themselves. The whole amount of subject matter assigned was comparatively well mastered in one week, and the remaining time was then given to reviews or to additional matter on which the pupils wished to be examined at the time when the Superintendent came around. It was found by the time the second examination had transpired, that a new era had dawned upon the school, and the teachers, instead of being tyrannized over, as they had feared, were relieved almost entirely of the responsibility and vexation of governing their pupils. The interest excited by this plan of management was so all-pervading and stimulating, that there was no more tardiness or absenteeism, no more shirking or mischief. Indeed, every pupil was doing his utmost to secure the best grades, and the teachers had only to guide and advise in this endeavor.

Every subordinate teacher, in our weekly teachers' meetings, expressed herself well satisfied and exceedingly happy in the supervision thus carried on. Not only was twice the amount of work done which had been done previously, but it was accomplished twice as well, and yet apparently by little effort on the part of the teacher. If there was any complaint in the village, the only one I ever heard of was that some of the children were taking too much time out of school to prepare their lessons and in reviewing their work in expectancy of the semi-monthly examination.

My experience with my eight subordinate teachers was, to me, a beautiful success; and, at the end of the year, I felt prepared to resume my work as a teacher of teachers, if an opening should offer.

Of my personal dealings with my pupils I give but one instance. Among other pupils in the grammar school was a very pretty girl of fifteen years, whose mother was a widow in good circumstances. She indulged her daughter in attending all the parties in town, also in all sorts of rides and other diversions, that drew off her attention and interest from her school work. This very pretty girl was the object of general attention, and, being so much flattered, she had hoped to pass with her class to the High School the following year, in spite of her low grades in examinations. I informed her mother, by a note, that she could not pass, and requested to see her. She came immediately with her daughter. Apologizing as well as I could for the girl, in the fact that she had found more pleasure in parties and drives, and other divertisements, than in her school duties, and that I thought perhaps it was more the girl's misfortune than her fault, that she was so pretty that everybody wanted her at parties, nevertheless, I said that it would be doing a great injustice to all the school to let one pass who was known to be so deficient in her work as she was. Still, if the Directors were willing to let her pass, I could not, of course, prevent it. She went to the Directors, and returned with the reply that they left it entirely to me. I remarked that I was very sorry for the daughter, and admired her very much, and that if she would employ a teacher during the vacation of six weeks, I thought it very probable, if she would give herself very diligently to study, she might catch up in those studies in which she was more deficient (mainly arithmetic). I would take the trouble to examine her in the first week of the new year, and, if I found her examination satisfactory, I should be very glad to let her pass into the High School. The arrangement was seized upon by both mother and daughter, and I have no doubt the young lady improved her opportunities most vigorously. She took her place with her classmates the next year, and, so far as I know, afterward made her school work her chief enjoyment. My experiences with the good people of Salem were, for the most part, very pleasant and satisfactory, so far as I was concerned, but scarcely worth narrating. I may only add, that at the close of my year, the students and patrons, without my knowledge raised a subscription and bought me a handsome gold watch, as a testimonial of their appreciation of my labors. The watch was worn by my wife for many years, and is now in the possession of one of my daughters.

CHAPTER XV.

EXPERIENCES IN LEBANON, OHIO.

In August of 1855 I was invited by the teachers of Southwestern Ohio to join them in forming a Southwestern Normal School Association, the meeting of the Association to continue three weeks, and convene at Oxford in the buildings of the Miami University. I was invited to take charge of the special professional training work of this three weeks' institute. The leading teachers of the occasion were John Hancock and Prof. Rickoff, of Cincinnati; Chas. Rogers, of Dayton; C. C. Ellis, of Georgetown, and David Parsons, of Urbana. Quite a number of teachers and lecturers were employed in various lines of instruction. As the different courses of instruction proceeded from day to day, private conferences were held by the teachers for the purpose of presenting a plan to the Association for the permanent organization and establishment of a Normal School. When action was taken in the Association, I was appointed the committee to draft a constitution for the Association, including the principal object of the Association—a Normal School. The draft that I offered for a constitution was adopted, and a Board of Trustees was appointed for the selection of a site and for securing a Principal and the necessary facilities for opening a Normal School, to be called the Southwestern State Normal School. Notices were inserted in the papers of the plan and of the desire of the Board to negotiate with any localities which were desirous of furnishing the requisite grounds and buildings for the said Institution. Judge J. C. Dunlevy, of Lebanon, communicated with the committee, and Lebanon, through negotiations with the leading citizens of that place, was selected as the site of the school. Lebanon proposed to furnish the use of the Academy building, as long as the school should continue, with an average of eighty pupils, for five years, at such rates as the Board should adopt. Before the meeting in Oxford adjourned, I was elected Principal of the prospective Normal School, and visited Lebanon during the month of August, in order to become acquainted with the people, and to decide definitely as to the acceptance of the proposition made by the people of Lebanon. In looking around the town with Judge Dunlevy, I found at least a dozen very comfortable buildings, such as any family need not be ashamed of as residences, without tenants. My remark to Judge Dunlevy was, that these unoccupied buildings were the most desirable feature that Lebanon had to offer for opening a school. Although Lebanon was five miles from the nearest railroad, it still appeared to me that, all things considered, it was the best site that could be found, for many reasons. The intelligence of the people, the numerous churches which seemed to be well sustained, and the entire salubrity of the location, together with the interest which the people exhibited in pledging themselves to support the school by an attendance of at least an average of eighty pupils for five years—these considerations, with the special interest which Judge Dunlevy manifested in the enterprise, seemed to me satisfactory in their promise for the rapid building up and continued growth of a large and flourishing Institution. I had yet a term of nine weeks to teach in Salem, to complete my year. I visited Lebanon once during that time, and made some necessary arrangements, issued circulars and advertisements for the opening of school on the 17th of November, 1855. As the soon as my term closed in Salem, which was about November 5, I came at once to Lebanon, to make the necessary repairs in the school buildings and to secure boarding places for pupils from abroad, and, if possible, to arouse an interest in the town and country round about in favor of the new enterprise. I was very kindly received, and all my wishes were met. The Normal School Trustees held a joint meeting with the stockholders and Trustees of the Lebanon Academy, and a legal transfer was made to the Normal School Association, with the conditions before stated, for the support of the school, by the citizens of Lebanon.

My family were in Salem. My wife assured me by letter that it would not be necessary for me to return, as she, with such help as she could secure, would be able to pack and move, and take care of the six children, the eldest being about twelve years of age — that she preferred that I should remain in Lebanon, and get everything ready, as far as possible, for the opening of the school, and for the reception of the family. I concluded to take her advice, and left her with the burden and responsibility of making the removal. Notwithstanding we had a considerable amount of property, household goods and school apparatus, all of which had to be packed safely for transportation upon the railroad, with several changes by the way, Mrs. Holbrook managed the whole affair herself, having very little help, with entire success, arriving in Lebanon, with children and servant, in due time; very tired, but all in good health and good spirits. The sympathy she received from some of the good people of Salem, especially in their hospitality and kindness on the day and night previous to her departure, was a matter of frequent remark, and of continued and deep appreciation. One Quaker family especially, the Pinkhams, took the responsibility and labor, after our goods were removed and shipped, of lodging the entire family during the night previous to their starting, giving them their supper and an an-early breakfast, enabling them to leave Salem at 5 A. M.

Among the repairs it was necessary for me to make in the Academy was the furnishing of several rooms, whitewashing and painting several others. The largest room, which had been used for a Primary School, No. 4, I had seated and furnished for a chapel. It would hold about 150. This was the largest room and best adapted to the purpose. One of the rooms, with sliding doors, was arranged with desks and seats for a model school; another with desks for adults. All these arrangements and expenses were assumed by myself, the Board of Trustees taking no risks and advancing no means. In fact, they would venture nothing, and, when written to, rather advised me not to undertake it, provided I could not do so without depending on them. Not one of them was present at the opening of the Normal School. The agent, however, appointed to send in students, appeared in the course of time. The conditions on which I was engaged by the Association were that my salary should be limited to $1,200, and that I should have entire control of the school and make such regulations as appeared desirable. With such help from the Board of Trustees, and with no property of my own, save a library of three hundred volumes and an apparatus that had cost me $2,500, I assumed the entire responsibility, feeling that I had nothing to depend upon but my own efforts as guided and favored by Divine Providence. I felt, however, the conviction that such a school was needed in this location for many reasons, and that I should be assisted by the same good Providence that had hitherto blessed me and mine.

The Public School teachers, of all the country round about, I found inimical to the new enterprise, fearing, as they said, that it would bring such a crowd of teachers from other parts, and the price of teaching would become so meager that they would be compelled to leave the neighborhood and go elsewhere. The price of teaching at that time, in the most favored schools outside of the villages, was not more than $1 a day, so far as I could learn.*

Mr. Kimball, the worthy principal of the Lebanon Public School, was friendly to me personally, and certainly not openly opposed to the success of the institution. About the 13th of November my family arrived. I met them on the omnibus, and we took our first meal together, after our long separation, at the Lebanon House. From the peepings and whisperings that came to our eyes and ears, we were led to suppose that we were each of us objects of curiosity. The good citizens of Lebanon were sufficiently surprised that the new teacher, depending on them, as they supposed, for subsistence, had come with such a numerous retinue, and felt, as they have since told me, a number of them, no little misgiving as to whether we would find our bread and salt assured. The history of the four or five previous teachers who had occupied the Lebanon Academy since

---

*The pay of country school teachers is now from $2.00 to $3.00 per day, in this county and adjoining counties. This is a direct result of the Normal School, in furnishing better teachers.

its erection was sufficiently ominous. Nearly every one had commenced with a fair attendance, varying from 80 to 120; then the attendance diminished and diminished, until within two years the principal found himself involved in debt, unable to meet the demands of his creditors, and compelled to leave, in some cases escaping the sheriff's claims. A similar fate, they apprehended, might overtake me, in consequence of the burden of so large a family. Mr. Suydam, one of the most liberal and intelligent citizens, soon after told me that, had he known I had such a large family, he would not have permitted me to come to Lebanon, or would at least have informed me of the endeavors of the previous teachers to sustain a school. My reply to Mr. Suydam's well-meant condolence was about like this: "It is not my expectation, Mr. S———, that Lebanon will sustain me and my family; but it is my purpose, *Deo volente*, to build up Lebanon, and, to some extent, to sustain the town." Such was the confidence that seemed to possess my wife and me, the children then being too young to realize the nature of the undertaking or the extent of the responsibility assumed. It is due the good citizens of Lebanon that I should acknowledge their hospitality, and general and marked kindness of the first families in the place, of all denominations. At the time, the Baptists were, perhaps, in possession of the most of the property, of the most attractive homes, and were the most cultivated part of Lebanon society. This is not saying that there were not intelligent, educated, and refined families in the other churches, for there were many; but through the Dunlevys and Corwins we became more immediately acquainted with all the Baptists. Melissa and I were invited as frequently as convenient to parties, at each of the Baptist homes, where we met very many intelligent and refined ladies and gentlemen. It was, indeed, a great encouragement to us, under the circumstances, that we were received, and, as it were, adopted into the best of Lebanon society—than which no better is to be found anywhere.

The school commenced on November 17, 1855, about 100 pupils being present—70 in the Normal Department, and 30 in the Model School. This Model School was all secured through the personal activity of Judge Dunlevy and his immediate relatives. It was made up of children under 12 years of age, from all the leading families in Lebanon. My assistant teachers were Mr. J. N. Bonham, Mr. H——, from Kirtland, and Mrs. Holbrook in the Model School. There were two foreign students present during the first week of the school. These were Mr. Henry Venable, now of Chickering Institute, Cincinnati, O., and Mr. Crosley, since, for twenty-five years and more, a leading and influential minister of the Universalist persuasion. This was rather a small beginning for a Normal School, for these really were the only Normal students—the only ones who expected to make teachers of themselves. The attendance from Lebanon was that of a village high school. By degrees other students arrived from the surrounding country, and several from Brown County, drawn by the influence of the agent of the Board of Trustees, who had been appointed to lecture and canvass Brown County and other counties in the southwestern part of the State, for the purpose of securing students. No special accommodation had been provided for students from abroad, but, several coming in, I found it necessary to rent rooms and furnish them for self-boarding. I was hardly able, at this stage of affairs, to rent a building, and none of the citizens were willing to rent rooms in their dwellings for the use of Normal students; hence the rooms that I obtained and furnished were chiefly in abandoned shops or in some unused wings of deserted houses. The furniture and bedding were supplied by myself, and the rooms fitted up, under my own immediate attention, by my three boys, the oldest being 12 years of age. Such rooms, with their very meager furniture, including a bed and two chairs, a table and second-hand cooking-stove, were accepted thankfully by those who had come for the purpose of Normal School instruction. No comfortable board could be obtained in the place for less than $5 a week. This fact in itself, of course, prevented any very large attendance on the plan of hiring board and lodging. Several families in the neighborhood brought their children, rented furnished rooms, and brought in supplies for them. Thus the year went on; the agent sent in several, perhaps twenty, pupils from Brown County, and possibly some from other localities; but he secured their tuition money in advance, leaving me to furnish the instruction and to take care of their boarding accommodations on my own responsibility and at my own expense.

The experiment thus far, as I had my two teachers to pay, was not particularly promising. When the time of the summer vacation drew near, I advertised an Institute of five weeks as a part of the regular work of the Normal School. I had previously, however, secured the aid of several worthy gentlemen in conducting the Institute. A committee of young men from the school canvassed the town to ascertain how many could be accommodated during the Institute term, counting rate for board and room at $2.25 per week. Accommodations were promised for about seventy-five students at this price. The Lebanon House also would furnish board and lodging for $2.50, two in a room, or $3.00 per week, one in a room. Accommodations for about one hundred foreign students were thus secured. As the time for the Institute drew near, however, I was informed in various ways that this family and that family would not be able to take boarders as they had agreed. In fact I discovered that it was the general feeling that $2.25 was not sufficient compensation for the time, expense, and labor of keeping boarders.

This was a dilemma. My advertisements were out, my character was at stake, and the prospect was anything but cheering. Receiving word from various quarters of the proposed attendance of a large number of students, much larger than the boarding accommodations thus cut short could supply, I held a council with my wife as to how we should meet the difficulties in this emergency. My first step was to rent a large vacant building on the corner of Mulberry and Mechanic Streets, in which there might be accommodated possibly sixty students, two in a room. The building was somewhat dilapidated, had only been used in part for offices, and was wholly without furniture. Now, within four weeks, this building must be fitted up with bedsteads, tables, chairs, changes of bedding, washstands, and some few other conveniences. I proceeded to accomplish the object with the limited means at my command. I purchased a Wheeler & Wilson sewing-machine, for which I paid $110 in Cincinnati, the first sewing-machine of any value ever used in Lebanon. Arriving at home, and putting a girl to work making sheets and pillow-cases, etc., the machine would not work. Although warranted, it had not been properly adjusted at the manufactory. This made it necessary for me to take the machine entirely apart, and study all its arrangements and adjustments, and thus, having discovered the difficulty, to replace the parts and so adjust them that it would accomplish its design. The Wheeler & Wilson machine was at that time very complicated, and such was its bobbin and the circular finger that carried the thread around the bobbin with the proper tension, that it required some considerable length of time in experiment to accomplish the necessary adjustment. At length it was done; the machine worked well. But for my early mechanical training in Boston and New York, much expense and delay would have ensued. The girl that I employed to sew with the machine being utterly inexperienced, was displaced by my wife. She succeeded, however, with her own hands and feet, in fitting up thirty beds, making herself the ticks, sheets, pillowcases, bedcovers, and pillows. Thus this difficulty was, in a measure, overcome. I found myself prepared to receive students as they came in, it being supposed that most of them would occupy these rooms, boarding themselves, or that those who preferred would take their meals at the hotel. At the close of a week at the hotel, a committee was sent to me to inform me that the board at the hotel was unsatisfactory, and that better arrangements must be made, or the large number who were boarding there would be obliged to leave the Institute. I was then occupying the property owned by Dr. Elliott, opposite the Methodist Church. Consulting with my wife, we concluded it was necessary to offer these teachers table-board in our own house. Additional tableware must be furnished, and other arrangements made, in order to accommodate about seventy with table-board; and our dining-room and sitting-room were both crowded two or three times in succession at each meal with those whom we were striving to make comfortable. Most of them retained their lodgings at the hotel, but took their meals with us. Of course, this new burden fell upon my wife, with such untrained help as she could engage, extemporize, and manage. This difficulty being surmounted, the Institute proceeded, and, on the whole, was a decided success, in everything but the finances, most of the income having been absorbed by the agent of the Institute. In footing up the income and outgoes of the year, and the amount that I had actually received and expended for the support of my family, my wife teaching six hours and I seven hours per day, we found that we had only applied to our own use and support $320; whatever other income there was being used to pay the two teachers, or held by the agent as compensation for his services. This result of our first year's income was much worse financially than we expected, for we had assumed that the agent would receive a per cent. for his services, and that the school would be sustained by the bulk of his receipts. Instead of this, the agent retained all the money that he had received, and we were left to take care of ourselves, and give instruction to the students that he sent, without receiving any compensation for the labor and expense involved.

Many of the circumstances connected with the

action of the Trustees in regard to the continuation of the school I shall omit; but it is due, perhaps, that I should mention that I discovered a conspiracy, on the part of the Trustees, going on during the Institute, by which, according to their own acknowledgment, I, who had made a success of establishing the school, was to be ousted, and one of their number placed in charge. They had hazarded nothing, and expended very little. Now, the constitution that I had drawn up made the students in attendance electors for the Board of Trustees. Judge Dunlevy was the first one who revealed to me that the Trustees were determined to dislodge me. In fact, he had been consulted on the subject, and had yielded enough to the proposals and intentions of those in the conspiracy to get the whole matter out of them. I felt secure of the election of three Trustees favorable to my continuance, instead of those whose term had expired by the Constitution, and with such agencies as were at my command, made certain the election of such men. When the election came off, the result was as I had expected. Three of the old Trustees were dropped, and three new ones elected, favorable to my continuance. Thus occurred a tie in the Board. That I had left a good position, as good as any of the Trustees occupied; that I had risked everything; that I had even to risk my reputation as an educator, with little or no encouragement from them; that I had made a success in spite of one of their Trustees, the agent, taking a large proportion of the money, instead of putting it into the treasury,—were considerations of little moment. But that a good position was to be had, with little or no expense, or risk, on their part, which I had made by my own enterprise, was a matter of chief consideration. After the election, at the Board meeting, some unimportant matters being disposed of, the election of the Principal for the second year was in order. Judge Dunlevy, being one of the Board, arose, and commenced offering a resolution for my reëlection for the second year. He had been apprised of the course that the three in opposition would take when this measure was proposed, and was ready for the emergency. Their plan was this: Knowing that, with the President of the Board, I would be elected, they had agreed secretly to leave the meeting before the motion could be acted upon, and thus defeat my reëlection, even though it should destroy the whole enterprise. The moment Judge Dunlevy offered the resolution, the President put it to vote, and, before they could get their hats, and get out of the room, it was decided that Holbrook was elected for the second year. Those three gentlemen never appeared as members of the Board afterward, nor did they send in their resignations. The four members of the Board remaining continued, however, to transact the business, all that was necessary, until the election of the new Board, on the succeeding year. The agent was one of the recalcitrant members, and his labors were thus dispensed with, and whatever receipts came in from the students went into the treasury of the Institution.

It was then a custom, not entirely out of vogue now, among examiners to take an interest in party politics in the county in which they are elected. One of the Board of Trustees of the Normal was a county examiner in Montgomery County. Through the connivance of the other county officers of the same party, he was accustomed to sell the best positions for teachers in the county to creatures of his own, receiving a per cent. of the salary of the teachers so appointed, or, if you please, arranged for by himself. The six or eight best positions, that paid the most in Montgomery County, were those chiefly, as he supposed, under his control. If it should so happen that, in spite of his personal manipulation, the district or union school should select a teacher for itself, then such a teacher was usually prevented from filling his contract by those managing the county examination. One way in which this was done revealed itself at this first Institute in Lebanon. Without having any detectives, I had friends in attendance who were willing to keep me posted on the measures which were secretly going on under the direction or connivance of this first Board of Trustees. A certain student from Montgomery County entered, paid his tuition, but attended no classes regularly. I was told that he was using this time for the purpose of securing such teachers from

Montgomery County, or elsewhere, as would fill those leading places in that county, and these positions were, in a certain sense, set up at private sale, not at public auction, to those who would give the largest part of their salary. Men were selected from those present, with their written pledge that, if they obtained these positions, they would pay from ten to twenty per cent. to this Trustee, who claimed to be the leading examiner from Montgomery County. Moreover, those who had pledged themselves, in this manner, were assured that they would secure good certificates at the coming examination in that county, on the following plan: The questions of the examination were in the hands of this agent of the Examining Board, and copies were given to all of those who were expecting positions. They would thus have opportunity to prepare especially on those questions in the different branches for the examination; whereas, those who did not have the questions in advance, because of the difficulty or unfairness of the questions, either failed of getting certificates, or received such meager testimony of their ability as would cut them off from the positions for which they had contracted. Mr. F—— was in attendance at the Institute, as pupil teacher, a gentleman of fine abilities, and very considerable experience as a teacher, at that time, thirty years ago. With a recommendation from me, he made application for the superintendency of the graded schools, at Germantown, Montgomery County. His application was favorably received, and a contract was made, conditional, of course, upon his success at the county examination, at Dayton. He attended the examination, but received, in due time, a certificate for six months, the least time that the law provided for. This was what Mr. F—— and I expected. The salary, at Germantown, was $1,000 a year, and a matter of some consideration to most teachers. When Mr. F—— received a certificate for six months, the longest time being for two years, he brought the certificate to me, and we held a consultation. The result of our mutual opinions and views, was that he should go to Dayton, and secure the services of the best lawyer of the party in power, and, through his influence, obtain justice from the Board of Examiners. Mr. F——, however, first went to the examiner, and demanded his examination papers, but they were refused, and he was very curtly told, that if justice had been done, he would not have had any certificate at all. He secured the services of a lawyer, who first consulted with the Judge of Probate, and then went with Mr. F—— to see the examiner again. After a short conversation between the lawyer and the examiner, the latter filled out a blank for a two years' certificate, and handed it to Mr. F——, without any remarks. The result was, that Mr. F—— secured the position, and the nominee of the Board of Examiners was rejected.

The narration of this case brings to mind a similar one which occurred in Chardon while I was teaching there. One of the examiners, Mr. G——, was conducting a private school at Burton, and it was his custom to bring several of his students to the examination, who had evidently been previously carefully drilled on his list of questions in grammar and arithmetic. These were presented for the examination of the entire body of applicants for certificates. These questions were prepared for a special purpose of tripping those who were not in the Burton school. These questions involved no principles, but were made up of catches and ambiguities, which might be answered in this way or that way. The result was, that instead of increasing his school, the general indignation thus aroused, compelled his patrons in Burton to dismiss him from his position.

In those days, institutes were not conducted to any extent by examiners, nor was there any county fund collected from teachers, or provided for otherwise to sustain county institutes. The present arrangement of the accumulation of county funds under the control of the Board of Examiners has led to a very general abuse of the examiners' power in granting or withholding certificates to those whom they wish to favor or injure. The general complaint of this abuse has called for a law which forbids any persons who are teaching teachers to act as examiners. For lack of any provision for the execution of the law, or for any penalty upon the Judge of Probate for not enforcing the law, it is to a large extent inoperative, and the abuse is widespread, and in many cases largely detrimental to the educational interests of the county under the domination of a Board of unscrupulous examiners.

More recently this evasion of the law has been practiced: The examiner who wishes to conduct the county institute and secure the larger part of the institute fund, resigns just before his institute or normal begins, and is reappointed as soon as it closes. Of course, the Judge of Probate is a party to this evasion of law, and ought himself to be impeached, but party politics "cover a multitude of sins."

I have before stated that my wife took charge of the model school. Our united efforts in making the model school a means of practical and valuable training to the pupil teachers, were of little value otherwise than to convince us that model schools are worse than useless for any such purpose. Various objections developed themselves as our experiments proceeded. We felt that we had every possible advantage for conducting such a department. It is not necessary to enumerate them.

The first objection was, it seriously interferes with the regular study and training of the pupil teachers, while giving their time to training and observation in the model school. Second objection: It is impossible to place the pupil teacher under circumstances in the management of a class of children, which are in any sense equivalent to the management of a similar class of children in his own school. For the most difficult part of his work, viz., the sustentation of order, is necessarily withheld from the pupil teacher, and exercised by the training teacher, thus defeating the chief object of the training in the very act. Third objection: In the necessarily frequent change of pupil teachers, the children made use of in the model school or in a model class, become so accustomed to the *régime* of the acting, rather than of the reality, that such children never behave as real pupils do when under the real instruction of the teacher to whom they feel themselves responsible. Spontaneity of action is thus destroyed, both for pupil teacher and pupil. Fourth objection: In the very nature of the case, this line of training, if it were practicable and useful otherwise, could only be used for any one pupil, in one grade and for but one kind of class in that grade. The management of model classes, wherever they are tolerated, generally confines the training, so-called, to the lowest grade, and to that only, this class of children being those who are the most easily managed. Fifth objection: The assumed circumstances necessarily involved in this false relation between the children and the pupil teacher, have, even under the most favorable conditions, a demoralizing effect upon the conscience and honesty of the pupils suffering by these assumptions. Sixth objection: The expenditure of time on the part of the training teacher, and of the Principal, under whom these training exercises are conducted, make the whole matter involving the time spent with the model classes, and the time required for criticism, discussion, correction and improvement of the points made or not made in the training exercises, too expensive altogether, for any good results that can come from such a lavish waste of time and labor on the part of the pupil teacher, the training teacher, and the Principal. Seventh objection: The results from these training schools with model classes, or model schools, have everywhere, with, of course, a few exceptions, been such as to show that every pupil thus trained, has really had to learn the whole business of class management and all class instruction over again, independently by himself and for himself, and furthermore with the expense of overcoming and unlearning whatever ideas or practical trend he had acquired from a model school training under the supervision of the training teacher or teachers. On the other hand, the training classes which, for years, I conducted in Berea, Chardon, Kirtland and Marlborough, gave immeasurably better results, in the immediate success of those thus trained. Of the hundreds who had been thus trained, scarcely a failure had happened in their first experience in teaching and managing a school. Remark: The kind of mechanical training which model schools under the most favorable conditions can give, is without the true spirit of independent and enthusiastic management on the part of the teacher.

This kind of training may answer for the schools of absolute Governments like Germany, or possibly for the autocratic management of the charity schools of England, but is utterly abortive with the free spirits of Young America.

Our second year, opening September 1, 1856, was, on the whole, rather favorable. While we lost considerable attendance from the town, we gained almost as much in the attendance from abroad, in the Normal Department. The original Board of Trustees and their agent had relieved us of their control and absorption of the income from the sale of scholarships. Still there were many pupils attending, who had previously paid the defunct agency, and were instructed at my expense, yielding no returns, except, perhaps, their own good will, and their personal influence, so far as it extended, in bringing their friends to the institution. Mr. B—— had been hired by the agent of the Normal School Association. He had received but a moiety of his stipulated salary. Disgusted with the treatment he had received from the Board of Trustees, he refused to continue his relations with the school, and threatened to prosecute for his unpaid salary. On investigation, however, he found no property belonging to the Trustees, and whatever there was in the way of seats and desks, I had provided at my own expense, and whatever of library and apparatus there was, I had brought with me. The Association, as represented by the first Board, was thus virtually bankrupt and defunct. The financial responsibility, together with the entire control of all the interests of the institution, henceforth devolved upon me. The new Board, being elected by the students, asserted no control, nor did they assume any financial responsibility. Any action which they took or were inclined to take in behalf of the institution was such as to give me, however, opportunity to carry out my own measures, and to realize my own plans, and reap the harvest of whatever ingenuity, philosophy or labor I could bestow in the management of the institution. During the second year, several of my pupils in former schools came from the North, and I employed as teachers the second year, J. H. Reed, Miss Catherine S. Morris, and also Miss Margaret Morey, teacher of the Model School. Mr. Reed and Miss Morris had been pupils at Marlborough; and were still pursuing their education while acting as teachers, each about three hours per day. The number of pupils reported during the second year, including those in the Model School, was 257. The Model School supported itself during this year, paying the teacher and other expenses, but for professional reasons was discontinued at the close of the year. In all, seven teachers were employed. Lebanon furnished eighty pupils in the Normal School, besides twenty-six in the Model Department.

During these first two years, it was with much difficulty that suitable accommodations could be secured for dormitories. The citizens of Lebanon refusing to rent rooms to students, I was compelled to rent such buildings and rooms as could find no other occupants. I furnished these plainly, for self-boarding, and thus, most students coming from beyond Lebanon boarded themselves in these rented buildings. Others, however, paid at the rate of $5 per week, for full accommodations in private families.

It was during this year that a rather exciting conflict with the county examiners took place, on the subject of grammar. The member of the Board who had charge of this subject, contended that passive verbs were intransitive, while the pupils of the normal school, without exception, parsed them as transitive. He marked them as defective, continuously, and diminished their grades and their standing in view of this difference of opinion. This was not a little annoying to me, as the gentleman who had charge of this was one of the pastors of the town, and in every other way a competent and respectable gentleman. But it became a question in my mind whether I should succumb to his false views, as I considered them, or take such measures as would drive him from his position. I concluded to take the latter course. Having instructed Miss M——, naturally a very quick thinker, and of amiable and winning manners, I sent her in to the examination. It happened that the examination in grammar on that occasion was oral, giving Miss M—— an opportunity to present her views in accordance also with mine, in such a manner as to place the worthy examiner entirely at fault, both with the other examiners and with the large body of pupil teachers present. Our pupils thenceforth were never marked with unfair grades for calling passive verbs transitive. Those who have given any attention to this matter will realize at once, that this error of the learned gentleman came from the false and yet very prevalent definition of the transitive verb, viz.: a transitive verb is one which takes an object *after* it to complete its meaning. The word *after* in this case was the misleading point in the definition. Passive verbs always take their objects before them as their subjects.

During the third year, the Normal School proper enrolled 335 different pupils, of whom 85 were residents in Lebanon. The table of statistics, given as appertaining to the school, is as follows: The value of buildings, $10,000; the apparatus in use, $1,200; number of volumes in Reference Library, 300. It was during this year that the periodical called *The Normal Methods* began to be issued in quarterly numbers. This periodical continued for two years. I then published it in one volume, called *The Normal Methods of Teaching*. The State Commissioner, Mr. Anson Smythe, under authority of the State, purchased from me, as publisher, fifteen hundred volumes, to supply the schools of the State. A. S. Barnes & Co., of New York, who were already publishing some dozen different volumes upon pedagogics, then assumed the publication of my book; and I have been assured a number of times, by agents of that house, that *The Normal Methods* had secured a wider sale than any of their pedagogical publications, except, perhaps, Page's *Theory and Practice*. The wide sale of this book for Institute use, and for training purposes in Normal Schools, contributed very largely to the building up of this Institution in each successive year up to 1861. I find, by consulting the several catalogues of the respective years, that the school increased regularly in its attendance. The assembly room of the Academy, during the fourth year, proved too small to accommodate all the students at one time, thus preventing the full advantage of our general exercises. By a vote of the Town Council, I was permitted to use the Washington Hall as an assembly room, by agreeing to pay rent double of that which had been paid before, at the same time receiving myself all the avails for the use of the hall for evening lectures and other purposes. These receipts nearly or quite canceled the rent. During this, the fourth year, 1859, pupils were present from Maine, Massachusetts, Pennsylvania, Iowa, Indiana, Illinois, Kentucky, and Ohio. The whole number of different pupils was 360. The number of teachers employed 7. Several additional building were rented, and fitted up for dormitories. This became necessary from the increased attendance from abroad, while the attendance from town proportionately diminished (on the principle, doubtless, that "a prophet is not without honor save in his own country and among his own people"). The rent of a furnished room, without carpet, for each pupil, at this period, was sixty cents per week, the tuition being $8.33 per session of eleven weeks. In the fifth year, 1860, 375 pupils were enrolled, 10 teachers employed, and fifty weeks were occupied for the school year, viz., four terms of eleven weeks, and an Institute of six weeks. The tuition was raised this year to $10 per session. During the first year of the war, the sixth of the school, 1861, the number of pupils enrolled was 272; the number of teachers 9. This being the first year of the war, many of the male students volunteered, and left for the army, thus diminishing the attendance and the income. My two sons, Josiah and Reg. Heber, were among the first who volunteered, one being seventeen and the other sixteen years of age.

During the seventh year of the school, repeated calls from the President for volunteers, in behalf of the country's safety, reduced the entire attendance for the year to 220; the number of teachers employed, 6. During the eighth year, 1863, pupils enrolled were 304; teachers employed, 6. The income not being adequate to support the board of teachers, Prof. W. D. Henke, having filled the Chair of Mathematics for three years, left the Normal to take charge of the Lebanon Union School.

During the ninth year, 1864, pupils enrolled 472; teachers employed, 7. The first graduating class, nine in all, took their diplomas. The curriculum of this class was equivalent to that of our present College of Science. The Business Department was also established, giving a very full and practical course of business operations, including all the branches necessary in business correspondence, business calculations, and the management of any set of books, whatever, in any kind of business. During the tenth year, 1865, when the war closed, the number of pupils enrolled, 612; number of teachers employed, 10; scientific graduates, 14; business graduates, 47. During this year a full College Course was introduced, with 7 pupils in the Senior or Classic Course. This curriculum, thus introduced, was carried through successfully, and all of those who graduated secured at once good positions as teachers or business men. The tuition was raised this year to $11 for eleven weeks.

I have spoken before of John A. Norris, who, during 1866, in his canvass for the State Commissionership, visited me two or three times. I was led with more confidence to adopt the full college curriculum in half the time of other institutions, as he had, without special effort or injury to his health, accomplished the six years' course at Kenyon in two years and a half. The number of students in the College Department for this year were: Graduates in the Classic Class, 7; graduates in the Scientific Class, 8; undergraduates, Senior or Classic Class, 8; undergraduates in the Junior or Scientific Class, 47. It was during that year that I commenced the publication of an educational monthly called *The Normal.* My son, Reginald Heber, was the editor. During this year I made my first purchase of buildings for dormitories—one in West Lebanon, that I named the "Eureka"; the other on Main Street, which I named the "Deuterian." The Eureka contained eight rooms, and was occupied by both ladies and gentlemen, with no teacher or other person in the building to whom they felt themselves responsible.

Leaving now, for the time, these statistical facts, I will give a few characteristic circumstances, endeavoring thus to exemplify the method of management pursued. In this building, the Eureka, at the time I am now speaking of, there were four rooms occupied by ladies and four by gentlemen, two in each room. One of the rooms was occupied by two ladies from the vicinity of Cincinnati, who had previously spent considerable time at a ladies' boarding-school, but, their father being embarrassed by going security for a neighbor, they had thought it necessary to prepare for teaching, in order to relieve their father of their support. I shall call these ladies Sarah and Susan Jones. There had been brought to me, by her brother, another young lady from a boarding-school at Oxford, the brother himself being a student of Miami University. From what I could learn from the brother, his sister had not been comporting herself according to his wishes, in her school relations, and had given her teacher and himself very considerable anxiety. It was evident, from his conversation, without his especially committing himself unfavorably to his sister, that she had been a pretty wild girl in her boarding-school experience. In reflecting on what course should be taken to correct, if possible, or to neutralize her boarding-school training, I concluded to place her in this Eureka building, entirely relieved from any supervision of any teacher whatever, thinking that it was possible that this boarding-school espionage and overdone watchfulness on her moral and social character had been the cause of her dereliction. I transferred one lady from this building to another, and placed Miss N—— with a sedate and reliable young lady as her roommate. In those days, when we used Saturday as our vacant day, our literary exercises occurred weekly, on Friday night, and often lasted until 10 or 11 o'clock. It was, perhaps, the first evening exercise of this kind that Miss N—— had attended, and, in walking from the Academy to her room, about half a mile distant, it was noticed by the other young ladies going from the same place to the same house, that one of the young men rooming there, in walking with Miss N——, was, by some means or other, walking with his arm around her waist. The ladies, of course, could say nothing about it while this transaction was going on; but, when they arrived at the Eureka, they called an indignation meeting in the room of the Misses Jones, and, passing proper resolutions, appointed Miss Susan a committee to wait upon me, to inform me of the conduct of Miss N———. Miss Susan called upon me the next morning, and, in the capacity of committee, laid before me the whole affair, including the indignation meeting of the young ladies in her room. I listened, with no little interest, to Miss Susan's statement. When she had closed her remarks, I sat deliberating, for a minute or two, as to what was the best course to pursue in order to help this boarding-school girl to recover her position in the esteem of the young ladies, and to restore her to the ordinary usages of good society. While I was thus reflecting, Miss Susan said: "Well, Mr. Holbrook, what are you going to do about it?" Said I: "Miss Susan, I am not going to do anything about it." Rising in her full height, in the vigor of her womanhood, she addressed me, as nearly as I can remember, in these words: "What! Mr. Holbrook, are we to understand that young ladies attending this school are to be tolerated or encouraged in such loose and disgraceful conduct on the open streets of the town? Are we, who have been better brought up, to be informed that we have no protection from a class of girls who, it seems, know no better, or desire to do no better? Is the building in which we are placed by your authority to suffer the reproach of such disgraceful conduct, and those of us who conduct ourselves properly to suffer under the reproach of such girls as Miss N———?" I replied: "Miss Susan, nothing could gratify me more than the remarks which you have just made. It is from the fact that you young ladies at the Eureka are well raised and well behaved, and are in my estimation perfect ladies, that I placed this boarding-school girl in that building, virtually under your influence; and it will prove very fortunate for her, that she has found sisters, classmates, who will have infinitely better influence upon her than any of her teachers have ever been able to exert. If there is any salvation for her, you will prove her best friends. You ladies of the Eureka, according to your own representations, have done what I wish you to have done. You have united yourselves in a band for self-protection, and have thus asserted your characters, and demonstrated that the conduct of young ladies and gentlemen in school need be no worse under school or college influence, than the conduct of the same ladies and gentlemen would be in their own homes, surrounded by the ordinary moral and social restraints of home life. I was satisfied when Miss N——— came here that, so far as she had retrograded from her home conduct, it was attributable entirely to her mismanagement at school, and for this reason I placed her in that building, entirely beyond the supervision of teachers, in order that she might be relieved of that kind of suspicion and espionage which evidently had been the cause of her misconduct. Now, Miss Susan, you no doubt were a lady (as you are now) in your school life, but you will certainly not say that all the young ladies conducted themselves properly under boarding-school rules and spies. If you please, what did you expect me to do, under the circumstances, in order to protect you from the further misconduct of Miss N——? Permit me to say what I suppose you thought I would do. It was simply this: That I would, in the first place, call Miss N—— to my office, and give her a serious lecture. In the second place, that I would bring up her case openly and personally at 'General Exercises,' and there give her another excoriation. Now, Miss Susan, this is the very course which has embittered that girl against school life, and has been the cause of her unfortunate conduct, and, if continued, it would probably be her ruin, as it has been the ruin of many other good and worthy girls. If you please, just let the matter rest right here. You young ladies have already made Miss N—— understand that you do not approve of it, and she, no doubt, is expecting some serious conflict with the authorities of the school, and she has prepared herself for it. Let us disappoint her, and, in due time, if the plan does not work well, report to me again. If it does work well, I should like to know, of course, and shall then give you the credit of having restored the girl to her right mind; for, in my opinion, Miss N——

was, before she left home, a good girl, but a very spirited one, and just such a one as would be injured by the ill-advised restrictions and regulations of boarding-school life."

Miss Susan replied: "Mr. Holbrook, I don't know but what you are right, but I am very much afraid it will not work. I am afraid she is a bad girl. I don't think she is a lost girl, by any means; but I am afraid she has gone so far in her lawlessness, that her case is almost hopeless." "Well, Miss Susan, if you please, let us try this plan. Tell all the young ladies that I thank them for their interest in Miss N——, and for sending you as their committee to report to me."

The result was that the young ladies had no further reason to complain of Miss N——. She behaved as well as any of them when she found that she was just as free to do right in her school life, as she was in her home life. The names here given, of course, are assumed, as the persons are all living, I believe, and only they are likely to recognize the line of incidents here described.

A circumstance occurred about the same time with a gentleman from one of the Ohio colleges. He came here to prepare himself for teaching, in order to get funds to go on with his college course. He entered the Teachers' Department about the middle of the term for eleven weeks. At the close of the term, when he had five weeks yet due him in the Normal School, I told the gentleman, whom I will call Mr. Smith, that I was about to form a class in Greek, of twelve pupils who had given their names for that purpose. Said I: "Mr. Smith, I have understood from you that you have been studying Greek six months at your college, and that you have made it a specialty somewhat. Now I want to ask you to be present at the organization of my Greek class, and see for yourself that no one of those who are commencing the study knows even the Greek letters.

At the close of the five weeks due you here, I should like to have you visit the class again, when, I think you, yourself being the judge, will be compelled to admit that this class will in six weeks know more about the Greek language than you have learned in six months." "Oh, that is impossible. Why," said he, "I studied Greek nearly all the time." "So I understand, Mr. Smith." "But I had the best teacher in the United States, save one at Harvard College." In fact, he was the first in his class, and was selected from college for that reason. "I grant all you say, Mr. Smith, and I will grant another thing, and that is, that you are intellectually as capable as any member of my new class. Still I have no hesitancy in saying, that if you will be present at two or three of my last recitations before you leave, you will be willing to say, upon what you yourself know of yourself and what you observe in the progress of the class, that they understand Greek in six weeks' training better than you do from the six months' study you gave under the best teacher in the United States. Mr. Smith was present at the organization of my class, and after a week, at my request, he visited it again, to observe what they had accomplished in one week. After another week, he visited us again, of his own accord, and perhaps his confidence in his own superiority, in his teacher, and in his line of instruction was somewhat shaken, perhaps not. During the last two weeks of his continuance in school, he became a regular member of my Greek class, and at the close of the sixth week of the term, when he was leaving for his school-work, he freely declared that the class in the Normal, under Normal instruction, was more advanced in the practical knowledge of the Greek language than he would have been under his college training in the whole forty weeks of the college year. Such exemplifications of college and boarding-school instruction and discipline were frequently, more or less every term, thrown upon us, in the Normal. Scarcely a term passes now that we do not receive individuals from some college or State Normal School from different parts of the Union. One year of college instruction, for the most part, enables those who come here from college life to enter our classes which have been under instruction one term of ten weeks, and a like proportion holds good for longer periods.

This kind of "let-alone" management, which redeemed Miss N——, has not, I admit, worked successfully in all cases. Some years ago, we had a young lady of about nineteen years, brought to us by her mother from Cincinnati, with the information that the daughter had been expelled from one of the ladies' colleges at Oxford, and that she brought her to us in the hope that under our management her daughter would be reformed, and would relieve her of her continued and increasing anxiety for her welfare. The young lady was assigned to a room in the Lyceum with another worthy girl, from Indianapolis. There were about twenty young ladies rooming in the Lyceum, besides several young men. I was occupying the lower story of the building as my family residence. Of course, these young ladies felt themselves more or less under our personal supervision. This Cincinnati girl, Miss Winans, I shall call her, very soon developed her boarding-school training by forming the acquaintance of the young men of town. She went so far as to invite one of these young men to her room; her roommate, however, being present. One of the young ladies who was disturbed by this breach of decorum, as she understood it, brought word to my wife, that this "town boy," as the girls called him, was permitted to visit one of the girls in the building in her own room, being invited evidently by the young lady herself. My wife took occasion, in her gentle, motherly way, not to reproach Miss Winans, or to scold her, or anything of the kind; but to speak of the impropriety of her course, and of the prejudice she would bring upon herself, even among the young ladies in the house, by pursuing that course of conduct. Miss Winans declared that it was a mere accident, she had not intended that the young man should go to her room, and it would not happen again. Leaving my wife, she ran up-stairs, and went around to all the rooms and to nearly all the girls in the building, and boasted of the ease with which she had got around the "old lady;" saying that the "old woman" was perfectly soft and green—she had not had so much to do with wild girls as some of her previous teachers had. Now, there were two courses of discipline to be pursued with this young lady. We were well aware that she had little sympathy. In fact, only one girl in the house approved of her conduct, even to her face. The one course was to take stringent measures, and put Miss Winans under the same *régime* that had resulted in her expulsion from the Oxford Seminary—in other words, to make an example of her in public, and to scold her in private, the very common method of dealing with such cases in most schools and colleges. The other method was to convince the other young ladies and students generally, that we were more anxious to save the young lady by patience, and submitting to her caprices and misconduct, than we were to vindicate our own characters for rigorous administration of discipline. Under the one plan it was plain to me, that we, instead of helping the girl, would have made her case still worse, by exciting the sympathy of the whole school in her behalf against our authority. By the second plan, we succeeding in securing the sympathy of every pupil, at least, in favor of proper conduct, and in full approval of our patience and kindness in bearing with the girl in spite of her waywardness and boast that she was coming it over us so easily. It is not to be assumed here by any means that we permitted the girl to pursue her own course, and in her wickedness to run over fellow-students and her teachers, and thus to taunt us to our face for our inability to manage her. After using all proper means, and finding that the girl was too far gone, had been too thoroughly trained in escapades and night-walkings and other improprieties, and her case becoming utterly intolerable to the other young ladies in the building, I wrote to her mother to come and take her away. Whatever became of the young lady after that, I am unable to say. I only heard of her afterward as a waiter girl in a restaurant.

During the twelfth year, 1867, the number of pupils enrolled was 751; teachers, 11; graduates in Scientific Class, 19; in Classic Class, 7; Business Course, 71. Up to this time, I had purchased six buildings for dormitories: Lyceum, Deuterian, Tertian, Tetartian, Pentonian and Hexonian. The town of Lebanon supplied the Academy and Washington Hall for the use of the school. During these first eleven years, the Normal School was managed under a definite code of laws adopted at the beginning of every session by a vote of the students, who, in voting for them, pledged themselves to sustain them by their compliance and influence. As individuals arrived, they pledged themselves also to the same rules. The growing prosperity of the school under these rules would seem to have warranted their permanence, but as continued relaxation in the rigor of discipline gave better results year by year, I decided to drop all former positive law and depend entirely upon the good-will of the students; in other words, upon the prevailing, popular feeling. The results justified the plan. Since that time, the popular sentiment has been in favor of order and diligence. This popular sentiment is sustained by the instrumentality of géneral exercises, of the monthly reunions, by the daily prayer-meeting, and by the interest always developed by the teachers employed in the management of their class recitations and drills, and by the free and genial intercourse of teachers and students in their meetings and greetings outside of class relations.

The chief reason, in any school or college, why popular feeling is found to be in favor of the violation, or at least in sympathy with the violator of good order, is in the servile position in which students are placed by the administration of law and discipline, and by the useless exactions and penalties imposed to secure diligent study. Since I have tried both plans, that of exacting study by pledges and penalties on the one hand, and by depending exclusively upon the interest excited by the teachers in their classes and otherwise, it seems to me altogether erroneous to impose laws on the large majority who, in any institution, will prefer to be right and do right, for the sake of controlling a very small minority who may prefer to do wrong. Since abandoning the idea of government altogether in the ordinary sense of the term, and relying upon management for good order and diligence, the popular sentiment here has been increasingly effective and controlling in its results. Private remonstrance with students, for want of diligence or for other derelictions, is very seldom necessary. From the first, no memorizing of definitions, rules, or other matter contained in the text-books, has been required. That kind of thoroughness which recognizes only the mastery of the precise words of the text-book in preparation for the recitations and examinations, we have ever held as abominable, as incompatible with the genuine love of study, and subversive of that general class interest which makes hard work exciting, fascinating, easy. I had always depended mainly on this class interest in study, for good order and decorum, both in school management and class management. I never tolerated, much less demanded, that kind of thoroughness which makes a verbal knowledge of the text-book the test or standard, so prevalent in most schools and colleges, nor did I ever depend on examinations, quarterly or annual, for giving any desirable or healthy stimulus to vigorous effort. So much skinning and coaching, and so many other dishonest tricks spring up necessarily with these college examinations in special text-books, that I consider the whole system vicious, and as training the student to shifts, expedients, deception and laziness, rather than honest, earnest work for the love of it as a life habit. I had always held it as a *sine qua non* in all correct teaching, that the teacher must be thoroughly in love with his business, and absorbingly interested in the subject taught, for how can a teacher excite a love in others for that for which he has no affection himself? My assistant teachers, all of whom I trained in the natural method of beginning every subject with the known, tangible and visible, and thus leading by easy stages to the unknown, from the concrete and sensible to the abstract and rational, succeeded for the most part in sustaining, each in his own work, that interest generally pervading the entire management of the school. This method never admits of following any text-book implicitly, and yet, text-books have, for the most part, been used as a necessary means of guiding the first efforts in class-study independent of the teacher, tending toward that stage in which the student becomes independent of his text-book altogether. This method involves, necessarily, the use of illustrations of every kind compatible with the subject in hand, and is the true object-teaching method, or in other words—the true "Normal Method" of teaching every branch. This has been the method of this institution from its origin, but improvements have been continually made, as no method can be "Normal" which is not making improvements upon itself continually. The first improvement was in passing from one text-book to the use of two or more. The immediate object of this was to break up the inordinate respect for the authority of the text-book, and to incite more extended and thorough research in study. The second improvement was in opening a general library of reference books to the free use of all students. The third improvement was in the use of outlines as a means of thorough investigation. Outlines were for many years prepared by the teachers, and copied by the pupils at the conclusion of the discussion of any branch, *e. g.*, Mechanics in Physics, or Gases in Chemistry, or Equations in Algebra. More recently, outlines are made by the pupils themselves, and in the emulation excited in business appearance, exhaustive investigation, and logical arrangement, in original or selected definitions, in original exemplifications and illustrations, these exercises prove to be a most healthful and permanent incitement, always cumulative in their disciplinary results upon the minds and habits of all who engage in their preparation. The free use of a full library is a necessary condition to any success in producing such outlines. It may be claimed, possibly, that this study in outlining, can give the student only the bare bones of a science, and that it can never improve the expression of a pupil's thought, or prepare him for any thorough discussion of the subject, or for any desirable position in life. The facts, however, are all against these assumptions. By proper adjuvant management, we find that exhaustive thoroughness in discussion is its immediate and always inevitable result, as these outlines are always followed by searching and thorough class discussion of all manner of points involved. It is found to promote both fullness and accuracy of expression in technical as well as popular language. The mutual class criticisms connected with the elaborate reports based upon their respective outlines, as given by successive pupils, have been found to have a positive and cumulative effect in enlarging the speaking vocabulary of pupils thus engaged, as well as increasing fluency and force in delivery.

During the fifteenth year—1870-71—the number of pupils enrolled was 1,065; teachers, 15; classic graduates, 5; scientific graduates, 17; business graduates, 47. It was found that the catalogue of this year contained names of pupils from thirteen States and one Territory, and since the patronage was thus shown to be national rather than local, it was proposed by some of the patrons that the name of the Institution be changed from the Southwestern Normal School to the National Normal School. This was accordingly done by a unanimous vote of the pupils and teachers the second term of the fifteenth year. During the sixteenth year, the number of pupils enrolled was

1,423; teachers, 14; classic graduates, 8; scientific graduates, 26; business graduates, 72; number in Engineering Department, 75. I purchased also this year several additional buildings for dormitories. These were the Heptoition, Octonian, Ennetian, Endetian and Decian. The citizens of Lebanon, more and more every year, opened their residences for the accommodation of students, and comfortable rooms were urged upon students at reasonable rates. Good table board was furnished at $2 a week by as many as six different families. I had, during several years, encouraged the formation of boarding clubs. These were generally managed by the student who formed the club. Any club of six or more were accustomed to hire a woman to do their cooking, who generally furnished their table, furniture, etc., while they divided the expense among themselves, paying the woman a certain rate per week each for her labor and the use of her furniture. The common price paid a woman for such services was 40 cents per week each. In order, however, to reduce expenses and make club-boarding more economical and desirable, I organized a club in the large dining-room of the Lyceum, placing it in the charge of Mrs. Holbrook, employing, also, a steward to manage the accounts and the coming and going of all those boarding in the club. The club price was about $2 a week for several years immediately following the war. From that time to this, I have controlled at least one club, keeping the price of board at a minimum. For several years it has been furnished to gentlemen for $1.25 a week and to ladies for $1. This club virtually controls the price of board in all the other clubs of the town, and is only sustained for that purpose, preventing that curse in most other college towns—a ring or combination of those furnishing board by which students are charged exorbitantly. I am satisfied that as good board is here furnished, as wholesome and varied, and as desirable in every respect, for from $1 to $1.50, as is furnished in other school or college towns for double these prices. A similar course has been pursued with regard to rooms for dormitories. Buildings have been purchased, rooms have been furnished, and great care has been employed to make these rooms comfortable, cheerful and wholesome, and at the same time to furnish them at the least possible expense to the students who may desire to occupy them.

It is hardly necessary to say that my chief care and responsibility and burden in the management of the Institution has been and is in the management of these rooms, in order to keep down the price of room-rent in town. It has been my policy always to have vacant rooms, so that any student can find accommodations at the advertised prices, leaving it to the judgment or taste of every one to occupy rooms which I furnish, or to select any which are offered in town. The competition thus sustained in the price of board in the twenty-five clubs, and also in the room-rent, has been so active and effective that students have little to complain of in their expenses here as compared to their expenses elsewhere. Although several other schools advertise less expense, we have tested this matter over and over again sufficiently to justify our saying that no other school, however managed, costs its patrons so little as the National Normal University. In fact, all the competing schools are compelled to put their tuition twenty per cent. less in order to draw students at all; and notwithstanding this apparent difference in their favor, by the management of every necessary expense we have always made this school less expensive to its patrons than any other. We claim, also, as we ever have, that the advantages and facilities for securing a thorough practical education in any profession or in any line of business are immensely superior here to those of any other school established and conducted by college men. The same holds true of any other school established and conducted on the principles which I have originated and brought into practical service for the advantage of the young at large. I have found in these many years of experience, that it is necessary, from year to year, to make changes in the teachers of our Faculty, for the reason that, it appears without exception, the teachers trained here, directly or indirectly, sooner or later fall back, more or less, into the routine of the old-fashioned college plans.

Thus it is necessary to replace those who are working, even here, with new impulse, as I conceive, from the fountain-head, from year to year, my children being the only ones who retain their vivacity, energy, originality and cumulative enthusiasm year after year in the management of our classes. For this reason, chiefly, I change off some teachers every year.

I find in the eighteenth year—1873—the number of pupils 1,613; teachers, 17; classic graduates, 7; scientific graduates, 37; business graduates, 92; number in Engineering Department, 97. The library, arranged in ten departments, for uses of reference, contained two thousand volumes, the latest publications in every department being added constantly; the library being always accessible to students and a competent librarian always in attendance. Much of the best study of the students is performed there.*

During the year 1872, the training of the Scientific Class in natural science being under charge of my second son, R. H. Holbrook, and having constructed a variety of articles of apparatus themselves, and having made extensive collections of minerals and fossils, Heber initiated and carried through our first school exposition. About fifty cabinets were displayed, each containing from fifty to one hundred and fifty specimens of minerals, fossils and other natural objects of interest, also many articles of apparatus made by the students, illustrating principles in chemistry,

*The library now contains 5,000 volumes, arranged in fifteen departments.

pneumatics, mechanics, hydraulics, etc. Many of these machines exhibited displayed decided mechanical ingenuity, as well as a thorough knowledge of the principles involved. The exposition also contained many extensive and beautiful herbariums, the sheets of which were displayed on the walls; also many large and fine maps made by the students in geography; also many well-executed drawings of objects made by the pupils; also a number of mechanical maps made by the Engineering Class, besides a large number of exhaustive outlines on rolls, rods in length. Each pupil having a cabinet, or any article of apparatus, was at his post, answering any questions proposed by visitors, giving explanations or performing experiments, as the case might be. Every subsequent exposition has excelled each preceding, and the materials in each have been entirely different from those in every other. Several of the cabinets, though collected mostly in the way of recreation and open-air exercise, have had sums offered for them varying from $50 to $500 each. Some of the best exhibitors in these expositions have been ladies, they themselves having collected the specimens or constructed the apparatus.

About this time there appeared a gentleman, in the short session, who had entered as a regular pupil, and who had evidently had the best opportunities, and had improved them; was polished, cultured, had much experience in the world, who was indeed in every way a gentleman, and who seemed to appreciate every movement in the classes, especially in the Training Class. At as early an opportunity as possible, I made it my privilege to form a personal acquaintance with the gentleman, Mr. Jones. I found that he was a member of the Friends' Society, that he had for many years been a preacher in that denomination, and that he had been a successful teacher of a Friends' boarding-school for about twenty years. In the course of my conversation, I ventured to inquire of the gentleman, after I had learned his position and his power, "What induced you to come here to our school?" He replied: "Of course, I came here to learn." "But, having been a teacher nearly as long as I have, I should naturally suppose that your success with the methods that you have adopted would have given you such confidence in their power and practicability, that you would hardly think it worth while to spend six weeks in another school for the purpose of learning other methods." "Well," said he, "do you remember three young ladies who were with you three or four years ago, by the name of Jones, sisters — Mary, Martha, and Elanor?" "Certainly, I remember them very well; they were excellent students, and very worthy young ladies; and, not only so, but quite attractive in their personal appearance. What do you know about them, sir?" "Why, those girls were nieces of mine. They were left orphans quite young, and I had raised them and educated them up to the time I sent them to your school in preparation for teaching as their means of support. When they returned to me from Lebanon, I formed an idea of your work here, not only from conversation with my nieces, but from your publications, and resolved at my earliest opportunity to spend a term with you, in obtaining a practical knowledge from my own observation and experience of your methods of exciting an interest in pupils in their studies." "Well, sir," said I, "have you discovered the power—learned the secret?" "Yes, sir, somewhat, but I am learning more and more of it every day; and I think that, by the time the term closes, I shall have possessed myself to a large extent of the same wonderful enthusiasm and energy and self-confidence that my nieces came home with." "But," said I, "was the self-confidence of your nieces in themselves and their methods misplaced? Did they not vindicate their claims to the possession of such qualities and gifts as would make them successful in their endeavors to be good teachers?" "Most certainly, sir," he replied. "I secured schools for all of the girls. They had never taught before, and their success has been such as I have never before witnessed, even in experienced teachers, in the management of public schools. And while I had some difficulty in obtaining schools for the girls, from the fact that they had no previous experience, every one of the three, in her first school, made an unexpected and beautiful success. And when questioned on their means and ways, they constantly affirmed that their success was attributable to their training in the Training Class at this institution. I think, from the success of these girls, that you may safely recommend those whom you have trained, and who have seized the spirit of your methods, as being better teachers than the great majority of those who have been teaching for years without having enjoyed the privileges of your Training Class."

I thanked the gentleman most heartily for his good opinion, and assured him that I hoped, as he became more and more familiar with the processes in the different classes in the institution, his judgment would be confirmed and strengthened rather than diminished. When he left, he voluntarily, at the close of the term, gave me for publication a very strong statement of his views and his appreciation of the work being done at this Normal School. This statement was published that year in the catalogue.

At different times during the history of this institution, we have been favored with visits from various gentlemen of good standing in different Normal Schools and Colleges. One President of a college spent a week with us, in observing the management of the various classes conducted by the different members of our Faculty. I proffered every opportunity for this continued observation; met him daily, and, looking over our programme, inquired "What classes would you like to visit to-day?" He selected from the general programme of fifty or sixty classes six or more of those he thought would be most useful to him in his line of observation. His custom was to take his place among the pupils of the several classes, and, with his note-book, to record points that he noticed in the management. He occasionally proposed questions to the teacher on his line of management, and asked the object of such and such proceedings, and sometimes, in a very gentlemanly manner, raised a point in criticism, and stated his objection to the course pursued; but teachers were instructed by myself to meet every reasonable requisition and desire of the worthy President. What use he ever made of his week's visit, and his continued and close application to the study of our methods, I am unable to say, as the institution over which he was presiding was even then in its last struggles for an existence. In my conversations with the gentleman, it was my opinion, although he raised no special objection to any of our methods, that it would be impossible for him, with the previous training he had experienced, to apply them to his own college government. His assumption, like that of most college men, was that boys and young men are necessarily sensual, and prefer idleness and self-indulgence to hard work and determined effort and self-denial. Such an assumption, or such an opinion, on his part would necessarily make all the methods practiced here useless and abortive, if not mischievous and destructive.

Another interesting visitor was a Mr. B———, from Sweden, Europe. He was sent here by the State Commissioner of Ohio, with a note of introduction. Mr. B——— stopped off a train, thinking he would stay, perhaps, two or three hours, and pass to Cincinnati on the next train. He remained here for a week, however, and, at the end of that time, said he should remain longer, had he not an engagement in the dedication of a Swedish College in Minnesota, that precluded the possibility of his continuance. Our Swedish friend, Mr. B———, pursued a course very similar to that of the College President, looking over the programme with me, and selecting those classes which he thought would be most interesting and profitable to him in the way of observation. Mr. B——— spoke English very rapidly, with considerable accent, but I found him to be a man of excellent ability, and of very broad and high-toned culture. After having graduated at the University of Stockholm, he had spent two years or more in a German University. He then, as he informed me, had spent a year at Rome, and was now on a tour of observation, travel, and experience, still pursuing this general course of education and culture. He was the son of one of the Swedish Bishops, who had the public schools of his diocese entirely under his own control. The son had been sent, at public expense, to America, to gain, as far as possible, the power to improve the Swedish schools under his father's jurisdiction. He had already spent some weeks in Boston, New York, and Philadelphia, and had intended to spend a week in the Cincinnati schools, but this week was spent with us. Of course the questions and remarks of this intelligent gentleman were in every case very apt, critical, and always polite, and not unfrequently very flattering, especially with regard to the management of this Institution without any laws. His repeated remark to me, after his day's work in the classes, was: "I have been watching and looking all the day in the classes, and in the recesses, for some appearance of disorder, or of disregard to good usage, and have in no case, in any class, or in any building, or time outside of the classes, discovered any tendency even of this kind. But, more than this," he added, at one time, "the perfect familiarity and equality of the teachers and pupils, in all their relations, both in their classes and out of their classes, is such as seems to me miraculous, impossible" (with a variety of other adjectives). "The students are everywhere seemingly controlled by some hidden influence which it is impossible for me to discover." Our Swedish friend had, doubtless, been reared and educated under a weight of authority; but he found no such crushing or coercive influence in this most orderly institution that he had ever known, as he frequently declared.

In answer to my inquiry, as to how much of

my management he could introduce into the Swedish schools, his reply was: "I have a great number of points recorded in my note-book which I shall most unquestionably use when I return home, and take my place as deputy to my father in the superintendency of schools in his diocese. They are chiefly on the management of classes—as I find that management practiced here, always varying in every class, by every teacher, but ever possessed of the same spirit." "But," said I, "what *is* the *spirit*, according to your view?" "Well, it is rather difficult for me to denominate it, but it does seem to me it is the spirit of mutual confidence and mutual respect, as far as I can get at it, between pupils and teachers. If I had been told before I came here, that there were no laws, I should not have come; but should have hardly thought it worth my time to visit an institution where lawlessness prevailed, as I should have then considered disorder and lawlessness the only probably permanent characteristics. But I am more and more astonished from day to day, and from hour to hour, at the prevalent interest, energy, devotion, of the large body of pupils that crowd your recitation rooms or hall, or the streets of the town. It is a growing wonder; the more I see of it, the more my astonishment increases. There is, however, one feature in your school which I shall not be able to take with me to Sweden, and that is the entire freedom of the sexes in their relation to each other. I shall not hesitate in attempting any other points in management that I have here noticed; but such is the established usage of our watchfulness over girls before their marriage, and its supposed necessity, that it would appear shocking and dangerous to bring the sexes together in Sweden with anything like the freedom from restraint which characterizes your dealings with that most difficult and delicate of all human relations." "But, Mr. B——," said I, "perhaps *that* is the secret power, more than any other, that has escaped your attention—the fact that this freedom in the mutual relations of the sexes is of itself a more potent factor in the management of this Institution without laws, and without spies, and without bad results, than any other one influence that can be found here." "Well, is that so?" said he. "It is most astonishing of all, that, in Europe, we fear the worst results, and, indeed, not unfrequently find them, in any relaxation of watchfulness over young ladies; yet, here with you, you proclaim what is our difficulty to be the cause of your marvelous success." "Well, Mr. B——," said I, "while you find it necessary, in Europe, to watch your girls (and what *do* you watch *for?*), we find them, in this Institution, the true source and chief power in sustaining propriety and courtesy. The ladies are left entirely without any guardianship, other than that which exists in their own hearts and consciences, implanted there by their home training. They are the guardians and servitors of order and propriety." "Do you never have any difficulty between the sexes? Never have any scandals, any escapades, any elopements?" "Why, no, sir; there is no occasion for anything of the kind, for I have a standing invitation for any that wish to get married to come to my house, and I will offer them every facility in accomplishing so worthy a purpose. Several different persons have accepted, at different times, my invitation, while numbers of others have preferred to be married in the home of the bride." "But do the parents never object to these arrangements of their daughters so far from their control and knowledge?" . "Oh, I have never known of any strenuous objection from parents, though probably many fears and doubts are experienced in regard to the choice of their daughters; but I have never known one match that has not met, sooner or later, the fullest approval of the parents, or that has not proven a happy choice."

In connection with this conversation, and the interest which our Swedish visitor took in this matter of the freedom of the sexes, and the fact of these school alliances, it occurred to me that his visit to America was not exclusively for the purpose of ascertaining the peculiar advantages that might exist in American schools, and so, Yankee-like, I proceeded along the line of interrogation somewhat in this way: "Mr. B——, I understand that you have come to this country to visit schools?" "Yes, sir." "Well, you have told me, furthermore, that the Swedish Government sent you here for the purpose?" "Yes, sir, I was sent here by the Swedish Government, at the solicitation of my father." "I suppose," said I, "this is the only object you have in view in visiting America—that you may introduce any improvements you may find into the schools under your father's supervision?" "Yes—not entirely so, either. I had other objects in view." "I suppose the general advantage of travel is one. Since you have become familiar with all European usages, you thought it possible there might be some wild, strange, uncivilized practices in America that would be interesting and amusing?" "Yes, sir; but I have found my sojourn in America exceedingly profitable, for it places me in a new relation with regard to the practices and usages of my own country. I see many things that I approve more fully than I could before I came. There are many other things that I would gladly have radically changed." "But you have no *other* object in coming to America than the ones you said—visiting schools, and the general advantages of travel?" "Well, yes, sir; I have several objects." "Well," said I, "there is no woman in the case, is there?" "Well, what makes you think so?" "Well, I don't know that I did think so; I only asked the question. Let me see, did you meet any American lady in Germany, or Sweden, or somewhere?" "Oh, yes, I met a great many." "Well, yes; but didn't you meet some very beautiful. maiden—different from the rest? I think you a very expert linguist, and that you speak the English language very well for a person who has been speaking it but six months." "I had a most excellent teacher," said he; "a young lady." "Well, will you tell me who that young lady was?" "Well, yes; I don't know that I have any objection." "And where did you find her?" "Well, we spent a year in Rome together." "And you taught her Swedish, and she taught you English; and you both learned Italian together?" "Yes, sir." "Well, which talked the best?" "She had been in Italy a year before me, and she talked the best." "And so you have come to America to renew your acquaintance?" "Yes." "And you are not going to take her back home to Sweden, are you?" "I expect to." "There, I understand it all; it's all right and clear now." "But," said he, "what led you to think there is a woman in the case?" "Oh, I don't know; there *is* a woman in almost every case that is desirable in this world." "Well," said he, "that is so."

A year afterward, I received a paper from Stockholm, most beautiful in its mechanical appearance, together with a letter from a Swedish lady, who had read an article in it, stating that she had become very much interested in our work from this article, written by Mr. B——, and that she had been very anxious to visit us* after having read

---

*Miss Cecile Gohl. She is now with us, as a student.

the article. She also stated that she sent the paper to me, thinking that I would be interested in the statement which Mr. B—— gave of his visit to Lebanon, and the National Normal University. It was written in English, although the lady was evidently a Swede. I called upon our teacher of German, a Danish lady, who translated the article in the paper for me. She demurred at first, saying that Swedish was quite different from Danish, and she had never studied Swedish. If it were the Norwegian language, she would understand it perfectly, as the Swedish and Norwegian books were used in both countries. But she made the attempt, and succeeded in translating Mr. B——'s article after some hesitation, for which she apologized by stating, that she had first to translate the Swedish into Danish, and then the Danish into English. We found it a very interesting and circumstantial detail of our plans, and of our peculiar management of our classes. The article, thus translated, was afterward published in our monthly.

HOW SICKNESS HAS BEEN MANAGED.

During the first several years of school it was customary for us—Melissa and me—to take any that were ill to our own home, and provide for them without making any charge. When, after several years, a young man, belonging to a wealthy family, had, from his own self-abuse and continued disregard of his health and my expostulations, brought upon himself a typhoid fever, and we had taken him to our home, as was our custom, and had taken care of him for about six weeks, boarding his father and sister also, and they, referring to my advertisement, declined contributing anything toward the long and expensive siege that we had undergone with him, and the expenses we had incurred for watchers, besides that of boarding his friends, I concluded that this plan would hardly be feasible any longer, and withdrew the advertisement, and made other arrangements than to take the sick into my own house and care for them, especially as the weight of responsibility and care and labor and anxiety and watchfulness came upon my wife, who was sufficiently laden, surely, with other cares. Now, it so happened that, after this arrangement, we had little sickness for a year or two; but, then, a married woman, whose husband was attending school, was down with continued illness for many weeks. She had exhausted the patience and health of the young lady pupils in the school, who had taken care of her. No other provision had been made in her several relapses. My wife interfered in her management several times, and, following her instructions, the patient had several times partially recovered, but she had fallen back by the same disregard of hygiene and the same imprudence that first made her sick. Thus she had several times called in medical advice, and at last had died in spite of, or, perhaps, in consequence of, medical advice and prescription. The husband secured the attendance of six young men—Normal students—to take the remains of his wife to her home burying-ground, in a neighboring county. In consequence three of the young men were taken down with the typhoid fever. Wife took much of the responsibility of nursing them. I secured watchers—chiefly from among the students. As a result of this long siege my wife herself came down with the same fever and barely escaped with her life, from the unusual fatigues and anxiety connected with her services to these young men. I then came to the conclusion that it would be necessary to say in public that, while we as a family would do whatever we could for the sick, it would be necessary for those who were suffering to employ watchers and obtain medical advice. In the few cases of sickness which followed this announcement we remitted no care or trouble in behalf of the sick; but the matter was taken up by the daily prayer-meeting, and since that time a committee has been appointed each successive term to announce to the prayer-meeting any cases of sickness or any need of watchers, and, save in a very few cases, students have been kindly and generously cared for by their fellow-students. Previous to this present year, the thirtieth (1885), there have been but eight deaths in the Institution among the 35,000 who have attended. As often as every other year the measles have been brought into the school, and when once introduced, they have never been checked until nearly every person in school who has not before had the measles has been attacked. Only two deaths from that cause have occurred previous to this year (1885). Five times during the history of the school the smallpox has appeared in town, or in the school, and in no one of these cases has it proved fatal or extended beyond the person who brought it here. I have remarked elsewhere that the excessive labor, anxiety and loss of sleep to which my wife was subjected in the care of the sick undoubtedly shortened her life many years. No expostulations on the part of her husband or children could deter her from taking a deep and personal interest in every sufferer in the school.

It is still customary for students to volunteer their services in case of sickness. Arrangements are still made in the prayer-meeting, through committees, to report cases of sickness and to provide watchers as far as may be possible. However, in all cases of protracted sickness, parents or other friends are sent for, and the case is then transferred to them.

The exceptional health of the school through these thirty years, the few deaths that have occurred, bear testimony to the entire healthfulness of the locality and to the effectiveness of the hygienic arrangements in the Institution.

MANAGEMENT OF WAYWARD BOYS.

As the reputation of the Institution extends, and as it is more and more insisted that there is less of dissipation and waste of time and of money here than in any other school, boys who were doubtless unmanageable at home have been sent here for the benefit of the moral influence supposed to be exerted here by both teachers and pupils. We have never claimed to be a "reform school," nor do I ever encourage parents or guardians to send any boys or girls here for instruction or moral improvement who are unmanageable at home. I have no fears of their influence in any direction upon the prosperity of the school, but the care and responsibility of one wayward, thoughtless, not to say reckless, boy, as any can see, is more wearing and exhausting than the entire management of the Institution in all the interests and diversity of employes and employment. I have, however, refused no one who has applied for admission; at the same time I am careful to state to every parent or guardian that I can not personally give care and attention or watchfulness to any such boy. If, however, the parent or guardian deems best to send or leave a child or ward under the general influences of the institution, not expecting me to watch personally over the diligence and good behavior of the pupil, I can accept the pupil with the understanding that the parent or guardian shall be informed whenever such pupil demonstrates that he can not be trusted with his own interests, and needs closer personal attention than I or any other teacher can bestow in his behalf. I have in some cases, however, been exceedingly tried, and have had my hopes and expectations in regard to some special boys, in whom I had a deep interest, on their own account as well as on account of their parents, continuously baffled; and after becoming discouraged time and again, I have still, at the request of the parents, held on and permitted the boy to have another trial, and still another. In some such cases the influences of the school have at last overcome the bad habits of the boy. In some other·cases we have not been successful, and the boy has been withdrawn from school by his parent or guardian without any public expulsion or disgrace. I could now enumerate several worthy business men of the former class, who, after several trials, have at last come to themselves, gone to work of their own accord and become interested in their own well-being and have been reformed—that is, made over again by the healthy moral and social influences brought to bear upon them by the power of their teachers and fellow-pupils.

EXPERIMENTS IN PHYSICAL TRAINING.

We have had a continuous session for the most part, from the first year of the Institution, of forty-eight or fifty weeks in the year, and our school exercises continue from 7 A. M. to 8 or 9 P. M., with an intermission of an hour at noon, and half an hour in the evening. It would seem necessary that students who thus voluntarily and earnestly apply themselves so many weeks in the year, and so many hours in the day, should, in order to retain their health and vigor, take at least one hour a day in physical exercises and recreation. I have initiated various forms of exercise at different times, at very considerable expense. During the second year of the Institution, I obtained and placed upon the Academy grounds, a thorough outfit of heavy gymnastic apparatus, and made such arrangements that every pupil in attendance could profit by the use of this apparatus. A sufficient amount of exhortation and of expostulation was given, to induce, if possible, every student to remit his mental application at least one hour in the day for this kind of physical training. After a few weeks, however, it became evident that the apparatus was not visited regularly by any pupil in attendance, and that no one at any time spent an hour, or a quarter of an hour, continuously in its use. It was eventually suffered through neglect, to go to wreck, the students all being too much interested in their studies to yield an hour, or, indeed, any time regularly, to the recuperation which such exercise might be supposed to afford. Some two or three years subsequently, a light gymnastic apparatus was brought here by Chas. S. Royce, and under his training and inspiration a large proportion of the school, ladies and gentlemen, were induced to give an hour a day to the use of this apparatus, and received, no doubt, many of them, much advantage from this kind of training. When, however, the incitement of the trainer was removed, and the pupils were expected or requested to purchase the apparatus, each for himself, and were thrown into groups for practice, it was found that comparatively few felt it necessary to avail themselves of this kind of relief from excessive application to their studies. The apparatus, then, for light gymnastics was laid aside, forgotten, no one feeling that he had time to make any regular or satisfactory use of the apparatus, even after he had been trained.

My next endeavor for physical training, a year or two intervening, was to introduce base-ball, and to divide the school into nines according to their times of recitation. The ladies, in sunbonnets and gloves, were permitted, if they chose, to form themselves into separate nines, or to join the nines of the young men, when they could conveniently do so. As a novelty, this plan seemed to be accepted, and promised to offer more continuous advantages than had been experienced from various previous attempts, but it soon became apparent that the interest was waning, and complaints were brought in that the nines were not full, and that the game, here and there, was prevented by the absence of one, two, or three from the nine at its appointed time. I then suggested in any such case that two or three nines should consolidate. This worked for awhile, but the nines soon became so few and so uncertain, and so few could be found upon the playground at any one hour, that a game was impossible, and this plan fell into desuetude, except, perhaps, with a few boys combining with town boys, who spent most of their time in base-ball rather than in their studies. So, for these reasons base-ball was laid aside.

The next experiment was in the way of croquet, and arrangements were made by which every student could have his croquet-ground, his croquet set, and his partners in the game at a definite time in the day accommodated to his recitations and studies. The experiment with croquet continued longer than any preceding one, especially as more ladies engaged in the several sets. But, before the season had gone by, very few were found availing themselves of the opportunity for exercise in croquet. Here and there, now and then, more and more frequently, this individual or that found it necessary to take extra time to get up a lesson, to write an essay, to prepare for a debate, or to make out an outline, or to get some other exercise ready to meet the demands of his own judgment in his regular school-work. Croquet gradually disappeared.

About six years ago, Mr. C. S. Royce removed his "Health Lift" apparatus to Lebanon, and being furnished with rooms at my expense, offered his services to any who needed them, and was at first patronized by quite a number of students as well as citizens. After remaining two years, however, the attendance of students at his rooms, although all who attended acknowledged the positive benefit they had derived from the "Health Lift," became so meager, that Mr. Royce was willing to accept an offer from a Water Cure to remove his apparatus there. This was my last experiment in endeavoring to give relief to the continued and excited application to hard study, which our Normal Course requires for its highest success. A comparison of our curriculum with the curricula of almost all other colleges, will show that a student accomplishes as much in one year, provided he meets the demands of our curriculum, as is accomplished in three years in most colleges. Now, this is *not* an *assumption*. It is not brought about by any "hot-bed process," or by any secret or patent-right operation; it is accomplished by the determined, earnest, voluntary work of every pupil here who keeps up with his classes and who receives a diploma from this Institution. Such work as is here ordinarily done, can never be done by any one who works from any other motive than his own choice, under the stimulus of his excited ambition, and under the energy of his own aroused faculties. The question then would rise from those who are not familiar with our operations, "How is it possible that while so many in colleges break down in their health without one-half the intellectual work that is accomplished here,—in the same length of time, the general health of those in attendance at the Normal is so unvarying, and in almost every individual case improved from the time he or she enters to the time he or she leaves?" My answer is: That college students rarely break down from hard study. The hard students are those who generally retain their health. Here, the change in the character of the mental application is so arranged as to make every study and exercise a rest and recreation for every other study and exercise. Again, our dormitories and recitation-buildings, about twenty in number, are so situated in the town of Lebanon, that a great deal of out-of-door walking is necessitated by the distance of the several buildings from each other. From the general habits and discipline of the school, and from the individual energy of the students, and the necessity of the utmost economy of time in passing from one class to another, these walks in open air are always necessarily of the most lively and exciting character. The step is very rapid, and the company is frequently that of the other sex in the walk, and the circumstances and environments attending these walks are generally such that a new Normal vigor seems to be roused in both gentlemen and ladies in this kind of jolly performance. Again, during the spring, summer and autumn months, sections are formed for collecting fossils, minerals, specimens from the strata and bowlders, over a wide area in this neighborhood. Sections in botany are also formed by other pupils, who make their excursions together in groups, generally of both sexes, and thus new interest in study, new incitement in social converse, and new powers of observation are aroused, all of which tend to the promotion of physical and mental vigor and social vivacity. Not only so, scarcely an exercise takes place in the Institution in which both sexes are not present, and participate in the work of the hour. Whatever most physicists, physiologists or fossil doctors may think concerning the mutual influence of the sexes, it is my judgment from years and years of observation, carefully compared and generalized, that such associations should be carefully utilized in the education of either sex, whether we look at their physical powers, their intellectual energies or their moral growth, and that those who neglect them, reject the most potent factor in the Normal development of either sex.

Not only do the sexes meet here in the regular work of class-recitation and class-drill, and all these walks and excursions, exerting their mutual influence upon each other, but they are accustomed to meet in regular debating sections, both sexes forming by preference, each of the fifty or more debating sections or literary societies always going on within the Institution. Not only so, but frequent reunions are provided for, of which the special object is to give the sexes, if possible, still better opportunities to become acquainted with each other, and to exercise, each upon the other, that subtle, social, healthful, moral influence which God has designed for the purity of the family, for the upbuilding of his church, and for the progress of society.

Some years ago, a gentleman of wealth and standing, who resided on the Ohio River, brought his three sons from a College Preparatory School. Their ages were from fourteen to eighteen. He said he had been advised to bring the boys to Lebanon for a business education, and that, as they had no taste for literary pursuits, and as his own business would give them employment in its different departments, and, as he hoped, they would share his business with him, he would leave them in my care, willing to entrust them to my judgment for their business training. I inquired: "Mr. S——, what is your idea of a suitable business training for your sons?" Mr. S——: "You may take your own course; I should like to have the boys remain with you and complete their education in your school, and when you have carried them as far as you think desirable, I will then initiate them each in his own place in my own business." "But," said I, "Mr. S——, you certainly have some preference as to the course that each boy may pursue in preparation for the department of your business that you wish him to enter." "No, sir, I don't know that I have any preference. I want my boys to be intelligent, competent business men, able to perform any business or any literary work connected with any ordinary business transaction." "Would you like them to continue their study of Latin?" "I will leave that, sir, entirely to you. If, in your opinion, Latin will prepare them better for buying and selling goods, and for managing men under their control, or improve their judgment in deciding the value of landed property, or stocks, or merchandise, then you will please let them continue in Latin just as long as you may desire." "You would like to have them prosecute their mathematics probably through the entire course?" "Yes, sir; if, according to your judgment, the training that you give in mathematics will make them more ready in calculation, and more acute in business transactions, you will please give them just so much and just so thorough a training in mathematics, as in your judgment will be useful." "Would you like them to study book-keeping?" "No, sir, if you please; it is the only study that I think would be of no special use to my boys in preparation for the different forms of business that I expect them to enter." "Why, Mr. S——, your views of a business education are somewhat peculiar. I had supposed that of course you would want them familiar with the management of accounts, and able to master and control any set of books whatever." "No, sir, if you please, don't let my boys study book-keeping; anything else according to your judgment. I have had so much trouble in my business in attempting to train young men to take charge of different sets of books involved in different departments of my business, who have come with their diplomas from commercial colleges, that I have, perhaps, a prejudice against book-keeping in any of its forms. I have never succeeded in training commercial college graduates into the safe and intelligent charge of any set of books in any line of my business." With these remarks of my worthy patron, Mr. S——, I assumed the responsibility of the business training of the three boys. The eldest, whom I shall call George, was, by nature sedate, industrious, and persistent in any work or study in which he felt it was right for him to engage. His success in all the different lines of study, comprising a thorough course of mathematics, a familiarity with the classics, with a mastery of English literature, with the power of analysis and expression in English composition, was from the first satisfactory to his teachers, and attractive to himself. Without the consent of his father, however, but according to his own preference, he took up, in due time, the study of book-keeping, and mastered it in all its varieties, principles and applications so entirely, that when, after three years, he left us, he was placed in charge of the books of his father's bank, and continues to the present time in charge of an immense business, in which a bank, iron-works, coal mining, and a railroad are involved. I have never heard any complaint from his father that his training in book-keeping was any disadvantage to his education. The second son was more volatile in his disposition, and less inclined to persistent effort in any direction; a young man of fine personal appearance, of amiable disposition, and rather unusual intellectual shrewdness, but seemingly unable to bring his energies to bear in any given direction for any great length of time. In his desire to correct his own failings, it was customary for him, term after term, to make new resolutions, and take up more studies than were desirable, and pursue them for a few days, or a few weeks, as the case might be, when, being attracted by social divertisements or other outside influences, and having an abundance of money at his control, he just as often relaxed and relaxed, dropping one study after another, until, again and again, before the close of the term of ten weeks, he found himself with one study, or perhaps out of all his classes. This course of procedure continued for almost two years, when at last, he came to himself, and seemed to realize that he had accomplished little for himself in comparison with what he ought, and that his preparation for life was, in a large measure, defeated by his want of persistence and grit, and by his too-easily yielding to this fancy or that. At the beginning of the third year, he made a firm and earnest resolution that he would retrieve his character, and hold on to any line of conduct, study or work that I would advise him to pursue. He never again failed in his purpose, and that year, his third, was a splendid success. He left us, as I believed, a man who would accomplish a great work in any direction, and in any kind of business in which he should engage. I have not been disappointed. He is a successful business man, and manages, independently of his father, an extensive business of merchandise and manufacture combined. The third son left us on account of failing health before his business course was completed. So far as I know, however, he is a worthy and successful citizen, engaged with his father, managing some department of his business. All of the sons, before they left here, took a thorough business course in our Business Department, aside from other studies which, in my judgment, would make them more intelligent and efficient business men. I bring up this example to show that the meager, narrow training given by most commercial colleges, is the worst possible preparation for a successful business life. In my opinion, to enter upon the immense and intense competition now raging in every kind of business, a young man, with or without capital, needs a good education in the broad sense, thus feeling himself competent to meet intelligent men, and to hold his position against all odds. On the other hand, the preparation for business which commercial colleges, so far as I know, are advertising, must be extended, corrected, and for the most part forgotten, before the young man can obtain any paying position, even as an employé in any business of any considerable extent or importance.

During the time that these young gentlemen

were here in training for their business life, there came a man from one of the Cincinnati commercial colleges to Lebanon, and gave a lecture in the Town Hall, upon the especial advantages which he declared, would follow from the business training in the institution of which he was the proprietor. A farmer boy in attendance at our school, was induced by the representations of this commercial college man, to enter there at the close of the term with us. How long he continued there and what he studied, I am not able to say, but some nine months afterward he returned to Lebanon, and reported his history for the nine months in Cincinnati, in language somewhat like this: "I entered the commercial college a few days after I left Lebanon, and continued there until I received my diploma. My expenses in cash—not all, of course, strictly necessary—were about $600; but when I received my diploma, with some others, and a public occasion was made of the conferring of diplomas, I imagined that my fortune was secured, and that I was then ready to reap the immediate rewards of my training. I received the highest praise for my diligence in study and for the mastery of all that was taught in the commercial college. I had been assured by the gentleman in his lecture in Lebanon, and from time to time, as I went on in my study, that I would find no difficulty in securing a good position immediately upon my graduation from this commercial college. A few days after my graduation, taking my diploma in its case, I started out on Third Street to find a position. To every application that I made, in every business-house, there was some objection presented, or some difficulty raised, or some doubt expressed, so that I failed the first day in finding a place for work. On the second day, I took Fourth Street and pursued a similar course, and somewhere along the line of application, some gentleman kindly told me that he thought if I would leave my diploma at home, I would be more likely to get a position; but so long as I made the diploma the ground of my recommendation, he presumed that I would meet with very little encouragement. I had previously come to the same conclusion, that the objections and doubts must arise from some one cause connected with my personality. The next day, I started out without my diploma, but canvassed other streets, went to other business-houses. The difference of my reception was at once manifest. Knowing from my appearance that I was a country boy, I was met with confidence and with encouragement, but no sufficient salary was offered for such services as a country boy would be able to render in a business-house in a city; but in several places, I was assured that if I would commence at the bottom of the business and work up, I would, in the course of time, obtain a good position, as country boys, ignorant of city practices, were always in demand. I am now in the employment of a heavy wholesale establishment, at wages barely sufficient to pay my necessary expenses, but I am encouraged to feel that I am giving satisfaction, and that I shall eventually rise to a higher position, and make myself necessary to the establishment. At least, I am making every effort to accomplish this end."

A few months ago, I was met in the streets of Cincinnati by a young man, Mr. R——, who had graduated in our Business Department. He came to me with great cordiality, and, at once, after passing the compliments, said: "Mr. Holbrook, do you remember what an effort you made with me to induce me to extend my education beyond grammar, and arithmetic, and book-keeping?" "I do, indeed, Mr. R——, most assuredly, remember all about it. I have had the same conflict with a great many other young men, endeavoring to elevate and broaden their views as to a necessary preparation for an ordinary business life. The narrowness and meagerness of business preparation has become so general, through the advertisements and practices of commercial colleges, that I feel it necessary, whenever I have opportunity, and I have had hundreds of cases to deal with,—I feel it necessary to prevent young men from making unworthy wrecks of worthy powers and opportunities." "But," said he, "do you remember how you urged upon me the necessity of studying English composition, so that I should be able to write a good advertisement, and a good business article for a newspaper, and thus become competent to manage the literary work of a large business establishment?" "Most certainly I do, sir; I have done the same thing with hundreds of others; with some I have prevailed, with others I have not." "But," said he, "it was that training in English composition, and in English literature, upon which you insisted, and which I for a time resisted, that has been the making of me. I am now engaged as chief and confidential clerk in a large manufacturing establishment. The correspondence, the advertising, and the literary work of the firm is all done by myself; and I have the satisfaction of knowing that the business, through my literary power thus exercised, is rapidly extending, and that I am become, as it were, a necessary, at least, a very useful, part of the establishment. I commenced with a small salary, but it has been gradually increased, until now I am receiving $100 per month, with some perquisites in percentages on sales, and I have the promise of still further advance in salary and in position, and I hope to be admitted before another year into partnership in the business; for all of which I have to thank you, Mr. Holbrook, for persuading me to go beyond my very limited ideas of a business education. My book-keeping I have never used, that is, in the way of keeping books, although the books of the establishment come daily under my supervision. But my literary power has been the means of my rapid advancement and complete success, far beyond my brightest expectations." "Mr. R——, I shall make use of this statement of yours as an encouragement to other young men, who seem to feel satisfied, coming to our school, if they can learn to keep a set of books." "I hope you will do so, sir; you are welcome to make any use of my success that you may desire."

Now, it is not true that every one who has completed a thorough Business Course at this Institution has met with the success of Mr. R——. But it is at the same time manifest, that every one who has had this broader and deeper training than any commercial college can possibly give, has the advantage of being able to enter any such opening that may occur. Yes, this literary training, in addition to the mathematical and business training proper, is immeasurably more effective and useful, and will prepare any young man to enter any business house, and apprehend more readily the great variety of business operations involved in such an establishment, than any possible training which he could secure in the miserable shams, pretensions, and operations of "actual business," advertised with such persistency, and urged with such assurances, and which seem for the time to draw into the meshes of those commercial colleges so many of the weaker sort of untrained, callow, and rustic youth.

(*Contents continued from p. 6.*)

CHAPTER XII.
EXPERIENCES AT KIRTLAND.

Rev. Truman Coe—A self-made man—Travels—A lady lecturer's triumph—John B. Gough's victory—Prof. O. M. Mitchell relates an incident of triumph over Harvard professors—New Orleans—Conversation—Northern and Southern views compared—Catholics evade the priest's control—A queer story—Attacked with cholera—Narrow escape with my life—Incidents of travel—Jenny Lind's power—One effect of enthusiastic teaching—A lesson in teaching arithmetic—An arithmetical contest—Withdrawal from Kirtland—Mormons—Incidents of overland travel in 1838—Tornado—The last of the wolves in the Western Reserve.

CHAPTER XIII.
MARLBOROUGH EXPERIENCES.

The question of the Bible in a public school settled—How I managed the janitoring—An infidel's views on the Bible—How dancing parties were managed—Scientific Institute held—Prof. Harvey and Mr. Loren Andrews employed as lecturers—Spirit manifestations—Mr. Harvey and tobacco—John A. Norris; how he accomplished a six years' college course in two and a half years—Story of a tramp—Removal to Salem at salary of $1,200—Narrow escape.

CHAPTER XIV.
REMINISCENCES IN SALEM.

Successful experimenting in school superintendency—A variety of difficulties overcome—How the subordinate teachers were won—A privileged character managed.

CHAPTER XV.
EXPERIENCES WHILE IN LEBANON.

How I came to live in Lebanon.—Invited to attend Teachers' Institute in Oxford to lecture on Teaching and School Management—Appointed a committee to draft a constitution for a

Normal School Association—Lebanon selected as a site of the Normal School—Conditions offered—Many unoccupied buildings—A favorable fact—Completed my year in Salem—Came to Lebanon to make preparations—Joint meeting of Trustees of Lebanon Academy and Normal Association—Family still in Salem—Mrs. H. packs goods and moves the family—Established in Lebanon—Repairs in the Academy—No help from Normal Trustees—Their agent takes all the funds he collects—My salary limited to $1,200, but all to be made by myself—Trust in God—Demands for a Normal School here—Public school teachers inimical to the enterprise: would reduce salaries—Arrival of family—Misgivings of citizens as to our support, arising from failure of five predecessors—Mr. Suydam's solicitude—My expectation not to secure support from Lebanon, but to build up the town—Hospitality of Lebanon people.

First Year of School.—Opened November 17, 1855—Pupils 100—Model School in charge of Mrs. H.—Judge Dunlevy's assistance—Three teachers employed—Prof. Henry Venable one of foreign pupils—Others soon sent in by agent—Provision for students from abroad—Vacant rooms rented—Fitted up by self and sons—Self-boarding inexpensive—$5.00 board in town prevented large attendance—Farmers' families furnished supplies for their children in attendance—Agent sent in pupils, but pocketed the funds.

Summer Institute.—Difficulties of obtaining board overcome—Failure of Lebanon accommodations—Large house rented and furnished by self—Purchase and invaluable use of the first sewing machine in Lebanon—My wife's counsel, sewing and keeping boarders—Success of Institute—$320.00 amount received in one year for use of family—Conspiracy of Trustees to dislodge me, and give my work, so successfully begun, to one of their own number—Judge Dunlevy's interference and failure of scheme.

County Examiners.—Dishonesty of County Examiners and schemes of county officers—Attempt to sell best positions in the county defeated—Similar case in Chardon—General abuse of Examiners' power—Their evasion of the law.

Model Schools.—Some objections to system—Developed by

actual experience—Results of system—Pupils must relearn the business of actual class management—Training classes the substitute, with immeasurably better results. Remark—M. S. are mechanical and destroy original enthusiastic class management. Suited to absolute government and autocratic management.

Second Year.—Opening favorable—Attendance from town decreased—From abroad increased—Agent and opposing Trustees withdrawn—Failure of unpaid assistants to secure salary from Association—My entire responsibility in the management of Institution—New Board elected, but assumed no control or financial risk, leaving me to make all plans and to reap all rewards—Former pupils from the North enter—Mr. Reed and Miss Morris teach and pursue studies—Refusal of citizens to rent rooms to students—Further difficulties in securing board overcome.

Conflict with County Examiners upon the subject of Grammar—Examiners defeated upon grammatical discussion.

Normal Methods issued quarterly during the third and fourth years—Published in book form by A. S. Barnes & Co.—Wide sales contributed to building up Institution—Larger assembly room secured—Rent of furnished room 60 cents per week—Tuition raised to $10.00 a term—Attendance diminished during War—Two eldest sons enlist—W. D. Henkle resigns the Chair of Mathematics and superintends Union School.

First Graduating Class—1864, nine graduates in Scientific Course—Business Department established—Full College or Classic Course introduced in 1865—Graduates, seven in number, secure positions—Tuition raised to $1.00 per week—Experience in college sustains me in shortening College Course from six years to two and a half years.

The Normal, an Educational Monthly, edited by R. H. Holbrook, 1866—Buildings purchased—Eureka and Deuterian occupied by young ladies and gentlemen—Management of rooms—Young ladies sustain order—Wayward boarding-school girl reformed without spies and coercion—Normal and College methods of teaching Greek compared—Forty weeks in College not equal to ten weeks at the Normal—Hard case disposed of without exciting sympathy of pupils—Results of coercion and enthusiasm compared—Absurdity of imposing laws upon the large majority for the sake of restricting the few—No laws result in increased diligence—College thoroughness hateful; true thoroughness exciting—Love of work an essential qualification of the true teacher—Methods of training assistant teachers—Independence of text-books—True object-teaching methods—True Normal method ever improving upon itself—Several improvements enumerated and explained—Use of several text-books—General use of library—Outlining by teachers, by pupils—Elaboration and discussion of Outlining System—Results—Exhaustiveness of investigation and cogency of expression—Data of succeeding years—Pupils from thirteen States—Institution changes its name—Purchase of five new buildings—Increased boarding facilities furnished by citizens—Boarding clubs established—Prices of board and rooms controlled by Institution—Cost of table board reduced to $1.00 and $1.25 per week—Rooms 30 to 50 cents—Advantages of Normal Course over College Course stated—Reasons for frequent change of teachers—Year 1873—1,613 pupils—Library arranged in ten departments—Contained 2,000 volumes—Always open to pupils—Competent librarian in attendance—Best study done here—First School Exposition—Displays of cabinets, apparatus, herbariums, drawings, etc., etc., prepared by pupils in charge—Ladies best exhibitors—Cabinets valued at $50.00 to $500—College professor attends the school—His inducements for coming—Success of our trained teachers—Statement of his opinions published—Visit of College President—His plan of operation—His inability to adopt our methods—Mr. Beckman sent to America by Swedish Government to study our school systems—Visits us—Novel systems of management appreciated—His astonishment at the good results of the freedom of the sexes—Exposition of our plans of government and instruction made in a Stockholm paper—Results.

Management of Illness in School.—Pupils nursed at our home—Plan relinquished for numerous reasons—Daily prayer-meeting assumes responsibility of nursing—Committees appointed—Services volunteered—Friends sent for—Prevailing good health—Few deaths—Measles—Smallpox—Healthfulness of locality.

Management of Wayward Boys.—Expenditure of time and money compared with other schools—Moral influence induces parents to send us unmanageable boys—Not a reform school—Healthful influence of school effective or otherwise—Worthy business men developed from the recalcitrant boys.

Experiments in Physical Training.—Physical exercise considered a necessity—Heavy gymnastic apparatus a failure—Light gymnastics under C. S. Royce—Base-ball for ladies and gentlemen—Croquet—Health-lift by C. S. Royce—Healthfulness sustained by judicious arrangement of studies and walking to and from classes—Under this management one year here equal to three at College—No "hot-bed" process—A fact accomplished by enthusiastic work—Health at College and the Normal compared—Advantages of botanical and geological excursions—Co-education conducive to health, morality and interested work.

Business Education.—Peculiar features of a true business education—Developed by examples—Success of thoroughly educated business men—Reform of wild youth—Normal business training compared with the shams of "actual business" and commercial colleges—Experience of commercial college graduate and our business graduate compared by actual examples—Broad education necessary to highly successful business man—Example—"Actual business" a fraud.

www.ingramcontent.com/pod-product-compliance
Lightning Source LLC
Chambersburg PA
CBHW020234240426
43672CB00006B/517